The Mind of Italo Calvino

The Mind of Italo Calvino

A Critical Exploration of His Thought and Writings

Dani Cavallaro

McFarland & Company, Inc., Publishers
Jefferson, North Carolina, and London

ALSO BY DANI CAVALLARO
AND FROM MCFARLAND

Magic as Metaphor in Anime: A Critical Study (2010)

Anime and the Visual Novel: Narrative Structure, Design and Play at the Crossroads of Animation and Computer Games (2010)

Anime and Memory: Aesthetic, Cultural and Thematic Perspectives (2009)

The Art of Studio Gainax: Experimentation, Style and Innovation at the Leading Edge of Anime (2009)

Anime Intersections: Tradition and Innovation in Theme and Technique (2007)

The Animé Art of Hayao Miyazaki (2006)

The Cinema of Mamoru Oshii: Fantasy, Technology and Politics (2006)

LIBRARY OF CONGRESS ONLINE CATALOG DATA

Cavallaro, Dani.
　　The mind of Italo Calvino : a critical exploration of his thought and writings / Dani Cavallaro.
　　　　p.　　cm.
　　Includes bibliographical references and index.

　　ISBN 978-0-7864-4766-4
　　softcover : 50# alkaline paper ∞

　　1. Calvino, Italo.
　　　　　　　　　　　　　　　　　　　20010004810

British Library cataloguing data are available

©2010 Dani Cavallaro. All rights reserved

No part of this book may be reproduced or transmitted in any form or by any means, electronic or mechanical, including photocopying or recording, or by any information storage and retrieval system, without permission in writing from the publisher.

Front cover ©2010 Shutterstock

Manufactured in the United States of America

McFarland & Company, Inc., Publishers
　Box 611, Jefferson, North Carolina 28640
　　www.mcfarlandpub.com

To Paddy,
with gratitude for inspiring me to embark on this project
— and for keeping me inspired

Contents

Preface	1
Chapter 1 — The World of Italo Calvino	3
Chapter 2 — Reimagining History: *Our Ancestors*	17
Chapter 3 — Eccentric Cosmologies: *Cosmicomics* and *Time and the Hunter*	41
Chapter 4 — The Endless Journey: *Invisible Cities*	66
Chapter 5 — Structures and Their Explosion: *The Castle of Crossed Destinies*	90
Chapter 6 — Science and Play: *Mr. Palomar* and *Numbers in the Dark*	126
Chapter 7 — The Universal Library: *If on a winter's night a traveler*	146
Chapter 8 — Empire of the Senses: *Under the Jaguar Sun*	174
Bibliography	197
Index	201

And as imagination bodies forth
The forms of things unknown, the poet's pen
Turns them to shape and gives to airy nothing
A local habitation and a name.

— William Shakespeare
A Midsummer Night's Dream,
Act V, scene i

Preface

> I am prisoner of a gaudy and unlivable present, where all forms of human society have reached an extreme of their cycle and there is no imagining what new forms they may assume.
> — Italo Calvino, *Invisible Cities*

The present study originates in a desire to provide a critical investigation of the writings of Italo Calvino, a writer internationally renowned as one of the most adventurous voices in the history of twentieth-century literature, both as an autonomous body of thought-provoking and affectively engaging texts, and as an invitation to embark on dispassionate radical thinking of a kind lamentably scarce in contemporary global culture. Calvino's works are examined in relation to relevant philosophical arguments advanced by the writer in the context of his theoretical and critical output. The book proposes that Calvino's works and philosophy alike bear witness to an extraordinarily versatile mind, keen on experimenting with a dazzling variety of fictional and nonfictional forms, and on approaching each successive experiment as a novel creative enterprise and a fresh contemplative foray into uncharted territory.

The book deliberately eschews chronological order by adopting instead a thematic focus. Relatedly, it does not aim to cover each and every one of Calvino's writings and deliberately concentrates, in fact, on a selection of those works deemed to epitomize particular aspects of the author's thought and to give them distinctive expression by recourse to a range of imaginatively handled forms. This approach is intended to make the book appealing and helpful not solely to readers interested in studying Calvino's evolution per se but also to students likely to encounter his work in the context of theme-centered courses — e.g., on postmodernist fiction, science fiction, folkloric tradition, magic realism, critical and cultural theory — as well as in the context of interdisciplinary programs in the arts and the humanities, the natural and social sciences, and philosophy. Thus, the book attends closely to the principal themes that make Calvino pertinent to a variety of discrete and interconnected fields of inquiry, and explores them in depth with reference to an appropriate selection of his novels, short stories and critical essays.

Chapter 1, "The World of Italo Calvino," offers a panoramic survey of the author's narrative output in the light of cogent theoretical positions advocated in his critical writings. Each of the subsequent chapters seeks to evaluate Calvino's engagement with a specific cultural discourse, discipline or philosophical perspective by concentrating on a text or cluster of related texts and assessing their most prominent themes, narrative styles, structure and imagery. Chapter 2, "Reimagining History: *Our Ancestors*," focuses on Calvino's approach to the multifarious processes through which lived historical events come to be textually encoded in accordance with variable ideological priorities. Chapter 3, "Eccentric Cosmologies: *Cosmicomics* and *Time and the Hunter*," explores the writer's endeavor to identify the mythical and fabulatory potentialities of various cosmogonic theories inspired by pioneering interventions in modern physics. In Chapter 4, "The Endless Journey: *Invisible Cities*," the discussion pivots on Calvino's speculative handling of urban space and architecture as signifying systems of unique, possibly unmatched, storytelling caliber. Chapter 5, "Structures and Their Explosion: *The Castle of Crossed Destinies*," examines Calvino's fascination with the potentially limitless narrative possibilities inherent in the interweaving of verbal and visual languages as storytelling tools. Partly complementing the analysis proffered in Chapter 3, Chapter 6, "Science and Play: *Mr. Palomar* and *Numbers in the Dark*," foregrounds the author's commitment to the collusion of scientific procedures and fantastic speculation. Chapter 7, "The Universal Library: *If on a winter's night a traveler*," throws into relief a concern so deeply embedded in Calvino's entire oeuvre as to operate as something of a leitmotif from beginning to end: the concept of narrative as a virtually inexhaustible palimpsest continually witnessing the metamorphosis of one tale or plot into innumerable other yarns. In Chapter 8, "Empire of the Senses: *Under the Jaguar Sun*," finally, the focus is on Calvino's poetic anatomy of the vocabularies, figurative repertoires and underlying philosophical implications of the often neglected languages of the senses.

Please note that when extracts from Calvino's writings as yet untranslated into English are supplied in this study, the translations are by the author of the present work.

Chapter 1

The World of Italo Calvino

> What we ask of writers is that they guarantee the survival of what we call *human* in a world where everything appears inhuman; guarantee the survival of *human* discourse to console us for the loss of humanity in every other discourse and relationship. And what do we mean by *human*? Usually, whatever is temperamental, emotional, ingenuous, and not at all austere. It is very hard to find someone who believes in the austerity of literature, superior to and opposed to the false austerity of language that runs the world today.
> — Italo Calvino, *The Literature Machine*

> "Existence" is an attitude ... the attitude of negation. We have the ability to withdraw from our condition (to "ex-ist") because we can take a negative attitude towards it. Such a withdrawal from the living world creates an imagined world, and makes the withdrawn existence into a subject of imaginings.
> — Vilém Flusser, "Key Words"

Italo Calvino (1923–1985) is today globally acclaimed as one of the most eminent and original authors of the twentieth century, as attested to by his status as a major candidate for the Nobel Prize for Literature and as the most widely translated contemporary Italian writer at the time of his death. Calvino's reputation owes much to his tenacious desire not only to engage with but also boldly reconceptualize a wide range of narrative genres. These include science fiction, political satire, romance, the epic, the folk tale, the fairy tale, the autobiographical memoir, the travelog, and the detective story—and this list is by no means exhaustive. Concomitantly, Calvino has deployed the critical essay as a supple means of addressing an impressive variety of philosophical, political, aesthetic, historical and broadly cultural issues, often blurring the boundary between fiction and non-fiction with great verve.

The versatility evinced by Calvino's opus at all levels is mirrored by a comparably broad frame of historical and theoretical reference. Thus, the works repeatedly hark back to the Classics, the Middle Ages, the Renaissance and the Enlightenment, while also engaging with recent and ongoing critical debates spawned by formalism, structuralism, poststructuralism, psychoanalysis, semiology and reception theory. This polyhedric disposition makes Calvino's works greatly appealing as interdisciplinary objects of study, as borne out by the presence on architecture and urbanology syllabuses, for instance, of his seminal *Invisible Cities* and by the fascination with *Mr. Palomar* or *Time and the Hunter* demonstrated by students of astronomy, chemistry and biology. In the realms of creative writing and theoretical analysis alike, Calvino unflinchingly demonstrates a desire to move on, to reassess and reimagine virtually ad infinitum all sorts of codes and conventions before they have the slightest chance of fossilizing or crystallizing. For example, even though Calvino at one stage harbored a passion for combinatorial play as a way of constructing mutable yet measurable and to some extent predictable structures, he soon turned his attention to the instability of all patterns and categories and, ultimately, their ineluctable dissolution.

An analogous position underpins the writer's attitude to science. On the one hand, Calvino is heir to enlightened rationalism in his commitment to the punctilious investigation of even ostensibly paltry phenomena. On the other hand, the imagination inevitably takes over, suggesting that science has more to share with myth than it would sometimes like to recognize, and that no all-encompassing metanarrative is therefore available. Empirical methods sustained by rational analysis are valid and desirable as long as one engages with the particular but presuming to then organize one's contingent findings within a likewise graspable grand scheme is lunacy. To resort to a metaphor, it could be suggested that even though one might get to know intimately an enormous number of individual cities and even arrange them neatly within an atlas, what will always remain inscrutable is the nature of the atlas itself. Being genuinely scientific, for Calvino, should not amount to attempting to quantify human knowledge within unchangeable systems. In fact, it should consist of reliving and recreating the hypothetical moment of the birth of knowledge and science a potentially limitless number of times. The honest artist is the one that starts all over again every time.

As an analytically selective assessment of Calvino's corpus, the present study works on the premise that this discloses a unique modern configuration of the eclectic encyclopedic mind, grounded in an intrepid engagement with radical thought. Seamlessly blending realism and fantasy with dexterity, yet retaining at all times a disarming sense of candor, Calvino's reflections drive deep, quizzing the political and metaphysical definitions of the real by which many of us live. Calvino's oeuvre is here examined in the light of a variety of theoretical perspectives implied or invoked by his prismatic output. Thus, the book does not seek to apply a set of theories to its object of study from an external standpoint of critical mastery but rather to pursue the clues proffered by the works themselves. It is one of the book's principal objectives to highlight the ongoing legacy of philosophical lessons of the late twentieth century commonly bracketed as poststructuralism, proposing that these have not been rendered irrelevant or anodyne by ideological incorporation but in fact retain uncompromising questioning power when they are teamed, as is the case in Calvino's opus, with adventurous speculation. Simultaneously, this study wishes to emphasize both the diversity and the coherence of Calvino's output. Hence, it shows how the author, in adopting a wide variety of forms and genres, has placed a very personal signature on each. The main factors lending coherence to Calvino's work are his consistent interweaving of realism and fantasy and his equally assiduous return to certain themes: identity, space, time, perception and, above all, the roles played by language and storytelling as means of giving shape to human experience. Underlying these themes is an awareness of the impossibility of ever grasping reality in its entirety. As a result, the motifs of invisibility, absence and incompleteness also play a crucial part in Calvino's work.

Calvino's vision is able to capture in one single inspired movement the sophisticated aesthetics of the most accomplished avant-garde trends and the purity of an atavistic poetic imagination, the exploratory acumen of the boldest post–Einsteinian physicist and the colorful intuitiveness of medieval troubadours. A mathematical formula can be lithely invoked as the launch pad for a flirtatious dalliance with the fantastic and a bizarre trope, conversely, be used to sustain a display of analytical logic.

Stating that reality is never fully present may seem a banal expression of the obvious. It is nonetheless something we frequently forget or ignore. We think of ourselves as possessors of physical and psychological properties, and of such properties as the measure of our presence. Yet, as contemporary cultural anxieties force reality to shift gears, we become increasingly aware that reality is distant from us. Our own reality, both bodily and mental, is haunted by that which seems not to be there. Exploring reality means confronting its invisible aspects, phantoms that are either deliberately excluded from view because they are too baffling or brutal to register, or inadvertently allowed to fall into reality's interstices. Calvino's writings throw these issues into stark relief. The shape of reality is continually sought for in its most elusive pockets, by tracing through time and space that which makes its mark by being there and not being there at one and the same time. The human characters situated in this world are themselves existentially incomplete, and their presence is accordingly shot through with reminders of inevitable lack. However, even though Calvino's world view may often seem dark, it never sinks into undiluted nihilism. In fact, humanity's flaws are seen to hold creative potentialities: a lacunary subject may function imaginatively, by negotiating a deal with its absences, and by reaching out continually into the no-longer and into the not-yet. The characters thus oscillate between past selves they cannot restore and innumerable other lives still to be entered, a boundless realm of imagined possibilities. In this scenario, plenitude is only ever a broken promise while the gap is the precondition of creativity. This tension is embodied in narratives where reality and unreality coalesce through the production, within any one picture, of contrasting viewpoints, multiple perspectives and interlocking dimensions. Calvino strives to create existential spaces capable of conveying a feeling of limitlessness and of metamorphosing unrelentingly into other possible worlds where neither conventional notions of depth nor the law of gravity apply. They are pictures of a floating universe, of a transient spectacle, of virtual histories and invisible destinies.

Two recurrent images in Calvino's writings that faithfully encapsulate his outlook are the kaleidoscope and the labyrinth. The former, in playing with a finite number of shapes to yield unfathomable diversity, epitomizes the intrinsically aleatory nature of human experience with colorful economy. Where labyrinthine structures are concerned, Calvino acknowledges and even welcomes their challenge: a defiant invitation to reconstruct their latent maps and hence dissolve their power. Nevertheless, what draws him time and again to the concept and image of the maze is not so much this challenge and the prospects of control it entails but rather the dizzy pleasure of wandering through the labyrinth and getting lost in it — the thrill of the endless and very possibly aimless journey over and above any conclusive destination. Calvino's universe, in other words, is the boundless land of the eternal *flâneur*. No less importantly, Calvino persistently emphasizes the inherently material character of writing. This activity is not conceived of merely as a means of expression or communication but rather as an immensely resourceful way of chiseling, sculpting and molding one's environment in ever-changing configurations and with an undying appetite for experiment. The words used by Calvino in his obituary of Roland Barthes, first published in *La Repubblica* on April 9, 1980, at the time of the French writer's death, are no less apposite to Calvino himself: "the one who subordinated everything to the rigor of a method, and the one whose only sure criterion was pleasure (the pleasure of the intelligence and the intelligence of pleasure) ... are really one, and it is in the presence of these two aspects together — continuous and variously dosed — that we find the secret of the fascination that his mind exerted over many of us" (Calvino 1987, 302).

This study, finally, emanates not only from a long-standing interest in Calvino's writings but also from a conviction that contemporary thought and its underlying political structures are so caught up in ossified ideas that there is an urgent need for fresh approaches to reality — for speculative models that offer hope for a frank reassessment of the many unexamined "truths" on which today's cultures rest. This need is confirmed by the dominance of educational systems on both sides of the Atlantic wherein a blind devotion to measurements and league tables routinely squashes any urge to encourage people to reason autonomously. Calvino's opus provides, typically by recourse to generous doses of childlike curiosity and ironical inversion, an ideal blueprint for the pursuit of such a questioning venture.

Calvino's first novel, *The Path to the Nest of Spiders* (1947), follows quite loyally the codes and conventions of social realism, the literary trend dominant at the time. The writer himself was dissatisfied with this early piece, regretting its failure to reflect adequately his experimentative vision. In fact, even in this context, Calvino was already playing with narrative elements alien to the realist ethos, and thus tentatively reaching toward the fantastic. For example, although the novel, in mirroring Calvino's experiences of the Second World War and the antifascist "Resistenza" through the eyes of a child, generally adheres to an *ordo naturalis* in the presentation of its pivotal events, it often disrupts linearity through non-naturalistic flashbacks and foreshadowings, while also deploying the image of the titular "nest" to great symbolic effect as a chronotope. Moreover, as Martin McLaughlin observes, "even at this early stage Calvino was nonconformist, preferring to avoid the hagiographic approach encouraged by the Communist Party.... Instead he went against the grain, eschewing the Manichaean portrayal of the antifascist struggle as a battle between good and evil" (McLaughlin 20–21).

The collection of short stories *Ultimo Viene il Corvo* (1949), most of which have been published in English as part of the collection *Adam, One*

Afternoon, and Other Stories, closely resembles Calvino's first novel in that it deals with war-related themes. Nonetheless, it does not abide by the dictates of social realism insofar as it gives priority, persistently and deliberately, to various aspects of quotidian life. Furthermore, reality crisscrosses with fantasy on numerous occasions. According to Beno Weiss, this is borne out by the short story "The Enchanted Garden": "The beauty of the story is that even when evil seems to be lurking in the background — i.e., the war and the foreboding garden — the fablelike quality of the narrative continues to work its magic, as nature with its positive side represents the positive in life. As Calvino himself has pointed out, the fantastic shows that the world is complicated beyond our comprehension" (Weiss 21). Even later writings exploring concrete political realities with gritty documentary exactitude tend to transcend the boundaries of realism. The story "The Watcher" (1963), included in the anthology *The Watcher and Other Stories*, exemplifies this proposition by addressing concepts of immediate urgency — such as ideology, engagement, consciousness-raising — yet defamiliarizing them through the protagonist's surreal exposure to an institution for patients with severe mental and physical disabilities.

As Jeanette Winterson emphasizes, "Calvino's instinct was elsewhere; he felt that social realism, as a literary method, had exhausted its resources." This perception was validated by the pained awareness that "The energetic remaking of every kind of creative expression — painting, music, literature — that had happened after the First World War was not repeated after the Second World War. A kind of 'utility test' became the standard method of judgment.... Imagination, experiment, playfulness, beauty, the personal search for meaning that every artist must follow, had a suspect and self-indulgent feel." These, however, are precisely the values which Calvino treasured and pursued against all odds, regarding creativity as pivotal not solely to art but also to the forging of any kind of human society based not on unexamined structures and relations of power but on authentic tolerance and harmony as the outcomes of both self-understanding and mutual acceptance. Creativity, for Calvino, is what allows the most genuine traits of the human mind — its randomness, labyrinthine intricacy, incongruousness — frankly to express themselves. Literature should mirror this state of affairs by positing itself as "a force ... that could encompass everything — science, history, politics, fantasy, but would be in thrall to none of these" and could, in fact, "unscroll the inside of the mind." Calvino himself lived consonantly with this world view: he was "brave because he sat down to write what interested him — not what might interest other people. He had a day job in a publishing house, and he sought neither celebrity nor wealth. He was the extreme other of the creative writing course wannabe" (Winterson 2009). The *Times Online* article felicitously titled "Invisible Author" corroborates this proposition, maintaining that Calvino's devotion to the "transforming powers of literature runs in harness with his hesitations over the newly extrovert role of the writer in society. His instinct was to let the work speak for itself" ("Invisible Author"). This is tersely borne out by the collection of autobiographical writings and interviews *The Hermit in Paris* (1994), where Calvino intimates that invisibility should be an author's ideal state and a name on a book cover the limit of his presence.

The qualities which Calvino deems axial to creativity are crisply, yet lyrically, documented in *Six Memos for the Next Millennium* (1988), a collection edited by his wife Esther and published posthumously containing the text of the Charles Eliot Norton lectures he was due to deliver at Harvard in 1985 when disaster struck in the form of a fatal cerebral hemorrhage. These encompass "Lightness," "Quickness," "Exactitude," "Visibility" and "Multiplicity." The intended sixth lecture, "Consistency," never reached the page. As a cumulative holistic ensemble, Calvino's works can be regarded as an ongoing — and by no means teleologically driven — quest to implement the tenets discussed in *Six Memos*. This is undertaken by refining their import each step of the way and encapsulating them in ever-changing textual formations that are also, inevitably, formations of knowledge and desire. The need for Lightness occurred to Calvino at a very early stage in his career, when he realized that were he to bow to the requirements of social realism, he would inevitably be swamped in a discourse he could not honestly subscribe to, and that the only way to avert this fate was to create both an alternate world and a language capable of matching it. Literature, he sensed, might be politically most salutary when it succeeds in exposing the gap between reality and perception. "When I began my career," the author reflects, "the categorical imperative of every young writer was to represent his own time.... Soon I became aware that between the facts of life that should have been my raw materials, and the quick light touch I wanted for my writing, there was a gulf that cost me increasing effort to cross. Maybe I was only then becoming aware of the weight, the inertia, the opacity of the world — qualities that stick to writing from the start, unless one finds some way of evading them" (Calvino 1996, 3–4).

Lightness, in this context, should not be mistaken as vagueness or superficiality for it actually requires great care and dedication. Calvino recognizes the vital role played by this principle in ancient texts such as Ovid's *Metamorphoses* and Lucretius' *De rerum natura*, where Lightness emanates from a world view grounded in philosophy and science, yet comes into being through poetic language more resonantly than through any theoretical assumptions — in other words, through the act of writing itself rather than through some preestablished doctrine or agenda. In recent times, an analogous message is pithily communicated, according to Calvino, by Milan Kundera's *The Unbearable Lightness of Being*. Science itself is deemed to be committed to the removal of weight, as attested to by its increasing concentration on the tiniest of particles and energy flows. Citing writers as diverse as Shakespeare, Cervantes and Cyrano de Bergerac, Calvino comes to perceive Lightness as concomitant with a type of writing that operates as a metaphor for the impalpable substance of the universe at large, and seeks out reality by commodiously adjusting to its infinite possibilities without ever presuming to possess it conclusively. Lightness repeatedly joins forces with Quickness as "an agility in reasoning" and "economy in argument" (43) capable of giving free rein to "the mental circuits that capture and link points distant from each other in space and time" (48). Paradoxically, Quickness does not automatically equate to physical speed for it actually encourages the writer to follow the Latin motto "*Festina lente*, hurry slowly" (48).

All of Calvino's works concurrently bear witness to a desire for Exactitude, to deploy human discourse as precisely as possible so as to evoke the minutest nuances of imagination and thought. Its archenemy is the "plague afflicting language" that "tends to level out all expression" and to deaden the "spark that shoots out from the collision of words and new circumstances" (56). A major model here proposed as a case in point is the poetry of Giacomo Leopardi: a methodical endeavor to capture the inscrutable and the indefinite through extreme precision and meticulous attention to details. However, Exactitude should not be seen as an attempt to suppress the chaos of the cosmos since its pursuit inexorably shows that rational argumentation and logical thinking can only end up disclosing vast webs of "multiple, ramified conclusions" (71). Hence, Multiplicity often proves inextricable form Exactitude, insofar as the writer's devotion to the latter cannot be sustained without his preparedness to engage with a sprawling scenario of ever-proliferating, unforeseeable and even mutually incompatible possibilities. Time and again, the text "comes to pieces in his hands" as its "structure" is exploded by an intricate "network of relationships" spawned by the writing's "own organic vitality" (110). Lightness, Quickness, Exactitude and Multiplicity are frequently held together, throughout Calvino's output, by the catalytic agency of Visibility, which posits the imagination as the ultimate receptacle of all conceivable (and even inconceivable) potentialities and hypotheses. In this context, reality and fantasy ultimately share the same ontological status insofar as both "can take on form only by means of writing" as the "polymorphic vision of the eyes and the spirit are contained in uniform lines of small or capital letters, periods, commas, parentheses — pages of signs, packed as closely together as grains of sand" (99).

It is with the trilogy *Our Ancestors* (1960), comprising the initially separate novels *The Cloven Viscount* (1952), *Baron in the Trees* (1957) and *The Non-Existent Knight* (1959), that Calvino's creative trajectory signals a veritable quantum jump in the direction of playful experimentation, as he begins to pursue in tandem the principles of Lightness and Quickness. The physical image employed in the preceding sentence, incidentally, is inspired by Calvino himself as he joyfully celebrates "the sudden agile leap of the poet-philosopher who raises himself above the weight of the world, showing that with all his gravity he has the secret of lightness, and that what many consider to be the vitality of the times — noisy, aggressive, revving and roaring — belongs to the realm of death, like a cemetery for rusty old cars" (12). In *Our Ancestors*, Calvino portrays human identity as a presence inseparable from absence. The trilogy's splendidly idiosyncratic heroes are indeed defined by what they lack: by mutilation (*Viscount*), unanchoring (*Baron*) or invisibility (*Knight*). The three characters are thus presented as intrinsically foreign to and from themselves. As a mock epic based on a pointedly unorthodox rewriting of history from the bizarre viewpoints of split, transient and disembodied figures, the trilogy supplies unique insights into Calvino's skeptical take on history and historiography alike.

While *Our Ancestors* constitutes an immensely enjoyable and, at times, no less harrowing experiment in worldbuilding in its own right, it also represents the springboard from which Calvino proceeds to elaborate incrementally prismatic universes wherein every place and character feels both out-of-this-world and normal — unlike, yet peculiarly very much like us — in equal measures. Gradually, weight — and, with it, the threats of stagnation and dogmatism — are removed from people, places, history, science, textuality and even language itself. Although, as argued in "Invisible Author," the three novels were termed "fantasy" at the time of their original publication, they were nonetheless acknowledged as innovative "works of the imagination. They make no attempt to document the real world; rather, they explain it by moving sideways from it.... Calvino's 'fantasy' is in fact a serious 'other-world' where, just for a time, we can be freed from the problems of gravity" ("Invisible Author"). By no stretch of the imagination is this suspension of weight tantamount to escapism. In fact, it is an existential choice requiring much courage, for it entails conscious self-severance from the readymade ideological certainties which, according to Calvino, can only help us feel safely moored by weighing us down — both intellectually and affectively.

The cosmicomic tales — *Cosmicomics* (1965) and *Time and the Hunter* (1967) — perpetuate Calvino's quest for Lightness through the alchemical interfusion of absence and presence. In this instance, the author proposes that objects and phenomena are never wholly present or wholly absent but actually come into being as variable admixtures of being and non-being, plenitude and vacuity, kinesis and stasis. Enthusiastically attempting to fathom the ongoing collusion of absence and presence throughout the universe, Calvino does not hesitate to yoke together preposterous fantasies and rigorous mathematical thinking in the overriding interest of creativity. In the segment of *Six Memos* devoted to Exactitude, he pursues this proposition by invoking Paul Valéry's idea of "cosmogony as a literary genre rather than as scientific speculation" and thus embarks on a radical interrogation of "the idea of 'universe,' which is also a reaffirmation of the mythic force that every image of 'universe' carries with it" (Calvino 1996, 67).

Bravely engaging with the concept of Visibility, *Invisible Cities* (1972) drastically destabilizes reality's officially recognized boundaries through one basic trope: the narrative's sole actual referent, the city of Venice, eludes articulation while countless cities unmarked in any canonical atlas are capable of evoking an entrancing plethora of protean worlds. Hypothetical or downright fictitious dimensions persistently displace recorded geography. Once more, any sense of presence evaporates in the face of absent yet imaginable possibilities which, ironically, end up feeling more real than reality itself. Calvino is not, however, merely playing hide-and-seek with his reader, as the text's final words make hauntingly clear. Averring that the "inferno of the living is already here," the protagonist here proposes that the riskiest, yet most worthwhile, task a person can hope to undertake is to "seek and learn to recognize who and what, in the midst of the inferno, are not inferno, then make them endure, give them space" (Calvino 1997, 165).

Confirming the importance of Visibility by positing the visual image as a major storytelling tool, *The Castle of Crossed Destinies* (1973) chronicles the passage from the philosophical valorization of the idea of structure to the radical questioning of that idea by recourse to the principle of structurality. In so doing, it figuratively mirrors the transition from structuralist to poststructuralist approaches. Classic structuralism posits the concept of structure as a stable system organized around a fixed center that transcends the endless play of language. Poststructuralism, conversely, advocates structurality as a volatile connector that only holds systems together in uncertain and ephemeral ways, preserving their dynamism at all times and acknowledging their self-dismantling proclivities. As initially centered patterns of Tarot cards, the narrative's lingua franca, incrementally give way to decentered or even random constellations, any guarantee of a reliable system is radically undermined. The book also reverberates throughout with echoes of Calvino's fascination with the epic genre, and specifically with the most flamboyantly meandering of all narratives in that mold, Ludovico Ariosto's *Orlando Furioso*— a work which Calvino endeavored to retell in the form of inspiringly chosen extracts concatenated by means of original bridging prose in 1970.

In both *Mr. Palomar* (1983) and *Numbers in the Dark* (1992), Calvino's poetics of Visibility leads once more to the seemingly opposite — but actually complementary — concept of invisibility. In these instances, the idea is harnessed to an alternately humorous and tormented, yet always dispassionate, exposure of the fallibility of analytical procedures. His personae tirelessly strive to deploy empirical observation and logic to reduce baffling realities to their basic constituents. In so doing, they hope to make the world more intelligible. Ironically, they achieve the exact opposite since the individual elements they manage to extract from the whole turn out to be not irreducible elemental data but rather multifaceted entities in their own right, prone to undergo endless metamorphosis and to foster the escalation of unforeseeable complexity. Thus, any sense of presence gleaned from analysis is inexorably undermined by a galaxy of latent possibilities. Concomitantly, the two texts bring to mind the principle of Exactitude in their dramatization of the "search for the indefinite" as an "observation of all that is multiple, teeming, composed of countless particles" (Calvino 1996, 60).

In *If on a winter's night a traveler* (1979), the value of Lightness effervescently combines with that of Multiplicity through the image of "the novel as a vast net," proposed in the essay devoted to the latter in *Six*

Memos (124). This synthesis underpins the production of a kaleidoscopic text encompassing disparate literary genres, formulae and styles and thereby conveying the idea of the cosmos at large as a boundless library. The removal of gravity is instrumental in enabling the novel (or rather, the numerous embryonic novels it consists of) to vault nimbly out of one form and into the next. It thus engenders a composite body of writing that could confidently be described as a paean to the spirit of Multiplicity. In addition, *If on a winter's night a traveler* confirms Calvino's commitment to the materiality of language by positing books themselves as literally sculptable materials.

In *Under the Jaguar Sun* (1986), the languages of the senses are both meticulously and poetically explored in order to foreground the lunacy inherent in any attempt to grasp conclusively the mysteries of perception and communication alike. Both sensations themselves and the metaphors, signs and memories they relentlessly spawn are woven from elusive traces of smells, tastes and sounds that are either no longer or not yet discernible. The principle of Multiplicity thus gains the limelight again. Although Calvino's fascination with the empire of the senses reaches its apotheosis with the never completed *Under the Jaguar Sun*, this interest also finds notable articulation in *Difficult Loves* (1957), *Marcovaldo or The Seasons in the City* (1963) and *The Road to San Giovanni* (1990). Both *Under the Jaguar Sun* and those collections underscore Calvino's passion for the materiality of expression, eschewing the Western tendency to privilege the sense of sight as a faculty allowing for physical distance and foregrounding instead the senses that bring the body most explicitly to the fore: namely, olfaction, gustation and hearing.

Calvino's emphasis on the material dimension of language and writing, highlighted earlier in this chapter, is compounded across his output with a lusty appetite for visuality and, specifically, the visual poetry of cartoons. This passion is economically communicated by the short story "The Origin of Birds" (*Time and the Hunter*), where the narrator encourages us to ideate the story he is recounting in the shape of a sequence of drawn frames. Inspired by Calvino's model, Robert Coover has configured the speculative journey traced by Calvino's thought over *Six Memos* as a comic strip. Coover proposes that the first frame, dedicated to Lightness, would feature the "poet-philosopher" leaping out of "tombstones" that symbolize the "world in a state of petrified agitation." The second frame, depicting the value of Quickness, would still feature the aforementioned stones but host "two leaping poets" as a means of suggesting "the speed of thought," or "two sides of the poet's nature, such as melancholy and humor." In the frame for Exactitude, the world reveals a profusion of "geometric forms, symmetries, numerical series and cosmological models" of the kind Calvino was so deeply drawn to. With the fourth frame, where Visibility is the focus, the central character is accompanied by a "cloud-like balloon representing his thoughts" accommodating "all the other frames of our comic strip like a diminishing sequence of television screens"—a succinct graphic "celebration of the imagination." Unsurprisingly, in the final frame portraying the principle of Multiplicity, "everything explodes," as the image is powerless to contain within its boundaries "the sudden proliferation of images and the infinitely complex web of interrelationships among them" (Coover).

It is when Calvino appears to be looking at the genesis and nature of stories—not only other people's stories but also his own—as an external observer rather than their creator that many of his preoccupations often come to life most vibrantly. In the process, as intimated above, he is presented with an almost limitless reservoir of variations on the themes of invisibility, absence and inconclusiveness. The tales come to constitute, in his eyes, a sort of mega-encyclopedia of narrative possibilities and narratological functions. While everything is ostensibly present in this formidable totality of textual options, what Calvino emphasizes is an irreducible element of emptiness. He is acutely aware that no story is unique and self-contained: what is might just as well not have been or have been something quite different. What a story is, therefore, ultimately depends on what it could have been instead. Stories are only visible as fragments against a context or background which is both necessary and obfuscating, illuminating and elusive. We see what is present, but cannot see the sources of presence. The present story may be visible but presence itself is invisible. The impossibility of ascertaining the origins of presence runs parallel to a deep-seated sense of the ineradicable disjuncture between the immensity of the cosmos which the writer yearns to explore and the paltriness of the tools available to him to accomplish that momentous task.

This state of affairs is memorably captured in *Mr. Palomar* by the sequence where the titular protagonist goes to observe the night sky through a telescope and instantly encounters a number of difficulties. To begin with, he cannot make up his mind whether to look at the stars with his glasses off or on. He fears that if he takes them off, he will not be able to consult properly the astronomy handbook that details what he is looking at. However, he suspects that if he leaves them on, he will create an undesirable barrier between himself and the heavens. He is then at pains to decide whether to focus on an individual star or on an entire constellation, not to mention whether to inspect the space between planets or the celestial bodies themselves. Even once he has addressed these conundrums, Palomar's troubles are far from over since he then has to figure how to deal with his eye's adjustment to the transition between light and darkness. The riddles experienced by Palomar are an apt metaphor for a problem which any honest writer faces but few have managed to confront with Calvino's ingenuity. This, ultimately, amounts to a brave recognition that the one irrefutable factor underlying any story is its implicit capacity always to become another story.

Chapter 2

Reimagining History:
Our Ancestors

The three novels *The Cloven Viscount* (1952), *Baron in the Trees* (1957) and *The Non-Existent Knight* (1959) — brought together as the trilogy *Our Ancestors* in 1960 — cumulatively yield an alternately delicate and flamboyant anatomy of what Calvino, in his introduction to the volume, describes as his "relationship with the problems" of his "own time" and his "own life" (Calvino 1992, viii). In so doing, they emphasize an existential condition of lack with reference to three interconnected realms. *The Cloven Viscount* explores the theme of dismemberment: "incompleteness, bias, the lack of human fullness." *Baron in the Trees* focuses on disconnectedness: "isolation, distance, difficulties in relationships with others." *The Non-Existent Knight*, finally, examines the ethos of disappearance: "themes of empty forms and the concrete nature of living, awareness of being in the world and building one's own destiny, or else lack of involvement altogether" (ix). Instrumental to the articulation of these ideas are three highly unusual protagonists: a medieval warrior perfectly dimidiated in the heat of battle; an eighteenth-century young aristocrat who spends the bulk of his life high up in the trees; and a knight consisting solely of an empty suit of armor. These three characters enable Calvino to elaborate complementary configurations of the interplay of presence and absence in the construction of human identities. Firstly, Calvino's self-divided characters could be regarded as allegories of the authorial function insofar as in the act of writing, as noted in the essay "Cybernetics and Ghosts," "the person 'I' ... splits into a number of different figures: into an 'I' who is writing and an 'I' who is written, into an empirical 'I' who looks over the shoulder of the 'I' who is writing and into a mythical 'I' who serves as a model for the 'I' who is written. The 'I' of the author is dissolved in the writing" (Calvino 1987, 15). Secondly, it should be emphasized that what is missing in and from the bodies of Calvino's three heroes is not some dispensable appendage. Their identities are in fact defined by what they lack: by their being mutilated, unanchored or plainly invisible.

Pivotal to the trilogy is the mock historical reinvention of past ages, an imaginary present woven from the traces of an absent past. Calvino's decidedly non-canonical rewriting of the past from the eerie perspective of disembodied or half-bodied characters offers useful insights into the writer's ambivalent attitude toward history, and toward the philosophies through which official history is transmitted. The temporal coordinates of Calvino's prismatic tales form a multidimensional chart in which the more or less remote past is intermeshed with contemporary concerns, such as "the problem of the intellectual's political commitment at a time of shattered illusions" or the repercussions of "mass society" on the fashioning of identity (Calvino 1992, x). Even though they were written in the 1950s and hence well ahead of the rampant mechanization unleashed by digital gadgetry, the internet and the tyranny of the cell phone, the three novels offer an almost prophetic warning against things to come. At the time of their execution, Calvino already sensed that technological massification was tied up with a dangerous phenomenon: i.e., a hegemonic dismissal of the idea that the acquisition of knowledge should be a process grounded in independent thinking, and a concomitant assumption that knowledge can be purchased in prepackaged bundles. This attitude, he felt, could render that process altogether obsolete. Ideally, history should trace humanity's attempt to gain intellectual and emotional freedom from an ever-developing awareness of its dignity. However, lived history's horrors, indignities and blunders show that its course hardly amounts to a rational construction and is actually at the mercy of forces that elude or even scorn humanity's control. Calvino's stance evinces a resolve never to turn a blind eye to the evils of history and, by extension, the world's negativity. In fact, it takes the acknowledgment of these inevitable facets of human experience as the starting point for a conscious and punctilious project of ongoing reflection and engagement.

Especially crucial to the imaginative reassessment of history delivered by Calvino is his simultaneous commitment to the enduring legacy of the Enlightenment ethos and to an anti-foundationalist and anti-rationalist perspective. Thus, in enumerating the sources of inspiration lying behind the trilogy, Calvino places two substantially different models side by side. While ready to acknowledge his debt to "the *conte philosophique*, chiefly Voltaire's *Candide*," and his general "liking for the eighteenth century," he feels simultaneously drawn to R. L. Stevenson and his knack of "translating an invisible text containing the quintessential fascination of all adventures, all mysteries, all conflicts of will and passion" (viii). In a similar vein, Calvino's essay on "Philosophy and Literature" highlights the character of eighteenth-century *contes philosophiques* as "acts of revenge against philosophy," as well as their historical coexistence with "the *conte fantastique* and the Gothic novel": namely, ways of unleashing "the obsessive visions of the unconscious" (Calvino 1987, 46).

The trilogy simultaneously upholds and undermines some of the Enlightenment's pivotal aspirations, and resulting attitudes to historical data, by pointing to the coexistence of daylight common sense, order and rationality with mystery, anarchy and chaos. "Two Interviews on Science and Literature" bears witness to Calvino's divided loyalties. On the one hand, he states that although the "Enlightenment is accused of being at the root of the technocratic ideology that wields power in the industrialized nations," he is nonetheless willing to "accept the label of an exponent of the Neo-Enlightenment." On the other hand, he is simultaneously keen on stressing that his fascination with that era does not spring from its reputed stability and optimism but rather from the recognition that the so-called Age of Reason is "rich and many-faceted and full of contradictory ferments that are still going on today" (35). The writer's interrogation of stereotypical accounts of enlightened reason is spotlighted by his conception of the operations of modern science as ongoing and provisional processes, unable to deliver absolute value systems and hence well-equipped to "teach" writers "the patient modesty of considering each and every result as being part of a possibly infinite series of approximations" (38). *Our Ancestors* warns us against shallow idealizations of scientific endeavor as the acme of rationalism by drastically relativizing its aims and functions. Science, it is implied, may simply amount to a series of routine operations whose monotony is only occasionally relieved by a challenging task. This is demonstrated, in *The Cloven Viscount,* by the scene where the appearance in the military hospital of Medardo's horribly mutilated body is met primarily as a promise of novel entertainment: "how pleased the doctors were! 'A fine case!'" (Calvino 1992, 10). The scientific ambitions of the medical profession are overtly satirized through the character of Dr Trelawney, who "bother[s] little about the sick" (18) and is filled with "dismay and disgust" by "human beings and their infirmities" (24), since "his scientific researches" are governed by self-professedly superior aims: that is to say, "his passion for wills-o'-the-wisp" (19). Calvino concurrently questions the supposedly beneficial repercussions of technological progress enshrined in mainstream historiography by suggesting that the most accomplished "masterpieces of carpentry and mechanics" are actually, in despotic dispensations, "instruments of torture" (21–22).

The writer's ambivalence toward the Enlightenment stems, fundamentally, from his suspicion that the Western metaphysical tradition has fostered an exaggerated conception of reason. He simultaneously warns us, however, against the temptation to suppress that conception altogether. It would seem that for Calvino, as for Jürgen Habermas in Mark Hohengarten's assessment of the German philosopher, "genuinely postmetaphysical thinking can remain critical only if it preserves the idea of reason derived from tradition while stripping it of its metaphysical trappings" (Habermas 1995, vii). Calvino underscores the necessity of grasping reason's contingent and relative status, instead of blindly upholding its transcendental validity, in order to subvert the uniformizing and unifying thrust of Western metaphysics. Thus, he strives to assert the importance of individuality and disunity not merely by marking their distinctiveness but by proclaiming them conspicuously through bizarre distortions and implausible aberrations. The version of subjectivity presented by Calvino, accordingly, is not based on the model of the putatively autonomous self beloved of liberal humanism, nor is it rooted to the Cartesian ego as the corollary of one's awareness of the ability to think. In fact, Calvino's individual is precariously bounded, peripheral, ironically indecisive, estranged from itself and from others. The capacity to be oneself is inexorably predicated on the ability to capture what is missing in and from oneself: self-emergence is concurrently a loss of self.

Relatedly, the trilogy repeatedly throws into relief split and double identities as the underpinnings of its radically decentered take on history. In *Baron in the Trees*, Cosimo is presented as something of an Enlightenment hero, endowed with an inquisitive mind which leaves no familial, societal or broadly ideological conventions unquestioned: he is tenacious, resolute and putatively all-seeing. Yet, certain crucial facets of his behavior evoke a Romantic sense of excess which would be anathema to orthodox Enlightenment thinking. The boundlessness of his feelings precludes the possibility of situating his quest into any definite pattern or category. Cosimo's brother hopes he will at some point say "something ... which would show a limit, a proportion to his protest. Instead of which he said nothing of the kind" (Calvino 1992, 98). The Baron's determination never to descend from the arboreal realm — redolent of the social destiny of marginalization associated with the Romantic artist par excellence — becomes something of an obsessive mission. He is even prepared to give up his beloved Ursula when faced with the prospect of having to touch the earth again for her sake. In Calvino's version of the Enlightenment and of the notion of history spawned by that creed over time, the glorification of reason as a unique human faculty must ultimately pave the way to a recognition of all human attributes, including emotions and imaginative powers outside the province of rational thinking. At the same time, Calvino is eager to emphasize the limitations of Cosimo's powers by exposing the problematic status of the character's visual capacities. The Baron is endowed with an all-mastering, all-encompassing gaze which, within the parameters of Western ocularcentrism, ought to exemplify limitless capabilities: Cosimo, we are informed, simply "saw it all" (87). However, Calvino also stresses that the ability to see everything requires a mountaintop detachment, or bird's-eye view, which may only become attainable at the exorbitant price of self-alienation. Seeing everything, holding complete control over the visible realm, may entail, paradoxically, one's disappearance from that domain. To see everything is also, ultimately, to become invisible.

Cosimo's aspirations to join the Enlightenment elite of utopian and encyclopedist thinkers, moreover, rapidly precipitate into a whirlpool of irrational fantasies. Having set out to leave an indelible imprint on history by penning "a *Project for the Constitution of an Ideal State in the Trees* ... as a treatise on laws and governments," he finds his intention subverted by an unforeseen "impulse to invent complicated stories ... a hodge-potch of adventures, duels and erotic tales." Not surprisingly, Diderot, upon receipt of a précis of the proposed work, merely thanks Cosimo "with a short note" (212). Medardo, in *The Cloven Viscount*, further problematizes Calvino's double take on Enlightenment thought. The Viscount is defined primarily in terms of a cynical, calculating mentality which, however, may unexpectedly degenerate into utter irrationality. Even passion is the product of a rational decision: "so he decided to fall in love with Pamela"; yet, the narrator warns, "thoughts thus coldly formulated should not deceive us" (35). Indeed, on the eve of Medardo's wedding, we are presented with the image of a romanticized lover, "prey to the excitement of the vigil ... moaning and sighing in anxious imaginings" (67).

The author stresses that any emancipatory move entails both the promise of fresh directions and the specter of a directionless, utterly random experience since, as maintained in "Cybernetics and Ghosts," all "games of orientation are in turn games of disorientation" (Calvino 1987, 25). In questioning the synthesizing mythologies beloved of Enlightenment thinking and its historiographical brood, literature may foster alternative forms of illumination which, however, do not yield rational landscapes of uncluttered visibility but rather labyrinthine constructs of occlusion and concealment. Knowledge, therefore, is predicated upon loss and, more importantly perhaps, on an awareness of dispossession: a self-conscious appropriation of negativity capable, paradoxically, of becoming an affirmation. The Enlightenment's penchant for analysis, systematization and selection promulgates an ethos according to which human beings are knowable to the extent that they can be manipulated within the confines of formal structures and formulaic vocabularies. Calvino's juggling with conflicting and ostensibly irreconcilable narrative ingredients explodes the rationalist ideal as specious: "the more enlightened our houses are, the more their walls ooze ghosts. Dreams of progress and reason are haunted by nightmares" (19).

In *The Non-Existent Knight*, the ambitions of rationalist philosophy and historiography alike are radically questioned through the juxtaposition of hyperrational attitudes and utterly illogical situations. The Knight himself is presented as a champion of refined reason, driven by "a mania to inspect everything" (Calvino 1992, 292) and to engage in all manner of measuring activities. Yet, Agilulf's taxonomic mentality does not stem from his confidence in the existence of a countable, quantifiable and classifiable reality but rather from uncertainty and doubt, from a recognition that like his own body, the world at large verges constantly toward non-existence. His rationalizing operations essentially amount to a form of self-therapy since it is precisely when he feels on the brink of "melting away completely" that he begins "to count; trees, leaves, stones, lances, pine cones, anything in front of him" (299). The idea that Agilulf's speculative gymnastics do not originate in any authentic belief in the superiority of reason but rather in the necessity of negotiating his non-existence is most humorously communicated by the deferring tactics he employs in order to keep Priscilla's erotic yearnings at bay. Thus, the moment the word "love" passes her lips, he plunges "into a dissertation of the passion of love" and "the mention of bed" gives him a pretext for delivering a pedantic lecture on "the difficult art of bed making" (352–353). Agilulf's quasi-scientific activities, therefore, do not point to an unquestionable, objective grasp of reality but are, in fact, symptomatic of a need to shield a reality which, as it happens, is an unreality — an existence based on non-existence. His insistence, at banquets, on having "put in front of him fresh crockery and cutlery, plates big and small, porringers, beakers of every size and shape, endless forks and spoons and knives" (335) although, of course, he is not in a position to consume even a single morsel of food, neatly sums up his need to buttress his absence with the paraphernalia of presence.

If individual histories unfold under the sign of uncertainty, collective history, the trilogy proposes, does not progress according to rational rhythms either. In fact, it is wholly dominated by the arbitrariness and blindness of power. In *The Cloven Viscount*, for instance, the instant Medardo is brought into the presence of the Emperor, the latter capriciously declares: "let him be made lieutenant at once" (6). History ultimately amounts to vacuous rituals no more meaningful than the "senseless clustering of insects" (298). Relatedly, it is time and again reduced to bureaucratic paperwork and the whims of senile rulers. Apparently "invincible paladins" spend their time sitting behind tables "covered with papers" (295) as Charlemagne himself, having "done so many wars," invariably gets "confused between one and another" and does not really even remember which one he is "fighting now' (337). Wars do not solve anything, nor do they advance any just, rational causes. As the skeptical Torrismund points out, "the war will last for centuries, and nobody will win or lose" (332).

Simultaneously, Calvino resolutely eschews the idea of historiography as a transparent window open onto the passage of time—and hence an immediate record of events—by emphasizing that the contents of a historical account, like those of any text, are inevitably mediated by language: namely, an arbitrary system of signs arranged on the basis of artificial codes and conventions. The meaning accrued by a history book is merely a contingent product of its textual encoding. This message is underlined throughout the trilogy by the presentation of the three heroes' experiences as inextricable from the fictional tapestry in which they are inscribed: in other words, as circumstantial effects of textuality. To drive this point home with incontrovertible vim, the writer accords writing a vibrant life of its own. It is not uncommon, in Calvino's narrative, for the fictional world of writing to take over so-called reality. In *Baron in the Trees*, for example, the subordination of the world of action to the world of writing is dramatized through the character of the brigand Gian dei Brughi who, having been introduced by Cosimo to the art of reading, becomes so engrossed in his books as to relinquish totally his commitments as an outlaw. Paradoxically, it is the domestic, bourgeois and cushy world of Samuel Richardson's novels that most fascinates Gian and indirectly leads to his undoing.

In this regard, Calvino's approach to history echoes Linda Hutcheon's assessment, in *The Politics of Postmodernism*, of the attitude to the past cumulatively exhibited by postmodern fiction with an interest in the relationship between raw events and textually constructed facts — between lived history and ideologically ratified historiography. Especially relevant to Calvino's own opus is Hutcheon's contention that in postmodern fiction of that ilk, the past is posited not as "something to be escaped, avoided, or controlled" but rather "something with which we must come to terms and such a confrontation involves an acknowledgment of limitations well as power." Crucial to this venture is the acceptance that human beings may "only have access to the past today through its traces — its documents, the testimony of witnesses, and other archival materials. In other words, we only have representations of the past from which to construct our narratives or explanations. In a very real sense, postmodernism reveals a desire to understand present culture as the product of previous representations. The representation of history becomes the history of representation" (Hutcheon 55).

One of the most distinctive strategies adopted by Calvino in the trilogy in order to articulate these ideas consists of his steady delineation of manifold parallels, analogies and correspondences between seemingly opposite personalities and forms of behavior. Relatedly, the writer tenaciously refrains from either censuring his villains with inordinate harshness or showering excessive praise on his goodies. Determined to steer clear of stultifying binary oppositions, he assiduously proposes that actions are more often than not determined by inchoate motives and inexplicable eccentricities, and are therefore more likely to be understood — albeit approximately — through imaginative intuition than through stern ratiocination. Like Bertolt Brecht, moreover, Calvino believes that any work (literary, dramatic, pictorial) that aspires to fulfill a social function should first of all aim to be entertaining. Without entertainment, no political or ideological message is likely to have any durable impact. In fact, the author maintains, there is nothing automatically objectionable about a work that even functions solely as entertainment. Commenting on *Our Ancestors*, specifically, Calvino has indeed stated that it "would fully satisfy" him "as a writer" if readers were to peruse the three novels "simply for enjoyment" rather than to "interpret" them (Calvino 1992, ix).

At the same time as they audaciously expose the inanities of history through humor and irony, the three novels also draw attention in a more elliptical fashion to the arbitrariness with which accounts of history are typically written. They do so by configuring the entire histories of their three protagonists' worlds in accordance with those characters' preposterous anomalies and quirks. Accordingly, each story is distinguished by specific rhetorical and iconographic effects meant to throw those personality traits into relief. The first novel relies throughout on images of maiming, crippling and splitting that build toward the metamorphosis of the whole natural domain into an assortment of splintered beings. Doctors, for their part, manipulate injured bodies as though they were simply pieces in a gruesome puzzle, metaphorically analogous to the *disjecta membra* of their barmy societies: "a saw here, a stitch there, leaks plugged, veins turned inside out like gloves ... what caused most confusion were intestines; once unrolled they just couldn't be got back" (9–10). In the wake of Medardo's excursions, moreover, pears, mushrooms, dandelions, daisies, squirrels, butterflies, bats, and jellyfish, to name but a few creatures, are all found cut perfectly in half: paradoxically, the Viscount uses the same strategy to inspire both dread and love. The second novel revolves around images of intermittent visibility, reminiscent of the flickers and glimpses of light one may catch among luxuriant foliage. The narrator recalls that prior to the felling of the woods, "leaves and branches" were at all times interposed between people and the sky above (102). The whole world is here figured as a tracery of prismatic glimmers, shifting patterns of light and shadow. The third novel hinges on tropes designed to quiz the reliability of appearances at the ethical and ideological levels no less than on the physical plane. The ghastly spectacle of morcellated anatomies that litter the plain in the aftermath of strife renders the solidity of corporeal reality at large questionable, as though everything material had been irreparably contaminated by Agilulf's own non-existence, and his "unseizable nature" had somehow "extended over the whole field of battle" (313–314).

Historiography's whimsical dogmatism deteriorates into undiluted totalitarianism when the drive to shape the whole of reality in accordance with a single privileged image turns into a manic determination to shackle human diversity to the dictates of sameness. In *The Cloven Viscount*, this state of affairs is metaphorically encapsulated by Medardo's warped world view. Torn between a feeling of resentment toward everything whole, conducive to a desire to bestow upon his fellow creatures the same fate of dividedness as the one allotted to him, and an arrogant sense of superiority, Medardo muses: "If only I could halve every whole thing ... so that everyone could escape from their obtuse and ignorant wholeness. ... there's beauty and knowledge and justice only in what's been cut to shreds" (34). Although the Viscount is driven by an insane agenda, there is something ironically salutary about his stance insofar as his exposure of the stupidity of wholeness adumbrates the failure which awaits any venture striving for totality in an alienated, ontologically divided world — the type of quest to which official recordings of history are notoriously devoted. No less importantly, Calvino intimates that a genuine acceptance of dividedness should not amount to a clear-cut split between a good half and a bad half but rather result in the dynamic dialogue of opposites within one and every form. As Giuseppe Bonura observes, "being cloven holds certain advantages: one may believe blindly in anything one does. Blindly, but not dialectically" (Bonura, 93). Hence, good and evil must eventually converge in the wiser and sadder figure of the sutured Viscount, as a reintegrated and heightened apprehension of the world's simultaneous foolishness and fascination. At the same time, however, the finale of *The Cloven Viscount* also functions as a trenchant metaphor for the limitations of historiography. Officially recorded accounts of events, Calvino proposes, do not make history either truer or more easily graspable, any more than the construction of "a whole Viscount" could ever be "enough to make the world whole" (Calvino 1992, 71). Healing one single rift in the fabric of society is obviously not sufficient to improve its overall structure. The novel's conclusion thus suggests that its protagonist's dismemberment cannot be smoothly exorcized for the reason that it inherently symbolizes the as yet incurable fate of alienation suffered by all individuals, and most pointedly by artists and intellectuals, in the cultural milieu that Calvino sought to explore at the time, and whose history he aimed to reconceptualize in unprecedented ways.

The Viscount's schizophrenic attitude to the world is echoed by Cosimo's inner conflicts in *Baron in the Trees*. The character's unparalleled "stubbornness" (Calvino 1992, 78) and herculean animosity "against the family ... society ... the world in general" (81) compound to form a picture of "superhuman tenacity" (85) which cannot, however, alleviate his ultimate loneliness: "I'm on my own, and each acts for himself," he dolefully comments at a climactic point in the adventure (131). Politically, the Baron's escape could be read both as a disengagement from reality on the part of the disillusioned intellectual or artist, and as a form of engagement, requiring critical detachment from the sphere of everyday affairs. Cosimo is thus cut off from the rhythms of political reality and, paradoxically, able to mobilize collective action, as borne out, for instance, by his anti-fire and anti-wolf campaigns, and by the miniature revolution he instigates among the people of Ombrosa. Yet, if Cosimo's experience is to some degree an allegory of political commitment, the tale's ending also reminds us that such an allegory is ultimately an insubstantial weave of ephemeral arabesques, no more tangible than a "thread of ink ... swarming with cancellations, corrections, doodles, blots and gaps" (284). The whole adventure's equation to a fantastical cavalcade of signs racing over the blank page casts a shadow of doubt over the viability of effective practical action. At the same time, the Baron's unanchored subjectivity metaphorically alludes to any individual's lack of reliable moorings in either personal or collective reality.

Just as the split Medardo is torn between jealousy and contempt for any whole entity, the incorporeal Agilulf likewise oscillates between conflicting perceptions of his fellow creatures: "the bodies of people with bodies gave him a sense of unease not unlike envy, but also a stab of pride, of contemptuous superiority" (292). However, even as he is filled with disgust at the grubby and unrefined appearance of embodied humanity, he is still prey to an acute yearning to participate in their natural, albeit animalistic, routines. At sunset, in particular, Agilulf feels "isolated" and "suddenly naked": he is a "model soldier; but disliked by all" (290). The Knight's daily pattern allows "no relief" for he cannot know what it is like to "shut the eyes, lose consciousness, plunge into emptiness for a few hours" (291). It is not altogether surprising that it should be the sight of bodies — particularly of unconscious, relaxed, and defenseless bodies — that triggers most intensely the Knight's contrasting emotions. The body indeed encapsulates humanity at its simultaneously most vulnerable and most delectable. Though human ambitions, values and ritual practices may be successfully counterfeited by the empty simulacrum of the Knight's non-existent being, the body itself remains stubbornly resistant to any strategy of simulation. Agilulf's armor is patently a mask designed to conceal not a presence but an absence. While it may successfully hide the non-existence of anything tangible within its gleaming surfaces, it cannot, however, disguise the Knight's awareness of the gaping absence upon which his very identity hinges.

What troubles Agilulf is not his lack of an objective body — the body probed, dissected and analyzed by anatomical science, so to speak — since, on the functional level, he is capable of operating far more efficiently than any of his physiologically concrete counterparts. Nor is he particularly concerned with his lack of an aesthetic body, as the physical surface from which one may derive narcissistic self-gratification and which inspires desire in others. Agilulf has, after all, his own highly accomplished, if remarkably unconventional, ways of experiencing pleasure. In fact, what the Knight appears to miss, at least in moments of dejection, is that facet of corporeality which Francis Jacques terms "the body-self, something so insistently *ours* that it is confused with the feeling we have that there is a 'substance of our presence'" (Jacques, 17). Agilulf's predicament, in this respect as in virtually any other, is obviously extremely ambiguous: deprived of a body-self which he may experience as an intrinsically personal property, he is dispossessed of the pleasure of self-presence. Yet, insofar as such a pleasure is inevitably delusory, given that nobody's presence has any unequivocal substance in Calvino's universe, and that the body's material being may only, at best, foster an illusion of palpability, the Knight is placed in a privileged position which allows him to transcend the trap of imaginary misrecognition. This may explain his lingering sense of self-worth.

Furthermore, Agilulf's scornful feelings of superiority over embodied humanity are largely justified by the fact that his aseptic perfection is the object of desire animating many corporeal subjects: primarily Bradamante, who is said to have "taken to the life of chivalry due to her love for all that was strict, exact, severe, conforming to moral rule and ... to exact precision and movement." However, while the Knight may actually attain to these ideals thanks to his non-existence, carnalized creatures may not. The amazon is herself a bundle of paradoxes: for all her devotion to strictness and morality, her sexual behavior is proverbially unruly and promiscuous, and her tent "the untidiest in the whole camp." Moreover, whereas "knightly chivalry is a fine thing ... knights themselves are coarse, accustomed to doing great things in a slapdash way" (Calvino 1992, 327): in other words, they cannot even begin to emulate but can only, at best, provide a farcical travesty of Agilulf's hypersanitized purity. The fundamental difference between Bradamante and Agilulf is that her cleanliness is only a superficial effect conjured up by her shimmering armor, whereas the Knight is "clean inside and out" (330). Torrismund insinuates the possibility of Agilulf himself being a ghostly projection of human fantasies, a "made-up job." When Raimbaud, alarmed by these remarks, asks whether Agilulf is then able to perform "by his name alone," Torrismund ripostes: "here the names are false too" (332). That Calvino views naming as an unreliable and specious procedure is exemplified by the presence, throughout the trilogy, of several multi-named characters. Medardo, for example, is known as "the Lame One, the Maimed One, the Bereft One ... the Sideless One ... the Half-Deaf One ... the Buttockless One" (31–32). Gurduloo's name "varies according to the place he's in" and "every name flows over him without sticking" (304). Sophronia is also "Azira; or Sister Palmyra," depending on whether she is "in a Sultan's harem or a convent" (372).

In its adventurous effort to reimagine history, *Our Ancestors* persistently throws into relief the empirical world's inherent inadequacies by emphasizing its protagonists' perverse, yet undeniable, charisma. This quality is ultimately responsible for placing the three heroes onto a much more complex plane of being than the one enjoyed by the putatively normal people in the tales. In comparison with the protagonists, the characters that surround them come across as intentionally formulaic cut-outs in spite of their putatively higher materiality. They are hence excluded from the possibility of experiencing anything — sublime or trivial as it may be — with the same degree of intensity of which the heroes are capable: "they're just paper, you can put your finger through them" (331). Agilulf, as already argued, is preternaturally immaculate: his embodied companions can hardly even begin to aspire to his unique ontological status. Even after Agilulf's legendary armor has been disassembled, his body remains unsullied since an obvious corollary of non-existence is the exemption from the process of decomposition. This phenomenon, citing Ernest Jones, could be interpreted in line with the "Roman Catholic pronouncement that the bodies of saints do not decompose." Yet, it could also, less flatteringly for Agilulf, be read in terms of the Greek Orthodox Church's "dogma that it is the bodies of wicked, unholy, and especially excommunicated, persons which do not decompose" (Jones, 401). The body's failure to putrefy, in the latter scenario, is taken as evidence for the soul's inability to rest, to be at peace. Immunity from the phenomenon of decay could therefore be read as an absence of death which also amounts, implicitly, to an eternal curse. Furthermore, it intimates the dead person's enduring power, albeit in concealed form, and its ability to go on haunting the living beyond the boundaries of human temporality. Indeed, Raimbaud obsessively begs many a knight he meets in his peregrinations to lift their vizards, in the hope "to find himself facing an emptiness" (Calvino 1992, 378). In *Baron in the Trees*, similarly, when Cosimo at last vanishes into the sky attached to a balloon, he leaves without granting his fellow mortals "even the satisfaction of seeing him return to earth a corpse" (283).

What makes Agilulf so irresistible, most notably to Bradamante, Raimbaud and Priscilla, is that his non-existence seems to allow everything, to offer no resistance. This is obviously a misconception on the part of the Knight's infatuated followers, as Agilulf does not or cannot fulfill anybody's desires: what he bestows on them is the dubious gift of absence. Paradoxically, it is precisely his unfathomable emptiness that allows the other characters to go on fantasizing about endless, unexplored and forbidden possibilities of sensual satisfaction, and thus increase with every move his unearthly attraction. Pursuing this argument further, it could be argued that awe, passion, dread and desire of the kind inspired not only by the Knight but, in fact, by all three protagonists of the trilogy, are metaphors for repressed sexuality and emotions. In this regard, Calvino's version of history stands out as a daring attempt to rehabilitate aspects of humanity that conventional historiography has routinely ostracized from its venerable tomes in the service of propriety, rationality and discipline. Repression and desire, it should be emphasized, are not exclusive attributes of frail humanity but extend to the heroes themselves. The bad Medardo's feats of greed, mindless aggression and calculated cruelty, for example, are intersected by a morbidly possessive kind of love. Drawing on Maurice Richardson's suggestive account of the psychosexual features of vampirism (another powerful articulation of the interplay of presence and absence), it could be argued that in Calvino's chivalric world, "behavior smacks of the unconscious world of infantile sexuality with what Freud called its polymorph perverse tendencies" (Richardson, 418). It is through his reinscription of traditionally excluded or repressed aspects of human existence into the flow of history that Calvino ultimately engineers his most radical intervention in the domain of alternate historiography. Irrational fears, passions and longings of the type recorded by Calvino's off-center history indeed become the platform whence he launches a whole elaborate discourse woven from the interprenetration of textuality and eroticism.

Our Ancestors' take on textuality is informed by the practice of narrative deferral and by strategies of displacement which, though pervasive throughout the three novels, become especially prominent in their treatment of eros. Eroticism as articulated in the tales represents *en abyme* the embedding of experience in the act of writing since love, passion, lust and desire are fundamental means by which the characters construct their fictional roles, by which plots are conceived and advanced, and by which the compositional process itself is enabled. Medardo's decision to fall in love with Pamela, Cosimo's sudden awareness of his attraction toward Viola, and Raimbaud's mock-epiphanic vision of Bradamante are just a few examples of crucial turning-points in the stories in which erotic urges serve to define the characters' identities, supply them with roles within the overall yarn and, most importantly, sanction the forever postponed, open-ended and necessarily inconclusive nature of their exploits. A fictional identity predicated upon a character's erotic yearnings is also, inevitably, an identity constructed around lack, around the perception of an inexplicable and unpluggable gap. This is paradigmatically borne out, in *Baron in the Trees*, by Cosimo's inability to grasp, as he gazes upon the girls of Ombrosa, "why something that he was looking for was there in all of them and not there completely in any one of them" (Calvino 1992, 193). Even after the Baron has known love, the unacknowledged, repressed memory of Viola lingers in his unconscious as an intimation of the endless deferral of satisfaction, "of the waiting that can be prolonged beyond life" (220). Frustrating as this scenario of potentially eternal expectancy may be, it is also the case that such an unlimiting of the erotic experience constitutes a way of circumventing certain familiar obstacles with which writers intent on the faithful depiction of eros have to contend: namely, as Tommasina Gabriele observes, "the narrow morals and obsessions of a distorted societal view of sex; the mythicizing of sex in a desexualized society and the difficulty of avoiding tired, pretty clichés in trying to write positively about Eros; the human reaction to this primitive and frightening impulse; and the struggle to represent this sacred, unspeakable domain of human experience" (Gabriele, 63).

As noted by Calvino in the essay "Definitions of Territories: Eroticism," an amorous idiom capable of registering not only the tame and sentimental nuances of sexuality but also, more vitally, "laughter — systematic mockery, giggles of self-derision, the convulsed grimace" (Calvino 1987, 70) can ultimately produce a textual matrix in which eros is not the narrative's passive subject matter, but rather its actively structuring principle. In *The Non-Existent Knight*, Sister Theodora's authorial persona epitomizes the collusion of erotic impulses and textual productivity, for it is her very passion that guides, permeates and indeed shapes in a physical sense the act of writing. Sexual abstinence and unfulfilled desire are thus metaphorically equated to an inability to write, to let the words surge forth: "a time comes when the pen merely grates in dusty ink and not a drop of life flows" (Calvino 1992, 334). The unusual nun's predicament echoes Roland Barthes' assertion that the relationship between eros and writing is inevitably complicated by the disparity between the desire to write one's love out, so to speak, and the awareness that love can be neither contained nor indeed sublimated by textuality. This inconsistency is ultimately determined by the loving subject's otherness in and from itself, which results in an inability to make the text incarnate the unified identity which the subject patently lacks. *A Lover's Discourse* communicates this message most passionately: "I am both too big and too weak for writing: I am *alongside it*, for writing is always dense, violent, indifferent to the infantile ego which solicits it. Love has of course, a complicity with my language (which maintains it), but it cannot be *lodged* in my writing. I cannot *write myself*" (Barthes 1990b, 97). These reflections lead to the melancholy conclusion that "writing compensates for nothing, sublimates nothing ... it is precisely *there where you are not*— this is the beginning of writing" (100).

Theodora realizes that although writing may offer vicarious pleasures, it delivers no conclusive truths, for "life begins again at the end of the page, and one realizes that one knew nothing whatsoever" (Calvino 1992, 327). The unnegotiably incomplete nature of all writing, and erotic writing in particular, is here seen as a source of unrelieved frustration. However, the provisionality of the narrative experience also offers scope for practically limitless experimentation and for the construction and adoption of alternative roles. Calvino's tales highlight that none of these roles is ultimately truer or more dependable than any of the others, because all identities only exist insofar as they are embodied discursively. Thus, Calvino's spurious sister, a flagrantly unreliable narrator, repeatedly claims to have no knowledge of either sexual or military matters and to have undertaken her narration "as a penance." In fact, she turns out to be the female warrior Bradamante: a woman who, as noted, is well-acquainted with sex and war alike. The "frenzy" which goads her on writing "at breakneck speed" (380) is the indomitable hankering of the loving subject for the absent beloved. The apotheosis of the writer Theodora's narrative crusade comes to coincide with the culmination of the warrior Bradamante's erotic quest for, in reaching the book's end, Theodora simultaneously reaches the point of reunion with the object of desire in her Bradamante incarnation. The very pace of her writing has been dictated all along by her impatient striving toward Raimbaud, as though to suggest that loving and storytelling are virtually coterminous, that amatory pursuit equates to the curve of the written tale advancing toward its climax. Calvino deliberately leaves the story open, thus achieving two purposes at once: he highlights the unresolved character of a narrative experience predicated on the fluctuations of desire and, no less significantly, he succeeds in maintaining a sense of anticipation and tantalizing suspense, thus avoiding the trap into which erotic literature so often falls. "So-called 'erotic' books," Barthes warns in *The Pleasure of the Text*, "*represent* not so much the erotic scene as the expectation of it, the preparation for it, its ascent; that is what makes them 'exciting'; and when the scene occurs, naturally there is disappointment, deflation" (Barthes 1990a, 58).

That eros should provide the paradigm for a narrative of deferral in which identity and action are functions of the materiality of writing is perhaps not surprising, especially in the light of Barthes' important distinction between "reasonable" and "amorous" feelings: "*reasonable* sentiment: everything works out but nothing lasts. *Amorous* sentiment: nothing works out, but it keeps going on" (Barthes 1990b, 140). The capricious nature of erotic behavior is, moreover, intrinsically discursive, an offshoot of "*Discursus*— originally the action of running here and there, comings and goings, measures taken, 'plots and plans'" (3). Deferral is also, of course, one of the most salient features of chivalric romances. In this genre, the heroes' experiences do not tend, uniformly, toward a grand culmination, a sudden burst of stored-up energy, but rather err, episodically, from one partial dénouement to the next. Structural principles of duplication, repetition, recapitulation and symmetry, as clearly indicated by the closing pages of all three of the novels under scrutiny, are instrumental to the orchestration of such a multi-climactic narrative web. Calvino capitalizes on the attributes of flimsiness and transience conventionally ascribed to the romantic genre in the modern period but he also aims at recapturing its much more complex medieval connotations.

The spirit of the medieval romance is probably best defined by comparison and in contradistinction with the character of another dominant contemporaneous genre, the epic. As W. P. Ker points out in *Epic and Romance*, while the former is fundamentally defined by weight, solidity, sobriety and a sense of heroic defence of human values against all odds, epitomized by the coupling of feudal loyalty and the fight for Christendom, the latter displays a pervasive atmosphere of mystery and fantasy. Fighting itself, though central to the action of the romance, is prompted not so much by lofty spiritual ideals as by the unreasoned readiness of the Wandering Knight (Ker). More recently, David Lodge has likewise contrasted the epic and the romance with reference to an explicitly sexual analogy. "Epic," like "tragedy," is said to "move inexorably to ... an essentially *male* climax — a single, explosive discharge of accumulated tension. Romance, in contrast, is not structured this way. It has not one climax, but many, the pleasure of this text comes and comes and comes again. No sooner is one crisis in the fortunes of the hero averted than a new one presents itself; no sooner has one mystery been solved than another is raised; no sooner has one adventure been concluded than another begins. The narrative questions open and close, open and close.... Romance is a multiple orgasm" (Lodge 322–323).

The paratactical agglomeration of discontinuous and often incongruous episodes favored by the romance preempts the mapping of the narrative as a journey advancing toward a privileged center of meaning, pursuing instead a potentially infinite horizon. Moreover, the active and martial world of epic, peopled primarily by masculine or masculinized hero(in)es, is challenged by the realm of romance through the introduction of women and erotic affairs as pivotal textual components. In his evaluation of the poem *Orlando Furioso* by Ludovico Ariosto (1474–1533), offered in the introduction to his inspired retelling of the old tale, Calvino views the work as a pluricentric Renaissance pseudo-epic clearly indebted to the medieval romance's strategies of capricious aggregation and digressive complication. Calvino seems especially fascinated with the transition from "the severe military epos" grounded in the *Chanson de Roland* to the "romantic and adventurous" literature which makes Charlemagne's paladins and their exploits "popular" in an explicitly amative vein (Calvino 1995, 11). The writer identifies the nascent moments of this shift with the poem *Orlando Innamorato*, composed by Matteo Maria Boiardo (1434–1494). It is Boiardo's innovative move that transmutes Orlando — and, by extension, any classic epic hero — from a chaste, ironclad feudal warrior into a radically displaced entity swayed by passion and desire. Ariosto, however, is not simply elaborating on Boiardo's agenda when he turns Orlando, already suspiciously enamored with Angelica, into a raving lunatic whose absence from Charlemagne's army endangers the fate of Christendom at large. In fact, more crucially for Calvino, Ariosto's main lesson lies with his ironical attitude toward the ultimate significance of chivalric endeavor. Ariosto, argues the writer, "does not believe in chivalric exploits, and yet invests all his efforts, passions, and desire for perfection into the representation of skirmishes between the paladins and the infidel in a poem conceived with painstaking devotion" (19–20).

Ariosto's perspective on knightly excellence is clearly the inspirational force behind Calvino's own ambivalent representation of chivalric behavior as an unholy admixture of purity and altruism, on the one hand, and coarseness and solipsism on the other hand. No less influential, in the context of Calvino's reworking of themes and rhythms peculiar to the romance genre, is Ariosto's articulation of a picture of humanity predicated on the coexistence of irreconcilable extremes. At one end of the spectrum stands Orlando, a character traditionally deemed larger than life both in his military prowess and in his ability to withstand sexual temptation, yet also capable of descending into "the blindest bestiality." At the other end stands

Astolfo, the character responsible for retrieving the mad Orlando's lost sanity from the Moon, and for reintroducing it into the paladin's body so as to secure his rehabilitation as a Christian hero. As Calvino intimates, Astolfo's conduct and mentality mirror those of his Renaissance creator. At the same time, they also capture Calvino's own proclivities. This is suggested by his portrayal as someone who "never reveals to us anything about himself, about what he thinks or feels and yet — in fact, perhaps for this very reason — the Ariostesque spirit (this presence that does not let itself be seized or defined) is primarily detectable in him, the lunar explorer who is never surprised by anything, who lives surrounded by the marvelous, and avails himself of enchanted objects, magical books, metamorphoses and winged horses with the gracefulness of a butterfly but always to achieve utterly practical and rational aims" (23). Calvino's debt to Ariosto's iconoclastic poem will be discussed in depth in Chapter 5.

It is in reimagining the established genres of the epic and the romance that Calvino most ardently embraces the task of reconfiguring history itself through a synthesis of storytelling and eros by turning sanctioned ethical values on their head through carnivalesque disruptions and sleights of hand. By selectively appropriating elements of the romance form that suit his aesthetic and political vision and distorting them at will, the writer brings to fruition what Northrop Frye has termed "the central principle of ironic myth ... as a parody of romance: the application of romantic, mythical forms to a more realistic content which fits them in unexpected ways" (Frye, 223). Emphasis is consistently laid on the wayward and giddy rhythms of the wandering knight's movements. Errantry and erraticness combine, through their shared etymology, to seal the fate of perpetual mutability and displacement to which that character type is doomed. Writing specifically about "Amorous errantry," Barthes notes that although this amounts to "a fatality," it also, as Calvino's tales emphatically demonstrate, "has its comical side: it resembles a ballet, more or less nimble according to the velocity of the fickle subject" (Barthes 1990b, 102). The errant/erratic pairing conjures up a panorama of radical instability, wherein to err is both to ramble and to blunder, to rove and to be led astray, guided only by the capricious imperative of the moment.

The deferring thrust of the chivalric romance is, to a considerable extent, dictated by its involvement in the ethos of courtly love, a highly codified cluster of rituals according to which the hero may only worship the beloved from a distance, wander for her sake from one exploit to the next longing to please her, yet also aware that no victory, no show of courage or bravado, will ever make the Lady descend from her unapproachable pedestal. There are, needless to say, various ways of interpreting the psychosexual implications of this phenomenon. Barthes, for one, views the dynamics of courtly love in terms of a self-denying dedication to the loved object which makes any attempt at self-assertion on the part of the lover a transgression punishable by the least tractable of emotions — guilt: "any fissure within Devotion is a fault.... This fault occurs whenever I make any gesture of independence with regard to the loved object; each time I attempt, in order to break my servitude, to 'think for myself' ... I feel guilty" (118). Jacques Lacan, for his part, interprets courtly love as a twin phenomenon of displacement and sublimation. Arguing that the impossibility of satisfaction is the defining attribute of desire in any form, he suggests that an articulation of desire which deliberately pivots on, and legitimates itself through, notions of unfulfillment is a way of making a virtue out of necessity: namely, of rationalizing the reality of omission, unattainability and deprivation, on the delusory assumption that presence may only proceed from the appropriation of absence. Courtly love, in this perspective, is "an altogether refined way of making up for the absence of sexual relation by pretending that it is we who put an obstacle to it" and hence "the only way of coming off elegantly from the absence of sexual relation" (Lacan 1990, 141).

Calvino brings the guilt factor into play in his own distinctive fashion by insinuating that the devoted lover can never quite appreciate or do justice to the beloved's autonomous being, that what he pursues is a phantom and that, as a result, in aspiring to please the beloved, the lover is actually performing an autoerotic play likely to engender remorse and self-doubt. The lover is ultimately oblivious to the beloved's independent existence. At the same time, the trilogy estranges its heroes from the opportunity of "coming off elegantly" from the absence of self-fulfillment insofar as all of the male characters appear to be enticed not by etherealized icons of femininity but rather by full-bodied women. What is ultimately paradoxical, and possibly subversive, about Calvino's handling of romantic eros is that it simultaneously throws into relief the inconsummate desire of conventionally sketched errant knights, and the active, decidedly anti–Platonic sexual urges of the longed-for women: Pamela, Viola, Bradamante and Priscilla have clear aspirations when it comes to physical fulfillment, and it is the male heroes, if anything, who fall short of satisfying them or succeed in doing so only by circuitous routes. "If you want me," declares Pamela, "come and meet me here in the woods"

(Calvino 1992, 38); yet, Medardo wishes her shut up in his tower. "Come down and give me a push, now, do," taunts Viola as a child (94); Cosimo, however, is unable to leave his multifoliate domain. Later, "gossip has it that in Paris [Viola] passes from one love to another, in such a rapid succession that no one can call her his own and consider himself privileged" (237) and she becomes renowned for the "violent" character of her "demonstrations of love." Although the Baron can now partake of these favors, he is nonetheless unable to share one of her greatest loves, the "equestrian passion," which he can only observe from a distance with a mixture of "jealousy and rancour" (234).

Priscilla's explicit encouragement of Agilulf to take full advantage of her widowed status results, as mentioned, in interminable disquisitions about the nature of love and the art of bed-making: a spot of moon-gazing is the closest the couple comes to anything remotely erotic. Paradoxically, the widow, perhaps sufficiently replete with conventional pleasures to welcome less orthodox alternatives such as "entwining her legs and arms around [the] greaves" of her non-existent lover's armor (354), sums the whole experience up as "paradise" (356). (For fans of J. G. Ballard, it is worth pointing out that there is something elliptically Ballardian, and specifically *Crash*-flavored, about this description.) What Priscilla seems to be deriving pleasure from is precisely the metallic, rather than fleshly, texture of the Knight's body, its abstractly athletic and purely speculative robustness. The orgasms brought about by Agilulf constitute a text of physical *jouissance* woven through eminently non-physical procedures, of movement predicated upon motionlessness, of cracked plenitude. Barthes might as well have been reviewing Priscilla's sexual/textual pleasures when he observed that "The pleasure of the text is not necessarily of a triumphant, heroic, muscular type. No need to throw out one's chest. My pleasure can very well take the form of a drift. *Drifting* occurs whenever *I do not respect the whole*, and whenever ... like a cork on the waves, I remain motionless, pivoting on the *intractable* bliss that binds me to the text (to the world)" (Barthes 1990a, 18). What Priscilla seems to recognize, by default, is that "what pleasure wants is the site of a loss, the seam, the cut, the deflation, the *dissolve* which seizes the subject in the midst of bliss" (7).

The pleasure of the cut is virtually indistinguishable, in Calvino's alternate vision of history, from a riotous erasure of conventional distinctions between subjects and objects. As Medardo and his squire Kurt ride through the plague-ridden battlefields on their way to the Emperor, Kurt remarks: "one can't tell which died first, bird or man, or who tore the other to bits" (Calvino 1992, 4), thus intimating a gruesome coalition of human subjects and non-human objects. The erasure of conventional dividing lines between subject and object is tragicomically dramatized through the character of Gurduloo, who goes about cackling "Qua! Qua!" not because he thinks he is a duck but because "he thinks the ducks are him" (302); who, while fishing, identifies in turn with the net and with the fish; who finds it hard to realize that he is the one "who is to eat the soup, and not the soup" him (305) and that "the sea is not supposed to be inside him but he inside the sea" (360); and who will answer equally readily to the names of "goat" and "torrent" (304). (*Blackadder*'s unforgettable Baldrick comes readily to mind in scenes such as these.) Baffling as this may seem, Gurduloo, with his unbounded subjectivity, is the only character willing, or indeed emotionally furnished, to take stock of Agilulf's impenetrability:

"It's my master I'm looking for," says Gurduloo.
"In that flask?"
"My master is a person who doesn't exist; so he cannot exist as much in a flask as in a suit of armour" [378–379].

Erotic deferral and the collapse of conventional binaries are primarily dramatized through Calvino's insistence on the physical attributes of the written word. On one level, Calvino's emphasis on the material features of writing calls attention to the role played by the body and all its senses in the narrative process. It thus posits what Barthes terms an "aesthetic of textual pleasure" as "*writing aloud*": an act performed by "the *grain* of the voice" (Barthes 1990a, 66–67). Barthes' emphasis on the acoustic dimension of writing bears affinities with Theodora's effort to impress sound effects onto the page, the "tock-tock, tock-tock" of Agilulf's light horse, contrasted with the "tututum!" of Gurduloo's heavy gallop (Calvino 1992, 345). In more general terms, the analogy between writing and music is everywhere suffused throughout Calvino's descriptive repertoire, as borne out by the memorable passage from *Baron in the Trees* where "the silence of the countryside composes itself in the eardrum into a toccata of sounds" (142). Silence is presumed to contain, potentially, the whole polyphonic range which emanates from it, as presence may only emerge from a background of absence. Throughout *Our Ancestors*, writing is posited as the eminently material mechanism through which an uninterrupted, homogeneous continuum is broken up and symbolic articulation is accordingly enabled. Writing is a fracturing, spacing, rupturing and broadly differentiating process that occurs in nature no less than it does in culture.

In this respect, Jacques Derrida argues against the assumption that writing is an eminently cultural phenomenon to which so-called primitive peoples are oblivious. In *Of Grammatology*, he comments specifically on Claude Lévi-Strauss's study of the Nambikwara Indians, presumed by the anthropologist to be a genuinely primitive band of nomads unaware of the techniques of writing. Derrida highlights the importance of an apparently marginal detail in Lévi-Strauss's account — that is, the existence of a crudely marked trail traversing the Nambikwara's otherwise virgin territory — and proceeds to argue that the trail is itself evidence for the existence of a form of writing within the tribe: "one should meditate upon all of the following together: writing as the possibility of the road and of difference, the history of writing and the history of the road, of the rupture, of the *via rupta*, of the path that is broken, beaten, *fracta*, of the space of reversibility and of repetition traced by the opening, the divergence from, and the violent spacing, of nature, of the natural, savage, salvage, forest. The *silva* is savage, the *via rupta* is written, discerned, and inscribed violently as difference, as form imposed on the *hyle*, in the forest, in wood as matter; it is difficult to imagine that access to the possibility of the roadmap is not at the same time access to writing" (Derrida 1984, 107–8). Sister Theodora likewise draws attention to the act of writing as the creation of material spaces and differences by frequently referring to the pressure of the blank page which she must fill in order to bridge the gap between the world of chivalry and her own monastic existence. She does so by supplying pictures in which her literal writing (i.e., the organization of black marks on the white page) is equated to a sort of archetypal writing which manifests itself, as was the case with the Nambikwara, in the ruptures and cuts of the natural landscape: "To tell [the story] as I would like this blank page would have to bristle with reddish rocks, flake with pebbly sand, sprout sparse juniper trees. In the midst, on a twisting ill-marked track, I would set Agilulf.... With my pen I should also trace faint dents in the paper to represent the slither of an invisible snake through grass" (Calvino 1992, 357).

Writing as understood by Theodora is therefore a predominantly physical experience, the creation of traces and spaces, the intermingling of presences and absences on the amorphous blank sheet. Writing is also, by implication, the materiality of the line, an ideation of the entire world in the image of drawing. This vision fully validates Calvino's contention, advanced in the essay "The Pen in the First Person," that the graphic sign has a corporeality, indeed an "aggressiveness of its own" (Calvino 1987,

293). As the interrelations among Theodora's various subplots become increasingly complex and the pace of the characters' movements across the continents gains frantic momentum, the nun decides to turn the page into a "map" (Calvino 1992, 358), to indicate the "sea" by "scoring ... wavy lines" into its texture (359), and to outline various itineraries, incidents, encounters and crisscrossings by means of an intricate network of lines, arrows and icons. Her quest is redolent of Calvino's description, in the essay "The Structure of *Orlando Furioso*," of Ariosto's aforementioned poem as "the continual intersection and divergence of ... lines on a map of Europe and Africa ... [a] zigzag traced by galloping horses and the fitfulness of the human heart" (Calvino 1987, 166–167). Regrettably, though not surprisingly, Theodora's graphic universe yields no greater clarity than the non-visual ideation which the nun deems inadequate: by the time she has brought the interweaving adventures together and sketched their points of collusion on her map, the paper has turned into "a mess of lines going in all directions" (Calvino 1992, 363).

If Theodora's pictography may at first point to the possibility of bypassing the signifier's non-referentiality by resorting to a system capable of rendering the relationship between the signifier and the signified as a natural link, the text actually reveals, as JoAnn Cannon maintains, "the impossibility of that task. In an attempt to make the ink on the page coincide with the external referent, the narrator tells us she will resort to drawing.... In fact the narrator does not carry out her proposal; she only alludes to the pictorial mode through writing rather than actually making drawings on the page ... this representation of a representation is even further distanced from the referent" (Cannon, 45). The failure of the graphic experiment to embody reality in an immediate fashion ultimately foregrounds the inability of any symbolic system of signification to grasp and mirror a referent whose independent existence may be convincingly demonstrated. In fact, any degree of reality which may be attributed to the extra-discursive realm inevitably results from its construction in and by writing — historiography, as argued, is no exception. Calvino reminds us that the world captured and shaped by writing is a mobile construct without beginning and without end, animated by a centrifugal movement which continually causes it to expand from the inside, through a proliferation of unexpected incidents, intersections and digressions.

Chapter 3

Eccentric Cosmologies: *Cosmicomics* and *Time and the Hunter*

The cosmicomic narratives consist of ensembles of stories, endowed with variable proportions of action and description, recounting the genesis and subsequent evolution of the universe through the eyes of the preposterously named character of Qfwfq. The ultimate incarnation of a hybrid and polymorphous entity (for want of a better word) of the kind so dear to Calvino's heart, Qfwfq transcends space, time, the laws of physics and all conceivable biological classifications. Capable of acting as a supremely multiaccentual sign, Qfwfq could hardly be described as human, yet magically succeeds in coming across as not only human but also as a very distinctive type of person thanks to his unique narratorial voice — namely, a curious and impatient kid within a sprawling dynasty of likewise uncategorizable personae. Qfwfq is shapeless but feels tangibly full-rounded, wholly conjectural but also intensely corporeal. Weaving his way through a profusion of astronomically vast abstractions, Qfwfq's unmistakable voice enables the reader to enter the life and soul of the first mollusc determined to fashion a shell for itself, of the first crystal as the very concept of crystals begins to be formulated, of condensing or rarefying matter eager to contemplate its fate with dispassionate humor.

The pieces are prefaced by snippets of the actual scientific theories or hypotheses about the cosmos whence they draw inspiration. This strategy lends credibility to Calvino's premises with laconic robustness even as the symphonic poetry of creation is often allowed free rein. Furthermore, in Qfwfq's narrative world, recent developments in cosmogonic thinking are couched in such consummately human terms as to feel quite at home in the familiar world even though their conceptual immensity reverberates with notes so absurd as to verge not only on the comic but on the unnameably, immeasurably so — the cosmicomic indeed. The Big Bang and the moment when light first entered the solar system exude as much of a sense of immediacy as the here-and-now. The advent of organic life or the extinction of the dinosaurs appear to be as much a part of everyday reality as a regular human's quotidian routine. The first appearance of matter is thus associated by Qfwfq simply with the annihilation of his Granny's pillow, while the mind-boggling concept of space curvature is deployed to provide the narrator with a track onto which new-fangled atoms may be rolled like marbles. Originally published in 1965 and 1967 respectively, *Cosmicomics* and *Time and the Hunter* have recently been reissued in English as the integral part of the volume *The Complete Cosmicomics*, alongside a selection of pieces from other collections (including a few tales previously untranslated into English).

Both collections locate existence in unthinkable settings where impalpable density and a surreal hypernaturalism incongruously coalesce. In so doing, they convey both a sense of the arbitrariness of structure and an acute awareness of the intrinsic complexity of any apparently irreducible particle. Eager to bring out the sensuous qualities of language, the tales attest to a desire to retrace the fabulatory flight paths which connect disparate points in space and time. In fact, it could be argued that the fundamental motivating force behind the composition of *Cosmicomics* and *Time and the Hunter* is precisely a yearning to give narrative incarnation to immaterial concepts of space and time. Calvino is acutely aware of the incommensurability of infinity as absolute space and absolute time and humans' inexorably limited empirical grasp of both of those dimensions. To articulate this idea, the writer weaves a dense fabric of spaces and times (both present and absent, visible and invisible), now approaching one another, now branching off, at times longing to merge, and at other times oblivious of one another's very existence.

Linearity is rejected in favor of a spherical all-inclusiveness which condenses multiple zones into a dense mass of complications without these becoming, however, hopelessly entangled. In fact, although each tale multiplies from the inside its spatial and temporal axes, so as to suggest the boundlessness of galactic cycles and eras, this approach to the infinite is sustained by a concrete style that makes even the most surreal and Escheresque scenarios quite acceptable in terms of the narrative's internal logic of metaphorical compression and hence invests them with an aura of solidity. In the process, Calvino's cosmologies generate the type of sci-fi universe theorized by Casey Fredericks in *The Future of Eternity*—a universe where "speculative science and myth-making interact; the concepts, world views, and images ... are located at various points along a myth-science interface" (Fredericks 170). In this all-embracing network of spatial and temporal possibilities, the existence of any one individual element is posited as accidental and illusory, indeed potentially ridiculous — just as, Calvino ironically implies, one does not need to push a scientific or philosophical thesis very far before it becomes senseless. Calvino is not concerned either with the projection of utopian domains onto the future or with the application of precise mathematical principles to imaginary, alternative worlds but rather with unleashing a virtually inexhaustible progeny of hypothetical universes which, however primordial they may seem, actually resonate with contemporary intellectual preoccupations.

The approach adopted in the cosmicomic genre entails the amalgamation of glimpses of an atavistic past with a resolve to decipher critically an unintelligible present. By concentrating on processes of transition from one cosmic state to another, Calvino draws attention to those liminal aspects of the past which are least amenable to rationalization, and simultaneously highlights the uncertainty of the present itself as an unquantifiable dimension. Both the remote cosmos and our current universe, intimates Calvino, could be seen as latency phases (to borrow a phrase from psychoanalysis) that testify to the demise of one state of affairs while preluding to an as yet unknown novel condition. By suggesting lurking affinities between disparate temporal dimensions, moreover, the cosmicomic narratives indicate that the once-upon-a-time flavor of their creation myths is archaic in a purely morphological, rather than chronological, sense. Indeed, in its adoption of incongruous conjectures as viable triggers for narrative experimentation, cosmicomic fiction is ultimately concerned with a transtemporal and transhuman domain wherein the relationship between the beginning and the end of reality is always open to renegotiation.

The cosmicomic stories ooze with visual appeal, confirming at every turn Calvino's dedication to that aspect of the aesthetic experience. Furthermore, as Jeanette Winterson remarks, "the splendid and boisterous anarchy of Cervantes and Voltaire couples with the stripped-back beauty of the double helix. The writing explodes with the pleasure of its own creation" (Winterson 2009). This formal virtuosity, paradoxically, makes the narrative linkages proffered by the individual pieces appear most effortless when they have been most self-consciously engineered. At the same time, the stories benefit throughout from a unique sensitivity to the minutest detail that consistently manifests itself as a minimalist economy of expression, and as an ability to intimate that a whole world may be encapsulated in a single descriptive item. Thus, the tales bear witness to Calvino's ongoing pursuit of principles of concentration, conciseness of expression and compression, and to his fascination with the unsaid within the said, creating from scratch magic spells capable of working on the passage of time by contracting it and expanding it by turns. Concurrently, alacrity of pace and the ability to evoke disparate images simultaneously, stresses Calvino, testify to an intimate connection between physical speed and quickness of mind. Immersed in an atmosphere of fantasy, though not, given its internal coherence, of illogicality, each tale allegorizes the inextricability of the real from its diametrical opposite. Presence is an effect of the fabulistic ideation, assiduously reiterated and playfully varied, of an immense catalogue of invisible destinies. These are underpinned by myriad (often transgressive) interpretations of the concepts of strength and weakness, wealth and poverty, beauty and ugliness and, most vitally, by the penchant for transformation of anything into anything else.

A theme of pivotal significance to Calvino's articulation of his eccentric cosmologies is the universe's transition from undifferentiation to difference. Time and again, we encounter situations tracing the passage from a state of undifferentiation to a world of divisions, categories and compartments, from a fluid universe wherein everything merges with everything else to a schematized grid of neatly demarcated identities. Significantly, the cosmicomic characters' most painful and melancholy experiences coincide precisely with the shift from continuity to discontinuity, and with abrupt splittings of the inside from the outside. In the tale "Without Colors" (*Cosmicomics*), for example, the love between Qfwfq and Ayl is only possible as long as it is acted out in a gray, dawn-like condition of utter undifferentiation, where both living creatures and inanimate objects are harmoniously absorbed into the same non-chromatic cohesion of everything and nothing. With the introduction of colors, and therefore of difference, this Edenic state is abruptly brought to an end: "those pea-green lawns where the first scarlet poppies were flowering, those canary-yellow fields which striped the tawny hills sloping down to a sea full of azure glints, all seemed so trivial to me, so banal, so false" (Calvino 2009, 59).

"At Daybreak" (*Cosmicomics*) likewise insinuates that differentiated forms are "vulgar and out of place" in the sublime continuity of the pre-solar nebulae. Moreover, discontinuity implies vulnerability: one is more liable to get lost and go astray in a differentiated cosmos than in an undifferentiated one. In the latter, one may exist anywhere and everywhere and always remain in the same virtual place, while in the former, slipping out of one's compartment amounts to self-erasure. As Qfwfq and his family are caught in the transition from the nebular to the solar system, they feel "confused," encounter unprecedented difficulties and fall prey to that quintessentially human foible, the propensity for carelessness: "whereas before ... we were always careful not to scatter, now we had forgotten all about it" (24). "Death" (*Time and the Hunter*), additionally, suggests that discontinuity, while entailing the advantage of conceptual organization as a victory over the primeval continuum, the "swamp forest," also represents the human subjection to an arbitrary tissue of codes, a network of discordant "sounds, ideograms, morphemes, numbers, punched cards, magnetic tapes, tattoos, a system of communication that includes social relations, kinship, institutions, merchandise, advertising posters, napalm bomb, namely everything that is language" (239).

One of the most extreme exemplifications, put forward in "Blood, Sea" (*Time and the Hunter*), of the shift from undifferentiation to difference is supplied by a cosmogonic theory whereby the primordial sea in which all elemental organisms were at one stage supposedly floating is held to have had the same chemical composition as human blood, so that yesterday's exterior comes to constitute today's interior. The difference is that now, everything that once felt external to the self and could therefore be experienced in the open becomes relegated to a region of tenebrous interiority — an unfathomable and potentially deceptive domain: "the inside isn't changed, what was formerly the outside, where I used to swim under the sun, and where I now swim in darkness, is inside; what's changed is the outside ... which was the inside before" (190). The inside/outside opposition is also challenged in "The Spiral" (*Cosmicomics*) alongside the self/other binary once "sight" comes to be regarded not as a personal, internal awareness of being able to see but rather as an effect of external, extrasubjective channels of perception and recognition. An individual's identity is thus posited as a contingent offshoot of the gaze of the other, of its framing by extraneous eyes: "*our* sight, which we were obscurely waiting for," the narrator muses, "was the sight that the others had of us ... all of a sudden ... eyes were opening ... the swollen, colourless eye of polyps and cuttlefish, the dazed and gelatinous eyes of bream and mullet ... and at the bottom of each of those eyes I lived, or rather another me lived, one of the images of me" (150). "The Spiral," then, dramatizes the collapse of the barrier between internal and external dimensions by positing subjectivity as a kaleidoscopic product of the self's objectification by the non-self.

"Mitosis" (*Time and the Hunter*) likewise underscores the multifacetedness of identity through an allegory of asexual reproduction. The originally unitary cell, by splitting into two nuclei, both dies as an individual and enters alternative spheres of being in which the self is robbed of any intrinsic attributes, yet simultaneously enabled to embody polymorphous, if filiform, subjectivities: "I was for the first time aware of plurality ... I felt ... the sense ... of being lost in the innumerable world, and at the same time the still-sharp sense of being me" (221). The dividing line between inside and outside is also radically violated, to evoke a picture of multifarious subjectivity, in "The Chase" (*Time and the Hunter*). Here, the narrator and the unnamed pursuer out to kill him are fused into a seamless "us" (259) surrounded by an equally "single indivisible body" (261) of automobiles, trapped in the exasperating immobility of a jam. As the pursuer becomes the pursued and the sense of threat as an external dimension is progressively internalized while inner trepidation, conversely, is projected onto the outside, the narrator draws the following conclusion: "if I admit the existence of a chain of pursuits behind me there is no reason why this chain should not also continue through me into the part of the line that precedes me" (270).

"The Count of Monte Cristo" (*Time and the Hunter*) develops this theme by intimating that a menacing outside may be dispelled, once the inside has become enough of an outside itself to be able to defy the literal outside. This story supplies a critique of the analytical procedure based on processes of increasing penetration of the real. Instead of cutting through deceptive surfaces into a depth of authenticity, Abbé Faria is doomed to move from surface to surface, for any depth he may discover turns out to be a superficial façade, concealing countless more impenetrable layers. Edmond Dantès, by contrast, adopts a speculative approach based not on the endeavor to dismantle complexity but rather on hypothesizing its enhancement. Thus, Faria, in his attempts to escape from the fortress, goes on digging, "prising up the stone slabs ... perforating the rock with rudimentary awls," only to realize that each time, he finds himself "in a cell that is even deeper in the fortress" (281), that "his itineraries continue to wind around themselves like a ball of yarn" (283). In this dizzying proliferation of Chinese boxes, "each cell seems separated from the outside only by the thickness of a wall, but Faria as he excavates discovers that in between there is always another cell, and between this cell and the outside, still another" (286–287).

Dantès, for his part, embraces an ethos of survival, seldom far from

Chapter 3 — Eccentric Cosmologies   47

Calvino's cerebrations, based on a critically imaginative adjustment — if not exactly resignation — to the image of the world as a labyrinth. Survival, the writer surmises, does not pivot on the annihilation of the many obstacles barring the path to freedom but rather on an understanding of their stubborn impregnability. Hence, while Faria, in tracking irreducible truths, only unearths dumbfounding riddles, Dantès opts for an unsettling multiplication of intricacies and, paradoxically, ends up feeling more at "ease" (282) with the absolutely intractable than with any haphazard compromise. Just as Calvino toys with the idea of all-encompassing structures (the game of chess, the Tarot, the cybernetic model), ultimately to emphasize that any system, however thoroughly assembled, is riddled with inexplicable absences, so Dantès steers clear of all rational simplifications, conjecturing instead "more and more insuperable barriers" (286). He does so in the belief that if the construct he ideates is as inescapable as the real one, he will at least be able to put his mind at rest and give up on the possibility of escaping and if, on the contrary, that construct is even more inescapable than the real one, he will then stand a chance of escaping the actual fortress by exceeding its complexity in his own conjectures.

Calvino's problematization of the relationship between inner and outer dimensions, coupled with his emphasis on the irretrievable losses incurred by the subject upon entering a differentiated universe, raise issues of alterity and alienation. Difference is both an internal and an external state, forcing us to confront the reality of disparities within ourselves and to address the question of what exactly we are supposed to be different from. According to Fredericks, science-fictional articulations of the discourse of otherness are inevitably conducive to ideological and environmental quandaries: "will we really be able to experience the alien before we achieve the awareness that we are one human species, interconnectedly inhabiting one limited planet? Or before we understand and appreciate the non-human 'aliens'—the plants and animals—of our own planet? ... Or is it possible that the alien is the very image which makes us think out these problems of planet earth from a new perspective and on a larger scale? ... We do not yet know the outcome for our species and planet ... we aren't able to predict new knowledge (or we would already know it), but new knowledge will in itself constitute a large part of any new 'reality' of the future" (Fredericks, 181).

Calvino's cosmicomic explorations are consistently guided by a desire to understand, indeed feel, the texture of the cosmos precisely in the light of ever-changing cognitive configurations, wherein philosophical, scientific, mythological and aesthetic concerns are inextricably interrelated at all times. The essay on Visibility included in *Six Memos for the Next Millennium* offers insights into Calvino's aims and procedures which are specifically relevant to these issues. The essay is especially helpful in illuminating crucial aspects of Calvino's approach to scientific methods and terminology as a prismatic construct through which his preoccupations regarding time, space and language are endlessly refracted. The principle of Visibility indicates that in deploying as the starting point for each cosmicomic story an idea derived from the discourse of science, the writer can aspire to demonstrate that writing adopting images associated with fantasy and myth can originate in any terrain, even in a register seemingly divorced from the visual image in the way scientific rhetoric is often presumed to be in our times. Even the most apparently abstract or technically specialized text may unexpectedly proffer a phrase that kindles the pictorial imagination.

Calvino's emphasis on the interpenetration of scientific and literary discourses is explicitly foregrounded in "Two Interviews on Science and Literature," where he questions Roland Barthes' contention that while literature never treats language as a transparent vehicle for communicating facts, science views language as a neutral implement. Calvino, in fact, argues that "the science of today" cannot "really be defined by such trust in an absolute code of references" and that Barthes, therefore, "appears to envisage a kind of science far more compact and sure of itself than it really is" (Calvino 1987, 29). Scientific thought, in fact, is held by the writer to combine "precision" with a "poetic" element which is intrinsic to its "posing of conjectures" (32). Marco Porro persuasively reinforces the proposition that science and visuality are not incontrovertibly at odds. Calvino, the critic emphasizes, was a "scholar of the works of Einstein and Heisenberg since his years in high school," and hence well "aware that twentieth-century scientific advances had forsaken images linked to everyday perception." Addressing the outcomes of this undesirable repudiation of the visual, the writer felt that it "was necessary to separate imagination from visualization ... in order to reach an abstract imagination, modelled on mathematical structures. But even evocations developed as a result of logical constructions or deductive reasoning and found in mathematical or philosophical texts, can be translated into images" (Porro 61).

Moreover, as already pointed out in the chapter on *Our Ancestors*, Calvino regards modern science as increasingly devoted to the setting up, testing, and often discarding of hypotheses which are always, inevitably, part of "a possibly infinite series of approximations" (Calvino 1987, 38). This position is clearly corroborated by current scientific concepts which the lay reader may only, and partially, grasp through leaps of the imagination. What is a nonprofessional to make of the idea that 15,000 million years ago the cosmic egg blew up, say? And what of tachyons, particles deemed faster than light? What of naked singularities, namely, occurrences of matter so tightly compressed that they lack a horizon? And what of black holes and collapsing stars, given that scientific equations cannot as yet describe why infalling matter vanishes? The cosmicomic tales, in addressing creatively these sorts of ideas, warn us against two temptations: the inclination to accuse science of being oriented toward merely practical results likely to strangle free speculation, on the one hand, and the tendency to charge fiction with the crime of lacking any rational restrictions on the other. This is primarily achieved through the positing of a universe in which science and fiction coexist and reciprocally fuel their respective aspirations. For the cosmicomic writer, no world is ever closed, no conclusion predictable, no issue resolved. Cosmicomic fantasy, like contemporary science, seems willing to entertain any number of contradictory premises, perhaps in the belief that, as Robert Sheckley puts it, "the truth is to be stumbled upon in unlikely places" (Sheckley 192).

Cosmicomics and *Time and the Hunter* articulate in both literal and metaphorical ways Calvino's commitment to the cross-fertilization of literary and scientific registers. If scientific language lends literature a modicum of lucidity, exactitude and synthetic nimbleness (all being attributes of writing which *Six Memos* overtly praises), poetic modalities, for their part, typify the imaginative production of suppositions on which scientific inquiry thrives. Science, in this regard, may be associated not only with the atomistic acquisition of data but also with the shock produced by the envisioning of novel systems. Galileo's writings offer apposite illustrations of the physicist's response to discovery as a creative moment of epiphanic proportions from which mathematically verifiable principles may be subsequently extrapolated. As John Willett notes, the late–Renaissance scientist was most probably "amazed by the pendulum motion as if he had not expected it and could not understand its occurring, and this enabled him to come at the rule by which it was governed" (Willett 96).

The cosmicomic tales endeavor to infiltrate the vocabulary and assumptions of scientific discourses into the narrative's fantastic fabric and, conversely, to foreground the contamination of science by the magical and ludic moves of fictional writing. Both science and literature, in short, rely on images of a fundamentally rhetorical nature to explore the texture of human society as an irreducibly mythological construct, thus demystifying what Barthes describes as "the technical alibi proffered by our society in order to maintain within itself the fiction of a theological truth" (Barthes 1967, 897). *Cosmicomics* and *Time and the Hunter* mock the spurious religiosity and authoritarian stance of some positivist philosophical positions, often presenting evolutionism as their main target. For instance, in "The Origin of the Birds" (*Time and the Hunter*), the evolutionary ethos is parodied through the character of U(h), the reputed savant, who holds that the bird is simply a "mistake" (Calvino 2009, 168) in the chain of being: "hadn't we been told over and over that everything capable of being born from the Reptiles had been born?" U(h) wishes to sweep the bird away from the scene because the new species questions drastically his dogmatic tenets, particularly his conviction that evolution should necessarily lead to the improvement of existing species through a logical "succession of causes and effects" (170).

If both science and literature are implicated in the mythopoeic process, it must also be stressed that this process is inseparable from strategies of demythification and demystification of scientific and poetic conventions alike. Parody, as U(h)'s story suggests, is one available option. Alternatively, the writer may deliberately veer in the direction of a bathetic reductionism by relying on the irreverent displacement of conventional tropes and effects. Calvino's portrayal of the Moon in both cosmicomic collections is a case in point. "The Distance of the Moon" (*Cosmicomics*) satirizes traditional romantic renderings of the celestial body in question through the combination of semi-scientific observations and an almost blasphemously concrete descriptive register. The Moon is bathed in "a butter-coloured light" and is said to resemble "a black umbrella blown by the wind" (3), for instance. Furthermore, any potential claim to scientific abstraction is counterpointed by a minute attention to both highly evocative poetic images — the "violet-coloured fish," the "saffron medusas" (4) — and a relish in heightened, even repulsive, physical effects: the Moon's "underbelly" is compared to "the belly of a fish, and the smell, too ... if not downright fishy, was faintly similar, like smoked salmon" (5). The reason behind Qfwfq and his crew's periodic ascents to the satellite, moreover, is the collection of "lunar milk," an obviously imaginary substance whose characterization graphically encapsulates Calvino's corporeal imagery: "Moon-milk was very thick, like a kind of cream cheese. It formed in the crevices between one scale and the next, through the fermentation of various bodies and substances" (6). Likewise, in "The Soft Moon" (*Time and the Hunter*), the lyrical-elegiac tone which the writer inherits from a long tradition of literary idealizations of the silvery satellite is undermined by his equation of the Moon to some kind of heavenly goat, only capable of producing "a mud of acid mucus" (163). Calvino supplies a plethora of vaguely disgusting images, in his effort to upset stereotypical deifications of matter. The "incongruous substantiality" (158) of the soft Moon, for example, is contrasted with an equally fictional conception of the Earth as a perfectly aseptic planet, threatened by the corrupting agency of the satellite's "extended tumefactions ... like buboes or suckers," caused by "the swelling of the sublunary pulp which stretched its pale external tissues but made them also fold over on themselves in inlets or recesses looking like scars" (160). Calvino is concurrently highlighting, through these surreal images, the impossibility of fictionally describing the cosmos according to the rational procedures of a thoroughly systematized scientific model and the sentimentalist absurdities of conventional symbolism.

At the same time, Calvino is acutely aware of science's momentous impact on the construction of popular mythologies, thus echoing certain positions put forward by Joseph Campbell in *Occidental Mythology*, a text virtually contemporaneous with *Cosmicomics*: "No one of adult mind would turn to the Book of Genesis today to learn the origins of the earth, the plants, the beasts, and Man. There was no flood, no tower of Babel, no first couple in paradise.... Today we turn to science for our imagery of the past and the structures of the world, and what the spinning demons of the atoms and the galaxies of the telescope's eye reveal is a wonder that makes the babel of the Bible seem a toyland dream" (Campbell 520). It is precisely the cognizance of the extent to which people turn to scientific imagery to orchestrate, both individually and collectively, a sense of their environment and an understanding, however mythical, of their own embodiment, that lies at the root of one of the most debated cosmicomic issues: namely, that of anthropomorphism. In the aforecited "Two Interviews," Calvino responds to the suggestion that his "sympathies are directed more toward the cell than toward mankind" by stating that, in fact, his "cosmicomic stories might easily be reproached for exactly the opposite: that is, for making cells talk as if they were people" and thus "playing the old game of anthopomorphism" (Calvino 1987, 33). The writer is quite aware of the deleteriously colonialist implications of conventionally anthopomorphizing art, with its specious positioning of a human master at the center of the universe. This agenda is patently not what Calvino is pursuing. In fact, in populating the primeval void with quasi-human figures, in endowing amorphous matter with human language and human yearnings, he is neither advocating the primacy of the human form nor claiming to fashion inchoate and pre-human beings in the image of the presumably advanced mammal celebrated by some evolutionary dogmas. Quite the opposite is the case: the tales dramatize a "delirium of anthropomorphism." The "impossibility of thinking about the world except in terms of human figures" is parodied by situating the nominal superiority of such figures in the midst of fundamentally grotesque distortions of humanity, "human grimaces and human babblings." This strategy, argues the writer, could be seen as "a way of putting the laziest, most obvious, and most vainglorious image of man to the test: by multiplying his eyes and his nose in every direction until he no longer knows who he is" (34) — until, one could add, his very humanity, presence and visibility are hardly supportable.

The essay on Visibility from *Six Memos* both confirms and complicates the import of Calvino's assertions in "Two Interviews" by stating that while science interests the writer because of its sustained attempts to elude the constraints of anthropomorphic world views, he nonetheless insists on pursuing an anthropomorphic model of the imagination because such a model, in locating the human in a cosmos where humanity has never actually obtained, does not idealize presence but actually reminds us that "it seems extremely unlikely that man could ever exist in such a universe" and that our existence is, therefore, ineluctably traversed by absence (Calvino 1996, 90). Cosmicomic writing, by locating humanity in a context of unrealized, purely virtual presumptions, also underscores the character of creativity as the receptacle of potentialities, hypotheses and might-have-beens. Therefore, Calvino's experiments in anthropomorphism do not represent attempts to glorify the notion of humanized presence so much as allegorical reintegrations of a plethora of absent, marginalized or dormant lives. The dispersion of human or semi-human forms across a boundless cosmiscape corresponds to a particular perspective on the fantastic, the imagination, and the mind's analytical and synthetic faculties. The fantastic, in this context, constitutes a genre, an attitude toward people and objects and, most vitally, the ideation of the cosmos as an endless reservoir of shapes and images.

One of the principal fields in which pre-human life is overtly anthropomorphized is that of sexuality. This suggests the irreducibility of the erotic drive either to the realm of scientifically disembodied data — Qfwfq and company appear to feel very keenly when it comes to amorous passions despite their incorporeal or only pseudo-corporeal status — or to that of fully embodied humans since the cosmicomic characters are, after all, quasi-scientific abstractions despite their pulsational, palpitating energy. Calvino delivers an elegantly conceived double paradox whereby his speculative personae are disembodied yet carnalized, palpable yet abstract, at one and the same time. The enigma of a space-time construct wherein everywhere and nowhere, the present moment and eternity, seamlessly coalesce is thus duplicated at the level of the characters' peculiar ontology. As a result, science as articulated in the cosmicomic genre both confirms the all-pervasiveness of sexual impulses and marginalizes, indeed demystifies, their exclusive connection with humanity as we know it. Through Qfwfq, Calvino ironically anthropomorphizes eros as the impetus behind the evolutionary processes of development of non-human, no less than human, forms, thereby questioning the status of the human as the privileged locus for the manifestation of sexual desire and, concomitantly, relativizing any claims to anthropocentrism. Erotic desire implies a collusion of mental and corporeal forces, dominating the stories as the agency that enables civilization to unfold in the guise of a struggle to fashion a recognizably human form out of undifferentiated Nature. Simultaneously, Calvino evokes a powerful sense of continuity between the most elementary and the most sophisticated modes of creation, thus echoing Northrop Frye's conviction that "desire ... is neither limited to nor satisfied by objects, but is the energy that leads human society to develop its own form" (Frye 105).

The aforementioned tale "The Distance of the Moon" supplies a paradigmatic example of Calvino's treatment of cosmicomic eros and the attendant experiences of unfulfilled desire, loss and nostalgia. The narrative brings to mind Jacques Lacan's theorization of human psychosexual development as a transition from the "Imaginary"— the pre-linguistic and pre–Oedipal domain of plenitude supposedly enjoyed by the infant prior to the attainment of a sense of its separate identity and to the entry into the sphere of language — to the "Symbolic Order"— the enormous ensemble of codes, conventions, laws and rules shaping adult behavior and regulating human existence within a society. Accessing the Symbolic Order inaugurates the possibility of cultural interaction and relationality but inevitably consigns the subject to a destiny of lack, since a rigidly codified and partitioned system will never appease its insatiable desire for unruptured wholeness (Lacan 1977). In Calvino's story, the amorous plot unfolds simultaneously at the level of the pre-Oedipal Imaginary and at the level of the Symbolic Order of language. Qfwfq's cousin is presented as something of a pre-Symbolic infant: he is deaf, which suggests a metaphorical detachment from the realm of so-called adult, encultured language and, no less significantly, nameless. His eroticism, moreover, is equated to a polymorphously perverse exploration of the mother's body: he is the most accomplished extractor of milk from the Moon's uneven and unmappable anatomy (a physical apparatus whose texture and smell are uncompromisingly feminine in a directly genital sense), and he probes the satellite's fleshly folds not only for strictly functional purposes but also for sheer entertainment: "There were places ... that he touched merely for the fun of touching them," occasionally inserting "his big toe" into a yielding crevice of the lunar body (Calvino 2009, 7).

Despite his Imaginary connotations, however, Qfwfq's cousin is also an instrument, whether witting or unwitting, of a Symbolic articulation of desire entailing a fate of unredeemable loss. It is Mrs Vhd Vhd's fascination with his cousin's nimble intercourse with the Moon that causes the protagonist to fall hopelessly in love with her, to follow her and live with her on the Moon when this is racing away from the Earth, only to discover that being with the beloved is the ultimate defeat, for the sole thing she now desires is "to become the Moon." Calvino does not elevate either Imaginary or Symbolic sexuality to a rank of preeminence. Both forms of eros must acknowledge the inevitability of change: even in the beloved's undivided company, Qfwfq realizes that his love is overshadowed by "the heart-rending nostalgia for what it lacked" (16). The object of desire, for her part, must come to terms with the recognition that the Moon is what Qfwfq's cousin truly cherishes. Unbridgeable distance is the destiny deliberately elected by Mrs Vhd Vhd in the belief that if the being she dotes upon can only love the remote lunar body, she will make herself likewise remote by remaining on the Moon. Qfwfq's fate, too, is one of intractable deprivation: in his case, this is experienced not as material isolation but as a concomitant of his reintegration in the web of trivial domesticity: "my return was sweet, my home refound, but my thoughts were filled only with grief at having lost her" (18). The deaf cousin is the only character capable of embracing loss as an inevitable and not unequivocally damning lot: while his fellows struggle to reach the receding Moon by means of "ridiculously short" poles (17), a comical metaphor for their puny erections and limited penetrative capacities, he uses his own pole to play one final lunar trick and pretends to juggle with the treasured satellite.

As an always provisional and deceptive promise of plenitude, eros is the vehicle through which Calvino repeatedly articulates the necessarily partial translation of nothingness into somethingness. The anthropomorphization of erotic attachments involving non-human forms does not, however, represent a form of humanistic imperialism meant to master the entire universe according to normative human priorities but rather an invitation to establish some kind of amatory communication with all the materials of our day-to-day lives and thus rescue both them and ourselves from the squalor of reification. In encouraging us to contemplate the sexual potentialities, the basic aliveness, of disparate aspects of our environment, both animate and inanimate, the cosmicomic narratives simultaneously ask us to confront our own mechanized objectification. In this respect, they echo an intriguing argument put forward by Philip K. Dick in *Explorations of the Marvellous*: "We humans, the warm-faced and tender, with thoughtful eyes—we are perhaps the true machines. And those objective constructs, the natural objects around us and especially the electronic hardware we build, the transmitters and microwave relay stations, the satellites, they may be cloaks for authentic living reality inasmuch as they may participate more fully and in a way obscured to us in the ultimate Mind. Perhaps we see not only a deforming veil, but backwards. Perhaps the closest approximation to truth would be to say: 'Everything is equally alive, equally free, equally sentient, because everything is not alive or half-alive or dead, but rather *lived through*'" (Dick 219). The anti-humanist perspective ushered in by cosmicomic writing with regard to notions of identity and subjectivity is, moreover, paralleled by a decidedly anti-teleological approach to history. The extinction of a unified, quintessentially human subject is interwoven with the disappearance of the concept of history as the incremental disclosure of reason. As Contardo Calligaris points out, "History appears as the work of a subject that infinitely transcends mankind in space and time, of a total 'I' (experienced, however, through its individual fragments) which, in a sense, is the materialist counterpart of the Hegelian idea; in fact, the term history seems obsolete, insofar as it evokes the space of a tension between subject and object which no longer obtains" (Calligaris 91).

Indeed, what *Cosmicomics* and *Time and the Hunter* offer is a perspective of sheer virtuality based on the stretching of spatial and temporal criteria beyond the very notion of origin and toward an indistinct dawn wherein anything may become possible *one more time*. There is no absolute present or presence in these texts, insofar as characters and readers alike are compelled to proceed tentatively or even blindly toward spaces and times whose existence is utterly undemonstrable. One of the central ploys through which the writer relativizes the ascendancy of the human lies with his treatment of language. This is persistently presented as the epitome of humanity's subjection to structures of signification which, with the assistance of legion unexamined assumptions, come to be ideologically upheld as guarantees of human preeminence. Qfwfq, acting as the organizing force behind both *Cosmicomics* and the first two parts of *Time and the Hunter*, emblematizes the arbitrariness of referentiality, suggesting that meaning, in fact, is the transient effect of the conventional investment of certain signs with the power to signify. His pseudo-scientific remarks do not follow any systematic arrangement, but rather meander casually from one hypothesis to the next: Qfwfq's narratives are no more grounded in empirical reality than his name is pronounceable. His protean nature — as primordial matter, eternal memory, tadpole, dinosaur, camel, creature of the electronic age — typifies the unanchored nature of the linguistic signifier as an empty label that aspires to be safely attached to precise and concrete existential forms but never reaches its goal.

Moreover, human discourse is exposed as utterly relative, for many of the expressions used by the cosmicomic characters only make sense in terms of symbolic differentiation and thus ring comically forced in a world of pre-linguistic continuity. In the previously cited story "At Daybreak," for instance, Qfwfq and his family have no reference points in the impenetrable darkness they inhabit — yet, they unexpectedly produce ambiguous utterances which insinuate the dawn of symbolization in a hilariously incongruous fashion. When his infant brother Rwzfs starts "slamming or digging or writhing in some way," Qfwfq is surprised to hear that the creature is supposedly playing since the concept is quite alien to his universe at this stage:

> "What are you doing?" And he said: "I'm playing."
> "Playing? With what?"
> "With a thing," he said.
> You understand? It was the first time. There had never been things to play with before [Calvino 2009, 20–21].

It is simply impossible to imagine whence these nebular creatures, now on the verge of entering a solar cosmos, could have derived the ability to conceive words through which to describe their altering, incomprehensible conditions. How can any sign mean anything if its referent is unknown? What Calvino's text may be here endorsing, in deliberately exaggerated terms, is the irreparable divorce of the signifier from the signified. A few lines later, the narrator explicitly draws attention to the absurdity of the genesis of symbolization in a cosmicomic scenario by pointing out that when Qfwfq's dad announces that they are "hitting something" (23), the statement does not in itself hold any meaning since up to that instant, there have been no instances of hitting whatsoever and the characters, therefore, cannot be expected to hold any knowledge of the notion of hitting, let alone possess a word to designate it.

Qfwfq stumbles repeatedly into puzzling illogicalities as he catches himself in the act of uttering sentences which, strictly speaking, he should not be capable of constructing and, moreover, of trying to explain their relevance to his extraordinary situation. This often gives rise to vertiginously elliptical passages and some amusing syntactical acrobatics. The cosmicomic characters' names likewise indicate the coexistence of conflicting attitudes to language. Their algebraic tenor and frequently orthographic symmetry would seem to point to a radical departure from the sphere of embodied humanity: we meet Vhd Vhd and Xlthlx in "The Distance of the Moon"; Bb'b, Hnw, G'd(w)^n and Rwzfs in "At Daybreak"; Kgwgk in "A Sign in Space"; and Pber^t Pber^d, Ph(i)Nk$_o$ De XuaeauX and Z'zu in "All at One Point," to name but a handful. It is worth noting, however, that these formulaic pseudo-equations are implicitly concretized by their association with decidedly human epithets and titles.

At times, momentous occurrences may be condensed into a single, unadorned sentence: "So the better part was done: the heart of the nebula, contracting, had developed warmth and light, and now there was the Sun" (29). At others, anachronistic switches of register patently mock any pretences of cosmogonic grandiosity. This is paradigmatically illustrated by the case of Qfwfq's sister, G'd(w)^n, who sinks so deep into the Earth's rapidly coagulating surface as to disappear altogether until the unthinkably distant day when the narrator (so he claims) chances upon her in Australia in the year 1912. A no less flamboyantly risible disclosure is the matter-of-fact announcement that Qfwfq has recently bumped into his old acquaintance Pber^t Pber^d at the "bar here on the corner" and been appraised that he now works for a "plastics firm, in Pavia" (45). This idiosyncratic admixture of spaceless and timeless zones and crudely localized occurrences, sublime and potentially tragic glimpses of the infinite and bathetic remarks of a decidedly provincial nature, also serves an ideological purpose. In "All at One Point," for example, Calvino infuses in his customary scenario of pre-human undifferentiation — the stage at which all the matter in the cosmos was condensed in a single spot — the topical issues of xenophobia, prejudice and the transtemporal naturalization of undeserved rights when the Z'zu family are branded as "immigrants" (45). Although the concept is meaningless in a universe lacking any clear spatial and temporal separations, the adoption of the derogatory term is defended by its users on the pretext that it carries absolute value beyond both space and time.

Calvino's interweaving of overwhelming sidereal immensity and parochial pettiness could ultimately be read as a tragi-cosmicomic recognition of the limitations of human discourse as a system incapable of expressing anything other than the human. Therefore, the relativization of human forms and modes of expression, constantly underscored by the writer's emphasis on what Calligaris aptly terms "our limited spatial and temporal horizon," our "measuring of time ... and of distances" (Calligaris 94), concurrently indicates a depreciation of symbolic signification. Although language attributes fleeting identities to its subjects, it simply has no unified identity of its own. Qfwfq's oscillation between technical registers and disarmingly direct, homely ways of describing unthinkable occurrences bears witness to language's amorphous flexibility. So does his approach to the production of signs, as exemplified by the story "A Sign in Space" (*Cosmicomics*). Ultimately, the protagonist is unable to reconcile the sign's aesthetic and functional dimensions: if his initial concern lies with the beauty of what he has conceived, his increasing concern with its communicative faculties flings him into the philosophical nightmare stemming from the need to distinguish not only one sign from another but also the sign from the non-sign.

Lacking any systems of reference on the basis of which to produce his sign, any implements with which to accomplish the act, and indeed any notions of form, visibility and dimensionality, Qfwfq is nevertheless dominated by an irrepressible creative impulse which testifies to language's purely accidental origins: "I conceived the idea of making a sign ... or rather, I conceived the idea of considering a sign a something that I felt like making." The protagonist takes pride in the thought that in the endless "circling" of "constellations and planets and clouds ... only the sign remained still" (33). Furthermore, he identifies totally with the sign's privileged status: "the sign was mine, the sign of me ... it was like a name ... my name that I had signed on that spot" (34). Qfwfq's fantasies, in this regard, echo Jacques Derrida's evocative description of the unattainable prospect of "a signifier that does not fall into the world ... that seems to depend upon my pure and free spontaneity, requiring the use of no instrument, no accessory, no force taken from the world" (Derrida 1981, 22). No sooner has Qfwfq contemplated the sheer possibility of the sign, however, than the latter's presumed uniqueness is lost in a plethora of other imaginable signs, and its plenitude fractured by an awareness of its composite nature: "I had lost by now even that confused notion of my sign, and I succeeded in conceiving only interchangeable fragments of signs ... signs-within-signs" (Calvino 2009, 35). In other words, as soon as the sign-making process is set in motion, we are forced to confront a reality of purely relational, differential and hence inevitably fragmentary identities, wherein both unity and individuality are totally irrelevant concepts. The myth of originality is accordingly shattered, as Qfwfq realizes that his putatively indestructible creation may, in fact, be erased, transformed into "a shapeless scratch, a bruised, chipped abrasion of space" (36) capable of turning the cosmos into a "nauseating" void once again or even be "copied," albeit carelessly and crudely (37). The shattering of Qfwfq's illusions regarding the purity and ineffable distinctiveness of his work opens up a vista of symbolic deferral in which the desire to transcend the logic of the sign is inextricably interwoven with a troubled recognition of one's dependence on signs for expressive purposes. Tortured by the fear that his enemy, Kgwgk. may see his sign, find it pretentious and dated, and mercilessly parody it, the protagonist dreams of a signless world; yet, he comes to realize that it is only through signs that anything, genuine or fake, may be divulged. Merely in order to irk the antagonist, Qfwfq eventually begins to produce "false signs, notches in space, holes, stains, little tricks" (39). In this proliferation of haphazard traces, any individual sign rapidly loses its distinctiveness, its specificity, eventually even its power to signify at all.

In the final part of *Time and the Hunter,* Calvino leaves Qfwfq behind, to focus instead on a metropolitan scenario of dysfunctional relations. These reiterate the writer's preoccupation with the instability of identity borders by contemplating a spooky collision of human bodies and technology. *Our Ancestors,* it seems worth recalling, dramatized the deconstruction of the body in an apocalyptically baroque fashion by highlighting dismemberment and mutilation in an explosive vision of the human marked by both literal and metaphorical gashes, scars and excisions. In the final section of *Time and the Hunter,* the disunity of embodied subjectivity is foregrounded by rendering biological and technological bodies inextricable. Humanist notions of personality and personhood are concurrently thwarted and raised to an alternative level of meaning through their embedding in a thoroughly mechanized environment. By focusing on the relationship between the organic and the automated, particularly in the context of a car-dominated lifestyle, both the aforementioned tale "The Chase" and "The Night Driver" exhibit affinities with J. G. Ballard's writings. Calvino depicts an urban landscape in which individual subjectivities are transformed into the anonymous glimmers and luminous swathes projected by automobiles journeying endlessly along parallel highways or else reduced to prisoners of "the general system" of crawling cars, trapped in the rush-hour traffic (271). In Ballard, these same recurrent images evoke the merging of relentless movement and total stagnation, kinesis and stasis: "We had entered an immense traffic jam ... the traffic lanes were packed with vehicles, windshields leaching out the molten colors of the sun setting above the western suburbs of London. Brake-lights flared in the evening air, glowing in the huge pool of cellulosed bodies. ... the high wall of a double-decker airline coach formed a cliff of faces. The passengers at the windows resembled rows of the dead looking down at us from the galleries of a colombarium. The enormous energy of the twentieth century ... was being expended to maintain this immense motionless pause" (Ballard 151).

"The Night Driver" evinces especially intimate points of contact with Ballard's *Crash* in its emphasis on analogies between human bodies and cars and on the mediation of human relationships by technology. Close parallels between the human organism and the automobile are suggested in the very opening of Calvino's story: "I realize night has fallen. I turn on my headlights.... For night driving our eyes, too, must remove one kind of inner transparency and fit on another, because ... they have to check a kind of black slate which requires a different method of reading" (Calvino 2009, 272). Furthermore, amorous affairs, attendant quarrels, jealousies and trysts are utterly dependent on the characters' motorized existence. The narrator, who lives in "A," is on the verge of breaking off a liaison with "Y," who lives in "B," and in an extreme attempt to salvage the relationship, reckons he has no choice but to jump into his car and "dash over to B." Concomitantly, he suspects that "Z," his rival, might at that very minute be "speeding along" the same "motorway" and that "every car" he overtakes or is overtaken by could therefore "be his" (273). It is also conceivable, in the unnerving logic of the tale, that "Y" might have got into her car and be "now racing in the direction opposite" the narrator's along the very same route (274).

As in Ballard, cars and eroticism are closely associated, as the pleasure and excitement yielded by driving toward the object of desire far exceed those inherent in the actual "meeting" and its "inessential details" (276). The suspension of outcomes afforded by endless travel is preferable to any resolution. Ultimately, the symbiotic relationship between body and automobile is conducive to a metamorphosis of the human into almost incorporeal, beaming and flickering effects: "I felt the need to transform the things to be said into a cone of light hurled at a hundred miles an hour ... the Y I love is really that moving band of luminous rays.... And also with Z ... I can establish the proper relationship only if he is for me simply the flash and glare that follow me, or the trail-lights I follow" (276–277). Significantly, it is from this minimalist attenuation of the human body, of human language and human dispositions, and from an attendant recognition of the promiscuous interchangeability of identities in a world of undecodable signals, that the narrator derives a sense of equanimity and calm: "Everything is more uncertain than ever but I feel I've now reached a state of inner serenity ... we will continue, all three of us, speeding back and forth along these white lines, with no points of departure or of arrival ... freed finally from the awkward thickness of our persons and voices and moods" (279). This attitude is also redolent of Ballard's in *Crash*: if Calvino's narrator regains a sense of composure from the realization that the I may amount to a random flicker, Ballard's narrator eventually finds some peace in the awareness that he is only a cipher in the immense palimpsest of a car-saturated environment: "Around me ... along both ramps of the flyover, stretched an immense congestion of traffic.... Standing at the centre of this paralyzed hurricane, I felt completely at ease, as if my obsessions with the endlessly multiplying vehicles had at last been relieved" (Ballard 156). This sense of "ease" also recalls the state achieved by Dantès in "The Count of Monte Cristo."

Like much of Ballard's fiction, "The Night Driver" is heir to what David Punter has described as a narrative world wherein "the long tradition of enclosed and unitary subjectivity comes to mean less and less" as the emphasis falls on "the ways in which person is increasingly controlled by landscape and machine" (Punter 9). The ego is hemmed in by the desolate blankness of depersonalized signifying chains. Humans, metaphorically speaking, live on giant fairground wheels which may be stopped and dismantled only at the cost of halting the endless revolutions of their riders and hence consigning them to non-being. Nonetheless, the awareness of being surrounded by a seamless membrane of equally significant clues may be converted into a source of temporary comfort. Indeed, the relentlessly racing cars of "The Night Driver" provide a paradoxically reassuring image not because they guarantee some form of closure but rather because they confirm the endlessness of the tasks of pursuit and revelation.

Qfwfq's nebular and pre-chromatic worlds often posit the subject's engulfment in a web of largely illegible signals as a corollary of the primordial inability to distinguish a sign from a non-sign: if nothing is yet a sign, then anything could become one. "The Night Driver" would seem to offer a different picture by presenting an environment in which everything is always already a sign and incapable of being anything else, since existence and existence-as-a-sign have become coterminous. Yet, the gap between the two modalities is easily bridged if one considers that the regions inhabited by Qfwfq are not totally fictitious realms but rather ironical relocations of the present. There is barely any distance between Qfwfq's hypergalactic polysemy and the motorway of shimmering signifiers depicted by "The Night Driver." In both scenarios, "the individual hangs on to a discourse which he or she can own only with enormous difficulty, often in the end failing entirely to do so" (10).

Calvino's indefatigable pursuit of his aesthetic ideals in the cosmicomic stories is aptly complemented by the author's theoretical writings on folk tales and fairy tales (Calvino 1956; Calvino 1988). These constitute a metaphorical cosmology in their own right: a chronicle of the prismatic history of a galaxy of texts that have been progressively inscribed, displaced, mutated, reconfigured, reinscribed, grafted and superimposed on one another over many centuries. Calvino's exploration of folk tales and fairy tales supplies a particularly concise distillation of the writer's commitment to the articulation of an ongoing dialogue between the part and the whole, the individual detail and the broad structure — a quest pursued throughout *Cosmicomics* and *Time and the Hunter* by locating both actual and hypothetical singular entities within large or even limitless systems. Calvino proposes that any one individual tale offers a selection of items from a vast repertory of available images and that its meaning, as a result, is only measurable in relation to the untapped portions of the paradigm on which it draws — to what, in other words, is absent from the tale itself: "in any tale that has a meaning," the author maintains, "one may recognize the first tale ever told and the last tale, beyond which the world will not let itself be narrated in a tale" (Calvino 1988, 126). Calvino's reflections on the tale pithily attest to the writer's unremitting sense of both the arbitrary character of all structures and the internal complexity of any seemingly elemental detail. This is consistently allied to an unmatched perceptiveness to the materiality of language and to a desire to track the narrative trajectories that link diverse historical and geographical contexts. At the same time, he is attracted by the tale's proverbial sensitivity to the tiniest minutia — a quality that clearly manifests itself in a spartan succinctness of expression, and in the ability to intimate that a whole world may be encapsulated by a single descriptive item. No less appealing to the writer are the physical notes (of movement, of contact) with which traditional narratives typically reverberate and, last but not least, their flexible handling of time.

Calvino's remarks about the traditional tale in *Six Memos* bear witness to his ongoing pursuit of principles of concentration and compression, and to his fascination with the unsaid within the said. In this context, the author attributes his fascination with folk tales and fairy tales to the "economy, rhythm and hard logic with which they are told" (Calvino 1996, 35). Conciseness is repeatedly praised as one of the tale's most salient features, and an inevitable concomitant of its handling of the temporal dimension through alternating cycles of extreme swiftness and extreme immobility. The yarn that succeeds in achieving the most striking effects with minimum expenditure by means of variegated and protean worlds is akin to a magical talisman through which one may access a whole cosmos of narrative constellations in one single movement. Temporal displacements are also observable in the dilation of time caused by inner multiplications and ramifications leading from one plot to another plot of the kind most famously immortalized by the *Arabian Nights*.

Calvino is obviously familiar with the complex history of studies and interpretations of the fabulatory genre and aware of the importance of situating both individual tales and whole clusters of narratives in appropriate cultural, geographical, ethnological, anthropological and historical milieux. Indeed, he is especially eager to emphasize that any mapping of narrative possibilities on the basis of putatively universal deep structures should be critically contextualized, for reductionism ought not to conceal difference but rather help us grasp distinctive peculiarities of time and place. As he argues in his study of traditional tales, "reducing the tale to its unchanging skeleton contributes to highlight how many geographical and historical variables form the external casing of this skeleton; and establishing rigorously the narrative function, the place assumed within this scheme by specific instances of social existence, the objects of empirical experience, the implements available to a given culture, the plants and animals of a particular flora and fauna, can provide data which would otherwise elude us regarding the value which that particular culture ascribes to them" (Calvino 1988, 113). Though pluralistically respectful of the relative achievements of disparate approaches, Calvino is reluctant, however, to subscribe to any specific one, conscious of the multifariousness, obscurity and hazy origins of the subject under scrutiny.

The tale, for Calvino, is not so much a genre as a stratification of largely undefinable crosscultural products. Replicating Qfwfq's peregrinations through an accretional architecture of cosmogonic hypotheses, Calvino himself navigates the immense universe of traditional narratives. He thus finds, time and again, that any attempt to categorize all available tales on the basis of either generic or rhetorical criteria can easily induce an insatiable lust for more and more variations and variables, a feverish pursuit of comparative and classificatory models. Calvino detects the danger of passion degenerating into mania and ultimately comes to revel in the sprawling and unconquerable tentacularity of his subject as its most priceless asset. The tale, he argues, offers "an arabesque of multicolored metamorphoses that issue from one another," as patterns do in an Oriental carpet (146). Fairy tales and folk tales are, he concludes, both infinitely varied and infinitely repetitious. The pleasure yielded by unexpected variety in the circuit of repetition or by repetition manifesting itself in the guise of marginal differences is ultimately of paramount significance.

Calvino's simultaneous focus on difference and recurrence as equally vital mechanisms in the shaping of the tale echoes Vladimir Propp's views on the subject. For the Russian critic, too, tales are inherently repetitive, for the "functions" on which they pivot — namely, the acts which carry structural weight in the overall plot — and the "spheres of action" — character-types through which the functions are dramatized — are limited and stable and tend to recur in identical sequences throughout any one individual story. The idea that the number of available narrative ingredients is fixed and finite (the formalist critic enumerates thirty-one functions and seven spheres of action) may evoke a picture of dull reiteration. However, Propp, is eager to emphasize that uniformity of form, structure and pattern combines with a heterogeneous multiformity of variables, such as peculiarities of characterization and descriptive techniques, and that it is precisely with these shifting attributes, rather than with abstract systems of recurrence, that the tale's aesthetic appeal lies. Constancy and stability are essentially contributing but by no means despotically prescriptive factors in the moulding of a specific narrative (Propp).

For Calvino, analogously, it is only by consistently cultivating and sharpening one's awareness of the tale's sameness-in-difference and variety-in-repetition that the assiduous reader, in voyaging through forests and enchanted castles and contemplating at every turn of the page new spells, metamorphoses, monstrous aberrations and irrational passions, will experience not so much the promise of escapist routes as a defamiliarized version of her or his own reality whence some lesson may be gleaned. Calvino's critical project again mirrors Qfwfq's meandering exploration of the slowly evolving cosmos. The truth identified by Calvino resides, fundamentally, with a recognition that the ultimate system from which all possible plots may be extrapolated eludes us. Such a system asserts its authority by operating as some kind of irreducible blueprint from which individual stories can emanate but in so doing, it concurrently recedes into near invisibility. It becomes as insubstantial as a shadowy backdrop compared to the actual tales it spawns.

If presence is a product of absence, as argued at various junctures in this study, this is exactly what the popular tale unremittingly evinces. The "figures of darkness and the figures of night" (Calvino 1988, 137) interact dynamically with incarnations of radiance and daylight clarity, with a world "illuminated by auroral light" (129). Conventionally, fantasy may be situated on the side of absence (the empirically unverifiable) and lived experience on that of presence. Yet, suggests Calvino, it is from the hypothetical orbits traced by intangible voyages into the imaginary that the energy animating the creative act manifests itself as motion, as flow, and hence gives shape not to one reality but myriad realities. Like the cosmicomic stories, Calvino's writings on traditional tales tersely remind us that any story *is* by virtue of what it *is not*. Any story is always on the verge of metamorphosing into another story which might have, could have, perhaps should have been told instead or, more importantly, exists but might, just as feasibly, have never existed.

Chapter 4

The Endless Journey: *Invisible Cities*

Invisible Cities consists of a constellation of intensely lyrical descriptions, delivered by Marco Polo to Kublai Khan as chronicles of his journeys through the mighty ruler's sprawling empire, that gradually turn out to depict not actual locations visited by the explorer but rather nostalgic imaginary variations on Polo's home town, Venice. The Italian city itself remains invisible, dominating the text from its interstices as a ghostly presence that can only be inferred cryptically and indirectly in the form of fragmentary images, glimmers and hints. On the one hand, this suggests that the narrator cannot bring himself to frame Venice verbally for fear that he would lose it altogether were he to consign it to language: "Memory's images," he laments, "once they are fixed in words, are erased" (Calvino 1997, 87). On the other hand, Polo's narrative intimates that the city itself resolutely defies symbolic articulation due to its historically notorious accretional and fluid growth, redolent of the operations of organic tissue more than of those of stones or mortar. The broad implications of this paradoxical state of affairs incrementally emerge as the text unfolds. What humans most profoundly treasure, it is proposed, is easily marred by its textual encoding, and the safest means of protecting it is therefore to keep it outside language. Yet, language is ultimately inescapable and will always find a way of recapturing, however circuitously or surreptitiously, the contents of our thoughts. As Ludwig Wittgenstein puts is, "The limits of my language mean the limits of my world" (Wittgenstein 68), and "What can be said at all can be said clearly, and what we cannot talk about we must pass over in silence" (3).

Polo admits that the cities he describes to his employer are akin to ephemeral "ashes" he garners along the way (Calvino 1997, 60). This renders the seemingly most solid places included in his travelog strangely ethereal. Nevertheless, even though they lie beyond the atlas of referentiality, Polo's cities hold an undeniable power to fabricate limitless spaces and time zones. Harking back to the register of medieval compilations of real and imagined maps, Polo's visionary reports resemble a catalogue of emblems, wherein each entry is both a discrete narrative in its own right and the piece of a larger jigsaw puzzle. As instances of associative thinking based on analogical and metaphorical juxtapositions, the depictions of fifty-five cities portrayed in the text follow a non-linear, looping logic of displacement rather than that of rational argumentation, and therefore foreclose the possibility of arriving at any final conclusions. At the same time, Polo's cities are constructs of a phenomenal rather than noumenal kind, for what we discover about them depends on how they appear to a perceiver, not their absolute essence. Concomitantly, while they come across as quantifiable spaces, their coherence is purely contingent — i.e., a function of their ability to mobilize certain energies within a particular culture. There is no transcendentally agreed shape for any of Polo's cities; there is only, at best, a sense of the variety of activities that could or should go on in them and, in so doing, endow them with life.

The sense of a journey, route or trajectory gradually emerges from Polo's seemingly disjointed fiction: an adventure which, though it may bear no connection with the rhythms of external history and officially recorded facts, still manages to yield vibrant energy by unscrolling in the innermost recesses of the narrator's and the narratee's psyches. The text thereby obliquely engages with moral questions regarding the status of narrative truth and narrative falsehood. Calvino's ethics is an ethics of imponderables. It does not proceed from an accepted body of universally accepted obligations but rather from the experience of a lack: the absence of any anchoring definitions of morality, responsibility and honesty. Such concepts only emerge as context-bound inventions triggered by an acute apprehension of uncertainty and instability. In the absence of any verifiable certainties, Polo, like Jeanette Winterson's narrator in *Gut Symmetries*, comes to realize that "matter does not exist, with certainty, in definite places, rather it has a tendency to exist. ... our seeming-solid material world dissolves into wave-like patterns of probabilities, and these patterns do not represent probabilities of things but probabilities of connection" (Winterson 1997, 160).

Invisible Cities is an adventure of meticulous decoding where the reader, no less than the narrator and the narratee, is called upon to exercise his or her skills as a creative writer. Calvino underscores the interpenetration of readerly and writerly functions through the construction of a textual web in which no one party is assigned ultimate interpretative mastery. The text depicts a universe of tentative and experimental probabilities and connections, wherein the mind's imaginary projections are, by and large, often more real than what is experienced by the senses, and what is absent, extinct or as yet unborn often holds greater creative potentialities than the empirically realized. If Polo, to begin with, appears to be in control of his tales as the only fictional agent who has actually experienced the cities he itemizes for the Khan (or indeed the one city behind them all), it becomes increasingly clear that his authority is precarious because it is unlikely that he has really visited those places or indeed that they really exist. Polo's narrative authority is further called into question by his uncertain control over time, since the more he moves forward in his journeys, the more he is drawn back into the past, to "a little square of Venice where he gamboled as a child." The past itself, however, does not constitute a frozen dimension, consigned to the sealed space of an immutable archive since, as Polo keeps on moving, so does the past he carries with him: "what he sought was always something lying ahead, and even if it was a matter of the past it was always a past that changed gradually as he advanced on his journey" (Calvino 1997, 28).

Additionally, the paucity of information regarding the narrator's past, present and future actions and motivations makes him a dubious candidate for the role of fictional hero. Polo comes across, in fact, as something of a spectacle based on an unresolved tension between activity and passivity, excitement and listlessness, involvement and detachment. This lack of consistency in Polo's narratorial acrobatics clouds any clear motive or purpose which could conceivably lie behind his compulsive storytelling, inducing us to wonder why exactly he is narrating anything at all. Polo's control over his narrative is most drastically challenged as the Khan gradually appropriates the explorer's narratorial faculties by weaving out of his own visions stories analogous to Polo's: "From now on I shall describe the cities" (43), he declares emphatically in the opening of Part III, and, by the end of the same section, he has developed sophisticated ways of describing the places he has dreamed of.

The subtle and incremental transfer of power from Polo to the Khan is paralleled by an intensification of the extradiegetic reader's role: we are encouraged to step into the narrative as active writers, capable of elaborating our own personal geographies and of establishing connections which the text itself leaves unexplained. *Invisible Cities* thus allegorizes the collapse of the inside/outside binary which conventionally locates the reader outside the narrative, either as a passive consumer or as a masterful critic.

The text asks to be experienced simultaneously from without and from within: we are both extraneous bodies cut off from the melancholy tranquillity of the Khan's legendary garden where the dialogues are staged, and instrumental presences capable of instilling imagined life into spaces which, in our total absence, would amount to little more than lifeless tableaux. If the dialogical sections of the book, in emphasizing the enclosedness of the setting in which Polo and the Khan interact, somewhat exclude the reader from the narrative sphere, the descriptive passages are so many invitations to the reader to fashion multiple plots out of Polo's sparse, albeit highly evocative and tightly packed, clues.

It is incumbent upon the reader to select any number of possible itineraries through the narrative, aided only by a series of branch points supplied by the interactive fictional web. As Christine Boyer observes, in this respect, "*Invisible Cities* represents a network much like the matrix of a hypertext, in which the reader can select multiple routes and draw a variety of conclusions" (Boyer 142). Relatedly, navigating Calvino's text "bears a similarity to travel within the informational matrix ... where borders are crossed by a hypermedia navigator who guides travelers in riding, traversing. browsing, playing the links between different texts, images, words, and graphs as they move across the grid of the electronic screen establishing new relationships in unpredictable ways" (30). Calvino thus portrays a quantum theory universe where nothing is fixed or definitive, and different elements are capable of occupying contradictory positions at one and the same time. Through measurement, quantum physics instructs us, it is possible to surmise that a particle may hold a certain position in space and time. Yet, without any calculations, a particle is the sum total of all possible states. The deterritorialized diffusion over space and time of the Khan's empire would seem to hint at precisely such a world of simultaneity.

In the city of Laudomia, for example, tripartite lives unfold as the living population is insistently enjoined to find the reason for its existence through excursions into the realms of the departed and the unborn; any sense of safety gleaned from the former is questioned by the anxiety transmitted by the latter. Calvino's quantum theory universe is both unimaginably complex, given each particle's virtual ability to occupy countless positions, and minimalistic, given each particle's potential to encompass a whole cosmos. The Khan is stunned by the cornucopian profusion of ideas discernible in the tiniest portion of his chessboard: his entire domain's most astounding "treasures," by contrast, feel no more solid than "illusory envelopes" (Calvino 1997, 131). Concurrently, the Khan's atlas challenges the apparent certainties of empirically measured space and stretches well beyond the confines of explored reality, to include invisible cities whose existence is unknown to either Polo or the geographers of his time and yet, in principle, ought to exist in a potential state as "forms of possible cities." Indeed, the hypothetical locations theorized by visionary cartographers are, in a sense, no less real than the ones which Polo is supposed to have visited, since these are distorted by the very experience of traveling, which causes all cities to end up echoing one another until "a shapeless dust cloud invades the continents" (137).

At the same time, the opposition between concrete experience and theoretical abstraction is rendered irrelevant by the notion that each apparently new city is a place which one has always already visited. This realization does not, however, yield any sense of ultimate fulfillment: in fact, the more one sees or has seen, the more acutely aware one becomes of what has been left out, what remains stubbornly unseen. The voyager is unrelentingly haunted by a nagging nostalgia for life's minute and irretrievable might-have-beens, as wrenchingly evoked by the description of Diomira: "the special quality of this city for the man who arrives there on a September evening, when the days are growing shorter and the multicolored lamps are lighted all at once at the doors of the food stalls and from a terrace a woman's voice cries ooh!, is that he feels envy toward those who now believe they have once before lived an evening identical to this and who think they were happy, that time" (7). Cities exist in the memories of travelers who, in recognizing their beauties, sense that they have experienced them before and yet resent those who, unlike the passing traveler, can situate their feelings within a stable pattern of emotional continuity. The city of Irene further dramatizes the fate of unfulfillment to which the eternal wanderer is destined: "Irene is a name for a city in the distance, and if you approach, it changes" (125). Both Diomira and Irene mock the traveler's ability to discriminate between reality and illusion by embodying, respectively, the unrealizable promise of stability and the challenge of relentless transformation.

Argia, for her part, proposes a radical suspension of both belief and disbelief, by presenting a topsy-turvy world in which the city's very existence is a matter of conjecture, if not faith, any evidence for its existence being only graspable by listening to the noises that issue from its underbelly in the middle of the night. The text thus offers a paradoxical approach to both space and time in which longings are constantly mutating into melancholy reminiscences, the experiences of the dead and the living uncannily coalesce, and fantasies are both sublimated vestiges of something which really took place in some more or less distant past and hallucinatory déjà vus fashioned by fear and longing in equal measures. Memory becomes a superfluous concept, if memory is to be understood as a reconstruction of reality. In fact, reminiscences are not effects deriving from the experience of a city but the causes or preconditions of its existence: "Memory is redundant: it repeats signs so that the city can begin to exist" (19).

Calvino's explosion of the binary opposition between the empirical and the conceptual is reinforced by the unsettling coexistence of discordant urban identities. The superficially visible city of Zaira contains, "like the lines of a hand," an invisible city traced in its many nooks and recesses (11). The city of Anastasia, for its part, simultaneously kindles and stifles its inhabitants' yearnings. Other cities display schizophrenic personalities. Leandra is the battlefield for its Lares' and Penates' mock heroic antics. Raissa, a doleful city, is nonetheless capable of nourishing a ghostly undercurrent of joy. In Berenice, strands of extreme injustice and extreme justice coexist in secret bondage, while in Theodora, the most aseptic of all imaginable cities, a banished but incredibly resilient fauna of forbidden species flourishes in the interstices of official urban life. The city of Baucis, perched on "slender stilts" akin to "flamingo legs," hardly touches the earth: no-one can ascertain whether the city's eccentric lay-out is meant to suggest an intense hatred or, in fact, a deep respect for the natural world on the part of her inhabitants. The only thing of which one can be sure is that the people of Baucis are continually engaged in "contemplating with fascination their own absence" (77).

Sophronia has a permanent and playful half, the fairground, and a transient and serious half, the domain of factories, palaces, schools and banks; dismantled and reassembled at regular intervals, it resembles Ersilia, a city made of "spiderwebs of intricate relationships" which is abandoned whenever "the strings become so numerous that you can no longer pass among them" and rebuilt somewhere else (76). Eusapia, another double city, contains a subterranean copy of itself as a device meant by its builders to render the jump from life to death less brusque. Beersheba, by contrast, has a specular counterpart in the heavens that houses its "most elevated virtues and sentiments" (111). A grim travesty of Beersheba, Perinthia is torn between the dream of the astronomers that planned her and the reality of her concrete existence: designed to mirror the "harmony of the firmament" (144), the city is actually infested by all manner of deformities.

Moriana, almost a parody of the Saussurean sign, is "like a sheet of paper, with a figure on either side, which can neither be separated nor look at each other" (105); yet, despite its two-dimensional flimsiness, it is capable of conveying the illusion of multiple perspectives. A city's own divided identity is further capable of initiating a proliferation of subject positions for its viewer. Faced with Maurilia, for instance, the visitor is caught between two incompatible requirements: the imperative to praise today's prosperous metropolis and the obligation to recognize the superior grace of the old provincial town as represented in postcards. Despina, arguably one of the most intriguing of Venice's fifty-five alter-egos, "displays one face to the traveler arriving overland and a different one to him who arrives by sea" (17).

A virtually limitless number of possible cities can be imagined on the basis of the permutational and associational mechanisms of *ars combinatoria*—a practice which, though traceable back to the Middle Ages, is deemed by Calvino to be particularly apposite to contemporary perceptions of the world. As he argues in the essay "Cybernetics and Ghosts," nowadays "The world in its various aspects is increasingly looked upon as *discrete* rather than *continuous*.... Thought, which until the other day appeared to us as something fluid, evoking linear images such as a flowing river or an unwinding thread, or else gaseous images such as a kind of vaporous cloud ... we now tend to think of as a series of discontinuous states, of combinations of impulses acting on a finite (though enormous) number of sensory and motor organs" (Calvino 1987, 8). Thus, Kublai Khan constructs his urban template on the assumption that all the existing cities consist of variable departures from a basic standard and he needs "only foresee the exceptions to the norm and calculate the most probable combinations." Polo, for his part, deduces his taxonomy of conceivable urban configurations from a model city consisting solely of "exceptions, exclusions, incongruities, contradictions" and then cutting down the incidence of "abnormal" factors to arrive at a modicum of probability (Calvino 1997, 69). Both methodologies proceed from the premise that any place, real or virtual, represents not a single place but a swirling galaxy of imaginable spaces. This multiplicity expresses itself in more or less codified and formulaic moves, through which a location's inhabitants endlessly enact the same basic play with purely marginal changes to the cast. Combinatorial relationality, therefore, is not only the principle governing the conception and design of the city: it is also, no less crucially, the mechanism that triggers human interaction and makes communication possible even in the most thoroughly dehumanized metropolitan environment.

In the illustrious city of Chloe, for example, people appear to be deeply alienated from one another; yet, whenever they come into even the flimsiest form of interpersonal contact, they instantly begin to fantasize about one another and the things they imagine create complex patterns of association and relation. It is by virtue of these unspoken and unrealized moves that a potent strain of voluptuousness resonates continually throughout Chloe, despite its reputation as the epitome of virginal purity, in the form of a colorful merry-go-round of hidden fantasies. Fundamentally anti-essentialist and contingent in both content and structure, Calvino's urban tapestry is inhabited not by tangible and individualized objects but rather by rhythms of ceaseless exchange and circulation — of architectural and ornamental elements, as in the case of Clarice; of narratives, as in the case of Euphemia; and, more pervasively, of signs. Tamara, for example, epitomizes a decidedly post-humanist culturescape where any notion of presence is necessarily founded on the absence of solid referents beyond the thicket of disembodied signs: only signs are discernible, though signs do not lead to meaning but only to other signs, ad infinitum. Hence, the traveler is drawn into a world of almost obsessional decoding, subjugated to the imperative to detect signs in any aspect of both the visible and the invisible, the present and the absent.

As the wizardly creator responsible for the majority of Calvino's English-language translations, William Weaver, has emphasized, the very planning of *Invisible Cities* testifies to the writer's passion for hypothetical schemata: "He liked to make outlines, lists, *scalette* — little ladders — as the Italians call them (and his chapter lists, in his spare hand, did resemble ladders). Thus his invisible cities are fitted into categories: trading cities, thin cities, continuous cities." However, what these characteristically neat distributions ultimately reveal is not a rational and measurable order beyond doubt or dispute. In fact, they are underpinned by a deeply "mysterious, Calvino-invented system that has evoked pages of exegesis by eager scholars" but thus far resisted conclusive explanation by even the most proficient of critics. Calvino's status as the "son of scientists" undoubtedly contributed in no small measure to his development and confident utilization of a comprehensive "scientific and technical vocabulary" but this never led to the formulation of coldly crystallized theories. What always retained paramount importance, in fact, was the accomplishment of an ineffable equilibrium. Weaver argues that this is just what *Invisible Cities* achieves: "with *Invisible Cities* all was harmonious, as it should be for a book that is pure music" (Weaver).

A pervasive sense of instability and change nonetheless characterizes *Invisible Cities* throughout, and this is paralleled by the shifting modes of symbolization assisting Polo's and Kublai's narrative journey. Binary thought is again drastically undermined — in this context, specifically, by Calvino's refusal to advocate the superiority of any one form of expression over any of the others. Speech and writing, verbal and non-verbal languages, sounds and silence, all display virtues and flaws which bind them together in mutual suffusion. The linguistic tools at the protagonists' disposal range from a non-verbal type of communication, based on the exhibition of material objects and the uttering of equivocal noises, through the elaboration of a spoken discourse, to a language of silence counterpointed by the codes of chess-playing. The initial, primitive register holds the advantage of practically unlimited interpretability: "the connections between one element of the story and another were not always obvious to the emperor; the objects could have various meanings" (Calvino 1997, 38). The unbounded narrative potentialities of any one object underscore the dependence of any contingently selected interpretation on the absent traces of all other possible interpretations floating in the vacuum left unfilled by Polo's words. The Khan, at this stage, is principally intrigued by the countless narrative options alluded to by his visitor's exhibits that remain necessarily unvoiced due to the explorer's inarticulateness.

As time goes by, Polo learns Kublai's language. Although this makes his discourse apparently more accurate, communication between the two parties becomes less gratifying, drained of creativity and suggestiveness, until Polo resolves to rely once more on his body language in preference to verbal discourse. The Khan himself, while recognizing the greater thoroughness of his visitor's verbal inventories once Polo has gained access to the local discourse, finds them only partially satisfying. The orderliness of the newly established symbolic regime is hence encroached upon by reminders of a pre-linguistic semiotic universe. Forced to confront the stultifying limitations of human language, Kublai Khan and Polo ultimately develop a mute and motionless dialogue. The value here attached to silence is redolent of Martin Heidegger's notion that only silence may be meaningful in the rampant inauthenticity and capriciousness of everyday language: silence is the precondition of language, the stillness against which language differentiates itself, ideally in the form of the revelatory poetic word (Heidegger). Yet, Calvino's text is more of a parody than a celebration of Heidegger's views, since silence, in *Invisible Cities*, springs not from a messianic faith in redeeming epiphanies but rather from a stoical recognition of the pointlessness, absurdity and farcical pretensions of the pandemonium we quotidianly roam.

At the same time as Polo and Kublai move increasingly towards a mute mode of conversation, the narrative powers of each of the objects brought back by the Venetian develop, to reflect not simply the specific attributes of individual samples but also their combinatorial connections with innumerable other objects. Polo thus proceeds to portray his adventures by placing the items in a particular arrangement on the giant chessboard of the Khan's black-and-white checkered floor. The transition from the individual item to the relational cluster is not, however, the final stage of Polo's and Kublai's discursive voyage. Little by little, the interrelated objects themselves lose significance, and it is the set of criteria on the basis of which they are arranged that becomes paramount in an oblique allegorization of the development of structuralist thought. Drawing an intriguing analogy between Polo's newly devised narratological procedures and the game of chess, the Khan dreams of the day when, having learnt to handle the rules which govern the city as confidently as he already deploys those which govern the chessboard, he will eventually master his empire. He is also aware, however, that knowing the rules of the city-game will not actually allow him to know all of the cities contained within the empire. In this respect, he voices one of Calvino's recurring concerns, namely, the disparity between the enclosed and relatively safe world of the code, and the infinite and baffling world of its possible applications. The aforementioned essay "Cybernetics and Ghosts" addresses the issue as follows: "Just as no chess player will ever live long enough to exhaust all the combinations of possible moves for the thirty-two pieces on the chessboard, so we know (given the fact that our minds are chessboards with hundreds of billions of pieces) that not even in a lifetime lasting as long as the universe would one ever manage to make all possible plays" (Calvino 1987, 8–9).

In the end, Kublai Khan and Polo are inexorably brought hard up against the realization that systematic moves, rational arrangements and sealed codes are illusory, if necessary, fictions. Permutations and combinations are primarily arbitrary and random processes, as evinced by the cycles of generation, degeneration and regeneration experienced by the city of Clarice. When the city has lived through so many centuries of splendor and renown that decay becomes inevitable, her inhabitants, in an attempt to salvage the specter of her former glory, simply grab every single scrap of material they can lay their paws on and put it to a radically alternate use: sumptuous fabrics are demoted to the role of lowly bedding; precious cinerary urns become pots for simple herbs; exquisitely wrought grilles once employed to protect the windows of harems turn into cooking implements for feline flesh. The awareness that any concept of order is accidental and temporary makes any journey a zigzagging movement along invisible itineraries traced among points stranded in nothingness. Indeed, all of Polo's cities, not only the ones explicitly classified as thin, compound to form an oneiric landscape so rarefied, tenuous and fragile as to become virtually impalpable. However attenuated, though, the dream-city stubbornly refuses to disappear: in fact, the dream element is responsible for imparting her with both form and beauty. Zobeide, for example, would strike anyone as a fairly hideous place, were it not for the fact that it was built out of a collective dream of pursuit, love and desire.

Upon first entering *Invisible Cities*, the prevalent atmosphere one experiences is that of a magical Orient. Gradually, however, the senses are bombarded by the shapes and noises of a contemporary metropolis threatening to engulf the entire planet. The Khan increasingly thinks of his empire as a territory "covered with cities that weigh upon the earth and upon mankind, crammed with wealth and traffic, overladen with ornaments and offices, complicated with mechanisms and hierarchies, swollen, tense, ponderous" (Calvino 1997, 73). Some of the cities portrayed by Polo overtly mirror this sense of bloated heaviness: Zirma, with its dire underground packed with overweight women, is a paradigmatic case in point. Others allude to that same atmosphere by recourse to circuitous figurative strategies, whereby they succeed in conveying the feeling of ponderousness, paradoxically, through a veneer of apparent refinement. Valdrada offers an apt illustration of this modality.

Practically all the cities categorized as continuous (and they are not the only ones) point to the image of an ever-proliferating metropolis — a city given to accumulating waste and detritus faster than it can expel them and so amorphous as to resemble an endless suburban expanse. All cities, in this perspective, are essentially the same: "Only the name of the airport changes" (128). What these cities predominantly evoke is the idea of an overdeveloped conglomerate that simultaneously offers the consolatory promise of an all-encompassing dwelling place and the threat of an environment where nobody can really belong anywhere. Spatial fluidity should not, however, be simplistically interpreted as an exclusively contemporary symptom of deterioration. In fact, the plastic nature of urban living has been for time immemorial one of the most salient features of the city as a construct wherein the dividing line between imagination and reality is never absolute. According to Jonathan Raban, "The city as we might imagine it, the soft city of illusion, myth, aspiration, nightmare, is as real, maybe more real, than the hard city one can locate in maps and statistics, in monographs on urban sociology and demography and architecture" (Raban 10). Calvino's increasing emphasis on continuity — what Raban suggestively terms softness — as a metaphor for the extension of the city construct over the entire planet may seem at odds with the claim that the world is becoming more and more discrete. But the contradiction is only apparent, for the sprawling city is both continuous and discrete at once: it is everywhere but in the form of fragments, at times "scattered" and at times "condensed" (Calvino 1997, 164).

The coexistence, throughout Calvino's invisible geography, of continuity and discontinuity, displacement and condensation, fragmentation and compactness is one of the most conspicuous characteristics of the postmodern metropolis. In this respect, *Invisible Cities* could be read as a commentary, prophetic at times, on urban life as it is conducted today in an environment soaked through and through with computer-generated and electronically processed information. As Nicholas Negroponte observes, our perception of the world is conditioned by the coalescence of contrary states: "From a macroscopic point of view, [the world] is not digital at all but continuous. Nothing goes suddenly on or off, turns from black to white, or changes from one state to another without going through a transition" (Negroponte 7). An understanding of this intermediate or provisional space is crucial to any investigation of the contemporary metropolis insofar as it underscores the double-edged character of the captivating comparison between the electronic matrix and the city.

While investing urban space with attributes of order and rationality, the computer model also serves to efface and repress those portions of the city map which are most blatantly indisposed to digital sublimation. As Boyer maintains, "the spaces of disjunction between the rows and columns of the data entries ... represent the forgotten spaces, the disavowed places" (Boyer 9). This schizophrenic conception of urban reality is encapsulated by Calvino's juxtaposition of neatly mapped-out spaces, governed by quantifiable relations of exchange and combinatorial possibilities, on the one hand, and boundless realms of unruptured and hence nearly illegible continuity and self-dissemination, on the other hand. His world thus mirrors the current metropolitan condition as an unwieldy mix of thoroughly sanitized virtual spaces and spaces of physical decay and anarchy: the immaterial geography of computer networks and the corporeal geography of the ever-growing, polluted and diseased city "with all its gaping wounds" (11).

The foregrounding of spaces of contamination and chaos serves to challenge the organizing powers of symbolic language. Calvino's urban typologies and related geometries abide by a structuralist conception of language as a compartmentalizing mechanism, a means of chopping up an otherwise uninterrupted continuum. Yet, they also remind us that the boundary between any two compartments is not a vacuum but rather a dense region inhabited by forces that official structures of signification deem taboo and hence endeavor to repress or occult. As Edmund Leach remarks, the "taboo inhibits the recognition of those parts of the continuum which separate the things" (Leach 47). By drawing attention to spaces of darkness and disorder, Calvino prompts us to acknowledge the taboo as an object not only of revulsion but also of fascination. If many contemporary theorizations of the metropolis tend to obliterate the tenebrous and inscrutable territories which stretch indefinitely within the city's boundaries, *Invisible Cities* seeks to multiply the murky realms embedded within the urban tapestry. Death, decay and corruption, squalid and malodorous subterranean spaces, grotesque shapes, ailing bodies, vermin and waste coexist with the intoxicating radiance of the bridges and balconies, balustrades and stained-glass windows, domes and fountains, precious stones and glimmering reflections of architectural dreams where everything is possible and the law of gravity itself may be defied.

Half-corpses crawling aimlessly in the dampness and darkness of the underworld, disfigured creatures and mythical prodigies may easily be encountered amid the charm of lustrous buildings crowned by bright flags and the hypnotic beauty of fragrant gardens or azure lagoons. The reader, therefore, is repeatedly invited to contemplate rotting and fragmented bodies, spectral apparitions and crumbling ruins alongside myriad scenarios of spectacular beauty. In foregrounding, rather than marginalizing, the power of tabooed forms, Calvino's geography, despite its etherealizing proclivities, endorses the idea of the city as a corporeal entity. The nature of Polo's task is in itself eminently physical despite the conventional association of the voyager's gaze with strategies of disembodied probing. As his eyes scan the superficial skin of innumerable cities, he is not simply intent on gaining a panoramic view of both their tangible and their immaterial treasures: he is also engrossed in peeling away, decomposing, dismembering and reassembling each successive layer of the palimpsest, each painfully volatile and particularized fragment of his optical experience, in a fashion that renders the activity of looking strikingly tactile.

Invisible Cities thus articulates various ways of projecting the body onto urban artifacts: it amalgamates architectural and biological systems, fictionalizes the notion of bodily needs according to cartographic schemata, and channels bodily rhythms into the animation of otherwise inanimate objects. By bestowing a sense of aliveness on inorganic matter, the text both panders to the anthropomorphic proclivities of Western humanism — here addressed in Chapter 3 — and makes space vulnerable to the whims of organic decay. In acquiring a corporeal identity, space must live with the consequences of this gain, however dire they may turn out to be. The anthropomorphic ideation of space points, as Elaine Scarry remarks, to a desire "*to deprive the external world of the privilege of being inanimate.... To say that the 'inanimateness' of the external world is diminished, is almost* to say (but it is *not* to say) that the external world is made animate" (Scarry 285).

Calvino's way of making space bodily does not seek to promote humanity's mastery by subjecting inert inorganic matter to the priorities of organic animateness. Rather, it engages with multifold processes of reciprocal enmeshing and exchange between the organic and the inorganic, the human and the non-human. In the process, architecture is humanized, while the human body is architecturalized, rendered virtually inextricable from the architectural structures with which it is unceasingly required to interplay. The corporeality of built space is allowed to manifest itself in an architecture which, to borrow Coop Himmelblau's words, "bleeds, ... exhausts, ... whirls and even breaks ... a cavernous, burning, sweet hard, angular, brutal, round, delicate, colored, obscene, voluptuous, dreaming, seductive, repulsive, wet, dry, palpitating architecture" (cited in Vidler 8).

Calvino's urban body is indeed patently at odds with the visions of seamlessness, purity, harmony and wholeness, advocated by classical aesthetics, veering instead toward the grotesque, in a graphic architectural adaptation of Peter Stallybrass and Allon White's sculptural model: "The classical statue has no openings or orifices whereas grotesque costume and masks emphasize the gaping mouth, the protuberant belly and buttocks, the feet and genitals. In this way the grotesque body stands in opposition to the bourgeois individualist conception of the body, which finds its image and legitimation in the classical. The grotesque body is emphasized as a mobile, split, multiple self, a subject of pleasure in processes of exchange;

and it is never closed off from either social or ecosystemic contexts. The classical body on the other hand keeps its distance. In a sense it is disembodied, for it appears indifferent to a body which is 'beautiful,' but which is taken for granted" (Stallybrass and White 22). *Invisible Cities* thus asserts itself, among other things, as an allegory of the city as a bodily construct. Its project is sustained by recurring parallelisms between urban constructs and bodily functions and processes. Calvino's city is born, grows, conceives, reproduces and dies; she has sex, as suggested by the idea of the city reaching a climax; she follows certain diets; she develops diseases, neuroses and disabilities, such as congestion, tumorous overgrowth, hyperactivity and the fear of alien infractions; she exhibits anabolic and catabolic processes corresponding to her creative and destructive moments; she has both naked and clothed facets, both sealed and leaky elements, and adorns herself, either uniformly or eclectically; she contains idealized and monumental body parts to be proudly flaunted and secret, intimate parts to be cautious and ashamed of; finally, she bears signs of the passing of time as so many indentations, folds, lines and wrinkles in the tissue of her architectural make-up.

Furthermore, Calvino's cities tend to come across as fundamentally female bodies. This could no doubt be related to classic historical accounts of the birth of the urban construct as a product of the transition from the male world of hunting to the female world of sedentary life. According to Lewis Mumford, the association of early urban existence with the female body is corroborated by the sexual symbolism of architectural structures: "the house and the oven, the byre and the bin, the cistern, the storage pit, the granary, ... the moat, and all inner spaces, from the atrium to the cloister" (Mumford 21). However Mumford, while granting woman a central role in the inception of city life, also emphasizes the enduring dominance of the male hunter, now metamorphosed into the mighty protector of the walled citadel. The reduction of female powers signalled by the reintroduction onto the scene of the virile, martial hero is mirrored, argues Mumford, by the demise of primitive mythological beliefs based on dominating female figures often endowed with "savage attributes" and the creation of myths that commend female "tenderness, beauty, erotic delight" (36–37).

In Calvino's world, gender positions in the city do not relegate woman to a condition of ornamental supplementarity. In fact, *Invisible Cities* draws attention to the existence of crucial links between notions of space and specifically feminine attributes: links, as Elizabeth Grosz indicates, that are encapsulated in the concept of *chora*. Plato's term for describing a "mythological bridge between the intelligible and the sensible, mind and body," *chora* "signifies, at its most literal level, notions of 'place,' 'location,' 'site,' 'region,' 'locale,' 'country': but it also contains an irreducible, yet often overlooked, connection with femininity, being associated with a series of gender-aligned terms — 'mother,' 'nurse,' 'receptacle' and 'imprint-bearer'" (Grosz 47–48). *Chora* is a metaphorical womb, "the space in which place is made possible" (51), and while this analogy may be seen to perpetuate stereotypical associations of woman with the image of a passive receptacle, it also acts as a reminder of the incontrovertible corporeality of lived space — of a bodily dimension which may only be conquered and suppressed at the cost of losing access to our own bodies.

Calvino opposes the containment of femininity within the decarnalized male citadel by offering scope for the representation of female pleasure as autonomous. This is indicated, for example, by the city of Armilla, the domain of aquatic female creatures of mythical derivation who spend their time luxuriating in all manner of baths and fountains, always keen to discover new sources of liquid pleasure. Moreover, the association of woman with gentle manifestations of eros does not preclude more dynamic expressions of female sexuality, as shown most explicitly by the women of Hypatia. The problematization of gender roles in Calvino's city-body does not fail to affect the characterization of the voyager: invested with conventional masculine attributes such as independence and adventurousness, the right to enter any city he fancies and move around her at will, his penetrative powers are nonetheless precarious, as no exploratory journey will ultimately uncover the secrets that all cities stubbornly endeavor to keep invisible. The city's bodiliness ultimately amounts to a sensual remainder which, though rejected, abjected or projected onto the ephemeral screens of veiled fantasies and desires, ceaselessly defies the presence of planned space through its borderline absences. As Henri Lefebvre observes, the current tendency to talk about space in terms of eminently social practices does not automatically equate it to purely political and economic factors, for social space is also, inevitably, a geography of passions, emotions, longings and affects: "Representational space is alive: it speaks. It has an affective kernel or centre: Ego, bed, bedroom, dwelling, house; or, square, church, graveyard. It embraces the loci of passion, of action and of lived situations" (Lefebvre 42). No less vitally, in Calvino's urban perspective, "Space is liable to be eroticized and restored to ambiguity, to the common birthplace of needs and desires ... by means of differential systems and valorizations which overwhelm the strict localization of needs and desires in spaces specialized either physiologically (sexuality) or socially (places set aside, supposedly, for pleasure)" (391).

Calvino's cities fully validate this proposition while also emphasizing the deterioration of the metropolis into what Mumford vividly describes as "a colossal, clotted, self-defeating mass" (Mumford 640). This double perspective complicates the sensual and sexual dimensions of urban existence by drawing attention to the shift from the idea of the city as an organic body to that of the city as a deterritorialized sprawl. The model of the city as a centralized body, endowed with a nucleus and a boundary, is superseded by the image of a diffuse and undifferentiated conurbation. Concomitantly, the notion of a hierarchical urban structure capable of replicating the human nervous system (the cathedral or the palace operating as an architectonic brain) gives way to the random layering of a precariously bounded tissue, where no clearly identifiable nucleus is able to govern the development of the periphery. This shift from structures of condensation to processes of dissemination lends itself to both pessimistic and optimistic readings, insofar as it hints simultaneously at apocalyptic endings and at novel remappings of urban reality. Mumford's study foregrounds the negative repercussions of metropolization by emphasizing the transition from a model of the city based on the principle of implosion — namely, the mobilization of disparate activities in the service of the human community — to a cultural scenario dominated by rhythms of explosion: "the city has burst open and scattered its complex organs over the entire landscape" (45).

This depiction of contemporary city life is certainly reminiscent of Kublai's perception of his empire as a sagging structure riddled with unfathomable absences. *The City in History* does not fail, however, to acknowledge the positive potentialities of explosion as a means of combating the obsession with totalizing unity so deeply ingrained in Western thought. If the "proliferation of metropolitan tissue" (598) is horrifying because it denies, cancer-like, the benefits of organic growth, it is also the case that the traditional city could often only function through blockage and exclusion: "in many instances the city tends to encase the organic, many-sided life of the community in petrified and overspecialized forms that achieve continuity at the expense of adaptation and further growth.... In the end it has made physical disintegration — through war, fire, economic corrosion or blight — the only way of opening the city up to the fresh demands of life" (599).

Therefore, while bemoaning humankind's subjugation to "the

requirements of the machine" (601), to the "Cybernetic Deity' (618) and to an environment where "flesh and blood are less real than paper and ink and celluloid" (623), Mumford nevertheless accepts that the new city "has brought together, within relatively narrow compass, the diversity and variety of special cultures" (639). Although *The City in History* does not overtly describe Venice as a prophetic vision of the deterritorialized urbanscape, its delineation of the city's developmental patterns implicitly suggests a parallel between the geographical self-dissemination of Polo's native city and the postmodern expanse. The creation of a group of refugees from Padua in the fifth century A.D., Venice is "a new urban constellation that promise[s] to transcend the walled container" (369), the city wall consisting, ironically, of a proverbially unstable element, water. Its only internal boundaries, moreover, are defined by the web of one hundred and seventy-seven protean canals. Venice is seen as the product of incremental, "cumulative urban purposes" and hence as irreducible to the intentions or aims of one single author: "the plan of Venice was no static design, embodying the needs of a single generation, arbitrarily ruling out the possibilities of growth, re-adaptation, change: rather, here was continuity in change" (370).

What becomes progressively palpable in navigating *Invisible Cities* is its unique emphasis on the narrative potential of the experience of journeying. Michel de Certeau's assessment of walking in *The Practice of Everyday Life* as a means of constantly remapping space by creating ever new routes through it without recourse to rigid identities and bodies supplies a relevant metaphor for Polo's narrative enterprise: namely, his ongoing struggle to find a place, both literally and figuratively. Voyaging through space becomes tantamount to turning it into a story or cluster of stories. In a structuralist perspective, moving across the city can be thought of as "a way of conceiving and constructing space on the basis of a finite number of stable, isolatable, and interconnected properties" (de Certeau 93). In this view, as Steve Pile notes, any one chosen itinerary "cuts up, parcels and names houses, streets, neighbourhoods, blocks, and so on" (Pile 226). However, *The Practice of Everyday Life* also offers a poststructuralist option by foregrounding "the innumerable ways in which walking in the streets mobilizes other subtle, stubborn, embodied, resistant meanings. The streets become haunted by the ghosts of other stories.... The city becomes a ghost town of memories without a language to articulate them because walking is a transient and evanescent practice.... Walkers are involved in the production of an unmappable space which cannot be seen from above" (226).

In this unchartable world, people drift through "spaces of darkness and trickery," constantly reconfigured by a "combination of manipulation and enjoyment" (de Certeau 18).

Polo closely resembles de Certeau's traveler, in both the structuralist and the poststructuralist modalities just described. On the one hand, he is unceasingly elaborating ways of cutting up the spatial continuum by reference to relational and differential networks of signification. On the other hand, each systematic mapping of space is bound to prove fleeting and illusory, one limited reading among countless virtual stories. In Polo's universe (as in Calvino's), everything is endlessly recombinable and interchangeable, and any contingent orchestration of objects or concepts may well have been something quite different. Moreover, the Venetian adventurer cannot, at any juncture in his voyages, step outside space and contemplate it from a privileged vantage point. He is inseparable from the places through which he moves, and the narratives produced by his perpetual wanderings are therefore both his and not his, both effects of his actions and entities over which he has no authentic control. All-seeing, yet blind, Polo incarnates the paradoxes of the urban "practitioner": "The ordinary practitioners of the city live 'down below,' below the thresholds at which visibility begins ... they are walkers ... where bodies follow the thicks and thins of an urban 'text' they write without being able to read it. These practitioners make use of spaces that cannot be seen; their knowledge of them is as blind as that of lovers in each other's arms" (93).

Clearly, de Certeau's walker is not just any walker but, specifically, a *flâneur*, the prototype of the urban voyeur strolling aimlessly around, seeing all while retaining his anonymity. While drawing a comparison between this emblematic figure of modernity and a medieval traveler such as Polo may seem wildly anachronistic, it could nonetheless be argued that many of the characteristics generally attributed to the *flâneur* are also discernible in Calvino's anti-hero. It is the ambivalence of the figure of the modern urban walker that makes him so startlingly akin to Polo. As suggested earlier, Polo's position is equivocal. His influence as an ambassador, his prestige as a creative narrator, and his sexual prowess as a penetrator of countless cities are repeatedly enfeebled by reminders of his disenfranchized status: of his subjection to the Khan's whims, of his limited narratorial authority, and of his powerlessness in the face of each city's nameless invisibility. Similarly, the *flâneur* is powerful and vulnerable at the same time: "on the one hand," as Pile stresses, he is "captivated by the movement and excitement of the urban modern; on the other hand, terrified of being swallowed up by the masses" (Pile 230). The *flâneur*'s uncertain condition is primarily a corollary of his relation to the urban spectacle. The ability to hold innumerable images within his masterful field of vision is also an implicit admission of lack, of a precariously defined self which, in the absence of those images, would plausibly evaporate. As Keith Tester argues, "*flâneurie* can, after Baudelaire, be understood as the activity of the sovereign spectator going about the city in order to find the things which will occupy his gaze and thus complete his otherwise incomplete identity; satisfy his otherwise dissatisfied existence; replace the sense of bereavement with a sense of life" (Tester 7).

The *flâneur* thus incarnates the ambivalence of the developing city: he is an apparently all-powerful observer, seeing everything while remaining virtually unseen, and a lonely and dispossessed onlooker, excluded from any human relationship other than casual contact with the formless crowd. While his ego is relentlessly flattered by the fascinating pageant of new commodities and inventions, it is concurrently dwarfed by his exclusion from active productivity. The spectacle does indeed exist but not for his sole consumption. His experience, according to John Lechte, can never be unique, for in "the collectivity of idiolects" that is the city, "the singular appropriation of space gives way to random distributions of all kinds, distributions which *are* people walking in the city" (Lechte 105). Moreover, as Elizabeth Wilson maintains, being a man of pleasure means both being able to take "visual possession of the city" (65) and, far less gratifyingly, being thrown into the urban whirlpool of forever unfinished fictions. The *flâneur*'s experience as a reader, or interpreter, is overtly reminiscent of Polo's and, by extension, of any erring decoder of metropolitan life: "we constantly brush against strangers; we observe bits of the 'stories' men and women carry with them, but never learn their conclusions; life ceases to form itself into an epic or narrative, becoming instead a short story, dreamlike, insubstantial or ambiguous" (73). Just as Polo's peregrinations could go on forever or, alternatively, might as well never have started, so the *flâneur*'s journey has no clear points of either departure or destination. Walter Benjamin reinforces this point by emphasizing that there is no obvious sense of direction in the *flâneur*'s motion insofar as he experiences urban life as a labyrinth: namely, "the home of the hesitant" (Benjamin 40). The image of the labyrinth invoked by Benjamin is especially relevant to the present context given its privileged status in Calvino's own metaphorical repertoire (as noted in Chapter 1). Another aforementioned image also close to Calvino's heart that likewise offers a fitting symbol for the eternal wanderer's dispossession is, according to Boyer, that of the kaleidoscope: "At each step the *flâneur* takes ... new constellations of images appear that resemble the turns of a kaleidoscope. But as these spectacles of the city are formed, the *flâneur*'s internal thoughts feel devalued and disordered, the result of figures that flow and blend into each other as if they were in a dream" (Boyer 51).

The closing segment of this chapter proposes that *Invisible Cities* addresses the issue of the translation, or indeed translatability, of physical space into images. Echoing many a geographer's preoccupations, Calvino's text explores the viability of any endeavor to distinguish between the phenomenal environment and the behavioral environment. The former is the so-called real world but also a human construct—the product of human action and perception. Hence, the phenomenal is penetrated by the behavioral, since what we perceive is clearly a result of social, cultural and traditional codes and conventions. According to William Kirk, "the behavioral Environment is ... a psycho-physical field in which phenomenal facts are arranged into patterns or structures (*gestalten*) and acquire values in cultural contexts" (Kirk, 366). In behavioral geography, a central role is played by the notion of the image (either as cognitive structure or as visual map), as the mental factor which mediates between behavior and environment. Behavioral geography, in attempting to theorize the relationship between spatial behavior and its causes, often — and regrettably — relies totally on the psychology of individual perception without taking into account social structures and patterns of conduct. The danger implicit in this approach, *Invisible Cities* warns us, is that it may become totally oblivious to the constructedness of spatial experience: to the fact that "forms of behavior," as Doreen Massey argues, "can never be taken, theoretically, as given; they are always 'produced'— that is they are the outcome of the structured context in which they occur" (Massey 202). No less problematically, behavioral geography also relies on a strictly antithetical distinction between consciousness and the subconscious. *Invisible Cities*, by contrast, stresses that this dichotomy is not tenable, for the subconscious cannot be realistically detached or sequestered from rational categories.

In a sense, even though the ambitions of behavioral geography are empirically grounded and positivist in their general outlook, they are also redolent, in their attempts to isolate human essences and cleanse them of all social interferences, of humanist essentialism. Humanist geography, too, is concerned with discovering Man's place in the world. The difference between the two approaches, according to Roger M. Downs and

James T. Meyer, lies in their divergent views on consciousness: "in the empiricist conception, mind means brain in the psychological sense. For the humanist, mind is much closer to the notion of spirit (*Geist*), of mind-in-the-world" (Downs and Meyer 67). In both cases, however, the central thrust is foundationalist and binary oppositional. *Invisible Cities* questions both the behavioral and the humanist formulations of geographical experience by bringing into play postmodernist and poststructuralist approaches that turn spatiality into a chain of discursive maps. These structures do not simply accommodate but actually produce subjects. As Pile evocatively puts it, "the individual becomes a longitude and latitude of various power-infused discursive positions" and is therefore "multiplied, dynamic, participating and determined ... the site of constantly changing mutations of difference, at once stable and dislocated, at once fixed and changing. The subject is never in one place" (Pile 74).

The invisibility of *Invisible Cities* may amount to precisely this: the subject's continual transposition from this place to another place, from the unified domain of the humanist self to a post-humanist landscape of dispersion and disavowal. The explosion and scattering of subjectivity over an unlimited landscape entails a simultaneous dissemination of vision that radically calls into question the status of all visible entities by underscoring the relative and contingent status of visibility. We are thus reminded that what we see in an object in any one place and at any one time is purely a snapshot capturing no more than a diminutive visual shred of its entire existence. We can only attach value to that ephemeral image by isolating it from its broad context and then believing that it can stand, metonymically, for the whole. In so doing, we convince ourselves that by grasping an object in the form of a fixed visual snippet, we can also possess the limitless world whence it emerges. In other words, we use the snapshot to conceal the existence of a vast and indeterminate reality that mockingly eludes us. Each of Calvino's cities functions as a metaphorical variation on that unquantifiable dimension, persistently drawing attention not so much to what Polo's descriptions encompass as to what they leave out. Therefore, the cities do not act as snapshots but rather as reminders of the spatial and temporal flow stretching forever beyond the frozen image. At the same time, the cities do not only invite us to contemplate their existence: they also challenge us to acknowledge that they might just as well never have been, that the reasons for which they have somehow managed to replace the void that would otherwise have been there are quite impenetrable. *Invisible Cities* foregrounds the marginality of visibility and presence, and their derivative status as by-products of invisibility and absence, of an incalculable number of might-have-beens that empirical reality struggles to keep at bay but cannot ultimately account for. The text underscores the radical contingency of any object by reminding us that, in a sense, no city — and, by implication, nothing at all — actually *needs* to be and that what is, therefore, is inevitably traversed by the nothingness which it may easily have been instead.

In articulating their fifty-five takes on the themes of absence and presence, Calvino's cities also symbolize those systems of signification which, though drained of content to the advantage of structure are nonetheless densely packed with vaporous traces of meaning. Inspiringly, Jacques Derrida comments on the divorce of content from structure precisely by reference to the image of the city. The paradoxical city envisaged by Derrida, a place forsaken yet not definitely abandoned, could plausibly have featured within Polo's taxonomy: "the relief and design of structures appears more clearly when content, which is the living energy of meaning, is neutralized. Somewhat like the architecture of an uninhabited or deserted city, reduced to its skeleton by some catastrophe of nature or art. A city no longer inhabited, not simply left behind, but haunted by meaning and culture" (Derrida 1978, 26). Pursuing further the architectural simile, it could be argued that the collusion of visibility and invisibility, of presence and absence, finds an apt parallel in a specifically postmodernist preference: namely, the dissolution of what Peter Eisenman terms "the traditional opposition between structure and decoration, abstraction and figuration, figure and ground," in the service of an architecture that explores "the 'between' within these categories" (cited in Norris and Benjamin 27). As discussed in the preceding pages, *Invisible Cities* challenges many conventional binary oppositions precisely by articulating an architecture of murky thresholds and ambivalent interstices. The decentering architecture extolled by Eisenman is predominantly intended to dislocate official perceptions of architecture as a concrete vehicle for the expression of order, stability and authority — a logocentric structuring of space which, as Mary McLeod argues, has recurrently asserted itself by contrast with the volatility and impermanence of the fashion system: "From the late nineteenth century to the outbreak of World War Two architects shunned the transient and commercial qualities of fashion, associating it with the superficiality of ornament, they viewed fashion, especially women's fashion, as frivolous, unfunctional, and wasteful, the antithesis of rationality and simplicity" (McLeod 39).

Chapter 4—The Endless Journey

Eisenman's proposed architecture, refreshingly, thrives on principles of discontinuity and superficiality, on the instability of spatial boundaries, on the penetration of the functional by the ornamental, of the essential by the supplementary. The epitome of this vision of the built environment is the balcony space: a site that metamorphoses the inside into the outside and the outside into the inside by stressing the flimsiness of any barrier. Polo is well aware of the tenuousness of the boundary putatively separating the inside from the outside — as attested to, for instance, by the city of Zoe as a place marked by shifting spatial attributes and a pervasive atmosphere of doubt. The balcony problematizes the conventional link between building and dwelling, for it is structurally connected with a building, yet it is hardly conceptualizable as a dwelling place. At best, it operates as a medium for interaction between the private and public spheres; it does not foster, clearly, the cult of space as protected habitation. Perversely, perhaps, the balcony simultaneously supports and shakes the pillars of domesticity. *Invisible Cities* abounds with balcony spaces, alongside verandas, balustrades, belvederes, patios and parapets, as most sensationally borne out by the cities of Thekla, Valdrada, Zenobia, Octavia, Armilla, and the quintessentially Venetian Esmeralda.

Calvino's fifty-five cities are as many transitional spaces that frequently resemble archeological digs strewn with architectural fragments and can only be understood as places insofar as they are capable of engaging their visitors in an illusion of space. They are invisible not only because they might not exist beyond Polo's narrative meanderings or because they might already have ceased to exist by the time the Venetian has got round to weaving his tales but also, more importantly, because they only exist thanks to their localization by abstract narrative and symbolic frameworks — in other words, to their conception as evanescent landscapes of the mind. The most daring — and inexorably endless — journeys always take place in imagination and thought. It is only logical, in this scenario, that the places they fleetingly touch should be invisible cities or perhaps invisible ideas donning the garb of multiform cities.

Chapter 5

Structures and Their Explosion:
The Castle of Crossed Destinies

The book bearing the title *The Castle of Crossed Destinies* actually comprises two texts — or perhaps two complementary tellings of the same basic narrative — titled *The Castle of Crossed Destinies* and *The Tavern of Crossed Destinies*. The former was first published in 1969 in *Tarots: The Visconti Pack in Bergamo and New York*. The whole book as it now stands was originally released in 1973. For both texts, the point of departure consists of a set of disparate characters — somewhat reminiscent of the sorts of motley crowds one encounters in Chaucer's *Canterbury Tales* or Boccaccio's *Decameron* — who, having lost their way in a treacherous forest and been concurrently robbed by unknown forces of the ability to speak, endeavor to recount their experiences by recourse to cards selected from a Tarot pack as an alternative linguistic code, and hence a means of communication. The resulting text, as Contardo Calligaris points out, constitutes a tantalizing "void filled by reading, a silent space questioning the reader" (Calligaris 102). In substantially diversified fashions predicated on the adoption and redefinition of different narrative forms, all of Calvino's major works deploy tropes inspired by the themes of lack, non-existence and invisibility — and cognate images of mutilation, intermittence and disappearance. In so doing, they aim to expose the instability of various structures of signification and perception.

As foreshadowed in Chapter 1, *The Castle of Crossed Destinies*, specifically, illustrates the transition from a structuralist notion of system to a poststructuralist image of structurality: as centered constellations of meaning incrementally metamorphose into decentered ensembles, the safety net of a present and solid structure is radically displaced and human identity itself becomes contingent on unpredictable narrative moves. While the combinatorial manipulation of the Tarot cards may initially seem capable not only of objectifying but also of satisfying the desire to establish the limits of the narratable, Calvino's main concern shifts increasingly

Chapter 5 — Structures and Their Explosion

toward the range of narrative possibilities that remain unrealized: namely, the permutational options that cannot find a place within the text's compass and thus act as potent reminders of the multiforking paths laid out before any embryonic tale that inevitably escape telling. The meanings accorded to signs which are actually present in the text depend on their implicit relation to a deluge of alternative absent signs, traces and traces of traces. No sequence of cards is given priority over any of the others. As the hierarchical ambitions of classic realism collapse, what gains prominence is the absence of any structural factor which could govern the narrative either etiologically or teleologically. Multiple narratives eventually overlap, crisscross and become entangled, as each of Calvino's mute narrators is driven on exclusively by the anxious longing to communicate her or his own personal predicament and by a subliminal recognition of the futility of the attempt. The play of combinations, to which Calvino is so consistently devoted throughout both his fictional and his critical writings, does not ultimately uphold the omnipotence of the concept of structure but actually reveals its inevitable collapse. Moving from a desire to map out experience and knowledge according to rigorous patterns and sets of binary oppositions, the game ends up highlighting the untenability of any program of unification and totalization. Calvino's departure from what would at first look like the orthodox structuralist faith in mutually exclusive opposites is signalled by his placing of the principle of lack at the core of human experience. Lack cannot be reduced to either of the extremes of a polarized construct, since it cannot ultimately be made to coincide with either plus or minus, either yes or no. That a sense of lack is what animates Calvino's narrators is clearly spelled out in the opening pages of *The Castle of Crossed Destinies*: "none of us seemed to wish to begin playing, and still less to question the future, since we were as if drained of all future, suspended in a journey that had not ended nor was to end" (Calvino 1978, 6). The second section of the text, *The Tavern of Crossed Destinies*, suggests that if lack is the point of inception of the narrative, as the striving toward the non-existent, it is also, no less crucially, its destination.

This proposition is lucidly validated by the experiences undergone, in tandem, by the characters of Faust and Parsifal as they confront the intractable inevitability of reality's absence. For Faust, this realization is a corollary of the discovery that anything one might term reality is only ever a precarious outcome of the mind's urge to combine given sets of items in ever-variable formations, some of which may temporarily gain significance in the midst of an otherwise meaningless and amorphous "dust cloud" (92). Reality as such, however, is nowhere to be found. Parsifal, for his part, avers that the world in its entirety revolves around a vacuous core, an absent signifier devoid of any mass or weight whatsoever — pithily corroborating his hypothesis by pointing to the blank space at the center of the structure generated by the cards laid out on the table by the speechless companions. The concept of lack gains significance progressively as we advance through the text. To begin with, Calvino could be said not to doubt the possibility of a narrative based on the articulation of a limited, albeit enormous, number of images, codes, rules, elementary entities or more sophisticated aggregates. Indeed, *The Castle of Crossed Destinies* initially presents itself as a practical application of notions already thoroughly investigated by Calvino in his critical writings. In his essay "Cybernetics and Ghosts," in particular, Calvino examines the tendency to articulate knowledge according to terms in a code that can be compared and contrasted and attributes this proclivity to the human penchant for assembling and disassembling linguistic units as though they were pieces in a mechanical apparatus. Having equated the multifold aspects of psychological life to linguistic fields with their own specific vocabularies and permutational properties, Calvino then goes on to assess their impact on the creative act. He thus surmises that at base, writing amounts to an ongoing chain of efforts to string words and sentences together in accordance with conventions that do not hold any immutable intrinsic value and merely acquire authority through repeated usage (Calvino 1987).

In *The Castle of Crossed Destinies*, the basic narrative ingredients consist of the various images contained in the Tarot pack, whose cards the storytellers arrange according to a more or less predetermined pattern. Each tale is designed to find its location within the tapestry of a square which includes all the tales in such a way that the disparate sequences can be read from the left to the right, from the right to the left, from top to bottom, and vice versa. The scattered images must be institutionalized, subordinated to a rigid code, in much the same way as Saussure's *langue* must be filtered through an ensemble of necessary conventions which will make communication possible, and exhibit the status of *parole* as the product of an individual struggle to impose some order upon the randomness of nature. As anticipated in this chapter's preamble, the cards objectify the desire to define the boundaries of what may and may not be told, and Calvino is far more interested in stretching and expanding these margins to their ultimate cosmic implications and complications than in delimiting them categorically.

The emphasis hence falls not on what is deliberately selected but on what is excluded, on "the particles of the possible discarded in the game of combinations" (Calvino 1978, 35). These, by sheer virtue of their exclusion, remind us that no ordering structure, however comprehensive and complex, can ever account for a welter of rejected solutions that inhabit — or even haunt — the actualized text as the absent vestiges of unfulfilled potentialities: "life" itself, the text at one point advocates, "is the waste of material thrown away" (57). Calvino's apparent faith in the ordering and sense-making competences of structuralist methodology gradually yields to a recognition of the artificial and decidedly non-foundationalist character of any imaginable structure. It is no coincidence, in this respect, that Calvino should have chosen to explore the scope and potential of schematic rigor by recourse to a medium which, by virtue of its association with esoteric knowledge and fortunetelling, is pointedly intuitional and visionary rather than logical. In this respect, the views of a couple of experts in the field of Tarot lore are worthy of notice. Sasha Fenton, in particular, observes: "Nobody knows for certain where Tarot cards originally come from but they seem to share the same roots as playing cards and the game of chess.... The image that they have of being slightly dangerous in some unspecified way, only serves to increase their attraction.... If the reader treats them with respect but does not worry too much about any one particular reading, then they can be entertaining, informative and a useful guide to future actions" (Fenton 14). As to the meanings accrued by specific cards over time, David Fontana reminds us that it is crucial not to attempt to draw finite lines of demarcation between established interpretations and personal responses: "Don't worry whether you are talking to an image that has objective reality or simply to an aspect of your unconscious.... The image is simply there, existing in its own dimension. Let the image do the work for you.... Don't allow personal preferences for certain cards to influence you unduly.... Don't regard some cards as 'good' and others as 'bad.' Each has its part to play" (Fontana 170). Both of these perspectives impact directly on Calvino's own approach to the Tarot.

Before embarking on a specific analysis of the procedures employed by Calvino to expose the arbitrariness of structural thought, some of the more general implications of his project seem worth considering. Firstly, it must be emphasized that the writer's acknowledgment of the eminently constructed status of all structures signals a significant point of departure from one of the pivotal tenets of classic Western metaphysics, namely, the idea that structure is not something deliberately fabricated but rather a natural or God-given category: that which allows us to grasp, through processes of abstraction and conceptualization, some mystical element that would otherwise remain unintelligible in the physical object of observation per se. In this philosophical perspective, structure reveals itself as a correlative for the presence of the divine in the natural world. Ideology thus gains legitimacy by reaching toward, and eventually merging with, theology through the claim that the world is structured on the basis of universal and transcendental principles. Yet, as Dick Hebdige points out in terms vividly reminiscent of Calvino's own imagery, such a claim obscures the fact that structural ordering is "the discipline of chess, not of angels" (Hebdige 17). Critiques of the metaphysical notion of structure conducted by several postmodernist writers tend to follow two parallel, if ostensibly conflicting, lines. On the one hand, the text may be devoted to a drastic unsettling of coherent presentation, to upsetting the boundaries of mimetic and hierarchical narrative constellations. On the other hand, writers like Calvino and J. L. Borges, to name but one of Calvino's favorite authors, seem keener on taking on board the idea of structure at its most rigorous and on pushing a system's organizing proclivities to their extreme. Structure is here envisaged in fundamentally geometric, mathematical and algebraic terms: it is concerned with endlessly varied and reiterated transformative operations which may be formulated in a scientific (or mock-scientific) fashion.

On one level, this strategy may appear to lend further authority to the theological ideal described earlier. On another level, however, the scientific strictness and accuracy with which the narrative is invested are presented in such a way that their effect is to portray the concept of structure not as something that objectively reflects a solid reality but rather something that contingently constructs anything we may choose to call reality—something without which reality would be simply absent along the lines pursued by Faust and Parsifal. Systematic narrative arrangements, therefore, could be regarded as a magnification of the structuring function designed to expose the non-existence or invisibility of the world beyond the artificial nets through which we attempt to seize it. The emphasis is not laid on the representational correctness of the chosen structure but on its purely fictional character. The appeal of mock-scientific tales, relatedly, stems from the ambiguous fascination of a construct which, in purporting to explain the nature of the real, eventually discloses the vacuity of the real outside the circumstantial laws of the construct itself.

All ordering patterns, Calvino insinuates, are inevitably torn between a dream of totalization of all the knowable and an entropic process of regression to infinity. As images impelled by the desire to tabulate an otherwise chaotic universe, these ambivalent structures operate as metaphors for reading and writing which simultaneously evoke the atmosphere of an enclosed — and thus relatively safe — ludic space and the open-endedness of the game which may take place therein as an indefinite proliferation of alternative configurations, classifications and taxonomies. This complicity, indeed symbiosis, binding together systematic programs and unpredictable play interrogates radically the conventional opposition between so-called rational and so-called fantastic structures. Indeed, it suggests that putatively reliable systems (philosophical, religious, scientific, cosmological) are fictional constructions, products of the playing mind and of its anarchic impulse toward chance. Conversely, it also surmises that presumably imaginary constructs (hallucinations, fantasies, visions, dreams) are systematic articulations of play's drive toward order, as no game may finally escape the logic, idiosyncratic as this may be, of rules and conventions.

Ars combinatoria exemplifies the uncertain status of ordering strategies which partake concurrently of scientific rationalization and of random ludic urges: combinations and permutations, however predictable or quantifiable, do not reduce the incidence of chance and disorder. In fact, knowing that the number of available moves is limited, albeit colossal, inaugurates the prospect of limitless transformations, revisions, variations and deviations, and this is more likely to induce a sense of dizziness than a feeling of sober control. The game of combinations thus stands out as a conflagration of finiteness and infinity, logical patterns and indiscriminate contingency, reminding us that no narrative formula is ever conclusive, for any plan will ineluctably branch into legion others. *The Castle of Crossed Destinies* endorses the idea that the data of experience can only be processed within an open form, insofar as virtually any tale could in principle be nesting within the Tarot's "network" (Calvino 1978, p, 89). Any apparently sealed system consists, in fact, of a confused and frenzied encounter of clashing possibilities: "each story runs into another story, and as one guest is advancing his strip, another ... advances in the opposite direction" (39). The tales do not unfold in the name of a superior necessity but rather out of a fussy, obsessive longing to bring the narrative experience to a satisfying end: a frantic resolve to round things off, tot up the accounts neatly, and exhaust all options. Concomitantly, the rigid geometric scheme to which the stories in *The Castle of Crossed Destinies* are seemingly subordinated is repeatedly challenged.

In the first novel, each character disposes of sixteen cards to be placed within the square. However, one card in each series remains outside the pattern and the first and last sequences include seventeen cards (plus the cards used by the tellers to introduce themselves), divided in both stories into seven Major Arcana and ten ordinary cards, with one card remaining outside of the square and thus destroying the symmetry and equilibrium of the overall construct. Calvino's tendency to undermine the concept of structure as a domesticating force effectively manifests itself if one compares the 1973 edition of the narrative with the 1969 one. The clarifying movement from disorder to order celebrated in the earlier version, sustained by detailed references to specific cards and culminating with a harmonizing image of uniformity, gives way, particularly in the finale, to an opposite movement from order to chaos which turns the conclusion into a fresh beginning. Therefore, while the 1969 text climaxes with the assertion that all stories told by the cards are ultimately the same story despite their apparent differences, the 1973 version stresses that at the end of the game, the only option left is to "scatter the cards, shuffle the deck, and begin all over again" (46). In *The Tavern of Crossed Destinies*, the geometric structure which, despite its precarious symmetry, still functions as something of a guarantee of order in *The Castle of Crossed Destinies*, disappears. The various stories overlap, clash, become entangled, as each teller is driven on only by an anxious desire to communicate his or her misadventures. Grasping the cards as their personal and precious possessions although, in fact, the deck belongs to nobody, the characters strive to identify the images that most faithfully capture their distinctive ordeals only to find, time and again, that the cards stubbornly refuse to cohere into a legible grid. No sooner has one character tentatively succeeded in aligning a few cards with one another in the quest for cohesion than the hand of a competing teller stretches out greedily to grab it and make it fit into quite a different tale. In the process, it becomes increasingly clear that the Tarot figures hide more than they reveal and that any dénouement reached by a yarn can only disclose a scenario of catastrophe and chaos.

While the characters' selfish and literally grabbing behavior dramatizes the quest for transcendental signifieds in a game that only affords ephemeral and arbitrary signifiers, it also points to the ineluctable otherness of meaning, to the fact that meaning is never identical with itself. Given the Tarot's secretive disposition, the interpreter's quarry consists of textual ambiguities, elisions, doublings, discontinuous and lacunary subtexts — a dimension which, like the unconscious, is at once revealed and concealed by a person's ordinary actions. The reading of the various protagonists' experiences is made increasingly arbitrary by Calvino's separation of the plane of the narrators from the metaplane of the narrator-interpreter. It is quite clear that the often convoluted, subjective and even far-fetched interpretations proposed by the narrator follow the utterly haphazard and wayward rhythms of personal association. Although a sense of structural balance is salvaged by the assertion that it is precisely when the stories appear to be most random and disconnected that they come together within a balanced tapestry, it is undeniable that at the center of the construct there remains a vacant space. This is the vacant vista described to the character of Astolpho by the poet-magician he meets on the moon, the abyss of illegibility, the nothingness which, as indicated earlier, awaits both Faust and Parsifal at the end of their respective routes. Calvino's acute awareness of the precariousness of structures in general, and linguistic structures in particular, is highlighted in a useful *Note* illustrating the processes of conception and composition of *The Castle of Crossed Destinies*. Here, the writer's obsessive pursuit of balanced geometrical patterns is shown to be inseparable from a recognition of the impossibility of ever attaining total symmetry and equilibrium. Calvino is especially eager to draw attention to certain crucial structural divergences between *The Castle of Crossed Destinies* and *The Tavern of Crossed Destinies*, emphasizing that while in the former, the "cards making up the individual tales are in clearly defined horizontal or vertical rows," in the latter, "they form blocks with more irregular outlines" (118).

The writer's passion for the progressive erection, questioning and dismantling of relatively stable structures of meaning is tersely conveyed by Calvino's own spatial representation, within the book, of tapestries of Tarot cards visualizing the patterns formed by the interlocking of distinct tales in *The Castle of Crossed Destinies* and *The Tavern of Crossed Destinies*. These templates bring together in miniaturized guise all the cards already depicted in the margins of the main body of the book to lead the written narratives. These reveal, upon attentive inspection, a basic set of structural tenets worthy of notice in the present context. *The Castle of Crossed Destinies* encompasses twelve stories. Six of these are individual tales consisting of seventeen cards each, with the first card in each set corresponding to the tale's protagonist. Any two interlocking individual stories share four cards. Each individual story thus overlaps by a total of twelve cards with three other stories. The other six narratives are designated as "Other Tales" and utilize cards already laid out for the purposes of the six preceding, individual tales, but also introduce seven additional cards: six of these correspond to the protagonists from which the six Other Tales proceed. The seventh extra card, the *Seven of Clubs*, is the only element which falls outside the symmetrical arrangement of the cards. If this card, to which Calvino does not explicitly refer in the written text, is taken to signify the forest—as Club cards do elsewhere in *The Castle of Crossed Destinies* and as suggested by the closing image of "the foliage of this wood" (46)—then its asymmetrical positioning should not come as a surprise, since the forest is the primary symbol of disharmony and confusion from which the narrative emanates. *The Tavern of Crossed Destinies* forms a pattern of seventy-eight cards, based on the interweaving of seven main and several ancillary tales. The intersections between various tales are not symmetrically mapped out by recourse to clearly demarcated rows and columns, as was the case in *The Castle of Crossed Destinies*. In fact, the structure of *The Tavern of Crossed Destinies* is desultory and the connections between any two textually sequential cards often require leaps and diagonal moves. A number of cards which do not feature explicitly in the written text and yet appear on Calvino's visual map reinforce the overall sense of structural arbitrariness. The cards most frequently referred to (notably, the *World,* the *Tower,* the *Moon,* the *Sun* and the *Wheel*) cluster around the central portion of the diagram. The center itself, however, is significantly a blank space.

In the aforementioned *Note* accompanying *The Castle of Crossed Destinies*, Calvino implicitly suggests that even the apparently tighter structural coherence of the first text by comparison with its successor may be illusory, considering its thematic reliance on a famously and deliberately chaotic source, Ariosto's *Orlando Furioso*, and especially, as a structural fulcrum, on the portions of the Renaissance pseudo-epic focusing on the titular hero's derangement and on Astolpho's retrieval of Orlando's lost sanity from the Moon. It seems worth dwelling, at this point, on Calvino's choice of Ariostesque motifs as pivotal devices, since some of the principal structural and thematic characteristics of the Renaissance poem pointedly illuminate central aspects of Calvino's own narrative techniques. For one thing, it is significant that the blank space left in the center of the construct by the time the table is virtually covered with cards, should be filled by a tale of madness, melancholia and regret. Indeed, the centrality of irrational emotions and behavior serves to underscore the limitations of logically orchestrated narrative patterns. The thematic correspondences between the tales of Roland and Astolpho in *The Castle of Crossed Des-*

tinies and the Renaissance source are explicitly conveyed by Calvino's chosen imagery. The images devoted by Calvino to the sudden explosion of Roland's mind — and, with it, to the shattering of the character's status as a paragon of chivalric excellence — instantly bring to mind Ariosto's depiction of the mad Orlando's mounting frenzy and grotesque displays of Hulk-like superhuman strength.

Moreover, Calvino's representation of Astolpho's task is clearly indebted to *Canto XXXIV* of Ariosto's epic. Particularly interesting, in both texts, is the characterization of the Moon as the repository of unrealized potentialities, broken promises, neglected options, unfinished projects and life's incalculable might-have-beens — in other words, "the stories that men do not live" (35). This is a theme which not only informs Calvino's interpretation and employment of the *Moon* card but also, as shall be noted later in the discussion of this Major Arcanum, determines his lasting attraction to the melancholy satellite as a metaphor for lightness, suspension and intangibility. The presentation of the paladin's preposterously turbulent actions and his savior's interplanetary voyage vividly echo, in a condensed and almost hermetic form, some of Ariosto's most celebrated lines. Both versions of the story, most importantly, derive much of their rhetorical and dramatic impact from the fusion of a tragic sense of waste and an ironically disenchanted perception of human foolishness which implicitly relates them to the tradition of the Absurd. What Calvino seems to find most fascinating about Ariosto's themes and poetic techniques is his felicitous coupling of rapidity and slowness: while his heroes and heroines pursue their more or less noble, more or less trivial, goals at breakneck speed, the poem nonetheless allows for countless digressions, embedded tales and anecdotes, minutely recounted at a leisurely pace. Thus, the celerity and indeed hastiness of the Ariostesque cast, with its frantic jostling, galloping and darting to and fro, ultimately generate a labyrinthine pattern of interlocking trajectories, a tangled and tortuous structure of both actual and virtual narratives counterpointed by the lightning flashes of an unbridled imagination. The digressive proclivities of Ariosto's narrative poetry clearly encapsulate Calvino's model, put forward in *Six Memos for the Next Millennium,* for a form of creative writing which deftly combines mental suppleness and postponing strategies, by capturing and linking disparate images. No less significantly, such preferences mirror Calvino's ongoing concern with the ultimate impossibility of structural unity. Indeed, like *The Castle of Crossed Destinies, Orlando Furioso* represents a complex tapestry wherein numerous interconnections, overlappings and parallelisms may be detected without these finally enabling the reader to totalize the narrative by recourse to a sealed structural compound.

As Barbara Reynolds observes in the introduction to her English translation of the poem, "critics are not agreed as to the central, unifying element in the structure of the poem [*Orlando Furioso*]. Some have seen it in the hopeless love of Orlando for ... Angelica," while others have located it with "a stylistic individuality, an aesthetic harmony, an ironic detachment." For Reynolds herself, the work's "fundamental unity is the concept of Europe ... as the fount of the creative and civilizing forces of the world" (Ariosto, Part I, 12). Others still have tended to select one of Ariosto's poem's most pervasive themes as its pivotal concern, be this the concept of chivalry, the nostalgic celebration of past ideals or indeed their debunking. Arguably, lack of agreement among critics on the issue of the work's unifying factor may point to the absence of any terminally cohesive structural or thematic element. Reynolds believes that "the randomness of the poem's structure is only apparent" since Ariosto is constantly in control of "all his stage properties, his magic paraphernalia and his immense cast of characters. He remembers who has the magic ring, where the magic shield is and who has won whose helmet" (25). Calvino endorses this assessment of the poem's latent coherence as a web of interrelated people and objects. Yet, he relativizes the ideal of structural unity commended by Reynolds by pointing out that any degree of cohesiveness perceivable in *Orlando Furioso* does not stem from individual properties, identities or substances but rather from relational patterns of exchange — patterns which, moreover, are by and large inscrutable, enigmatic and governed by magic. As he underlines in *Six Memos*, Ariosto uses objects primarily as links in a "network of invisible relationships" (Calvino 1996, 33). Hence, the rationalizing portrait of Ariosto as something of an all-powerful Master of the Revels, able to structure his narrative on the basis of clearly constellated interconnections, gives way, in Calvino's perception of his work, to a pervasive mood of inconclusiveness and mystery, where the energies which bind characters and situations together are fundamentally intangible, latent, absent from view.

Orlando Furioso's exuberant variety and cornucopian outpours of surprises, vitality, porousness, sudden and illogical jumps from one continent, mood or style to another, and, above all else, sensational fertility, argues Reynolds, must be grasped in relation to the widespread Renaissance penchant for startling juxtapositions of discordant elements, not only in literature but in music and cuisine, too. In creating *The Castle of Crossed Destinies*, Calvino was also no less pointedly aware of the specific historical context of Ariosto's work. His adoption of Roland's and Astolpho's tales as structural hinges, for example, is inspired by the common origin of *Orlando Furioso* and the Bembo/Visconti Tarot cards — used as black-and-white illustrations throughout the first text — in the courtly culture of the Italian Renaissance. However, the central lesson he wishes to inherit from Ariosto has less to do with historical realities than with the element of excess, the fictional remainder refusing to be accommodated within any closed circuit, which the Renaissance poem continually evokes. Calvino never denies the structural coherence of *Orlando Furioso* as an overall vision lurking beneath its profusion of episodes and digressions. Nor does he overestimate the controlling power of certain recurring threads which Ariosto unobtrusively weaves into the fabric of his poem. What interests him most is the extent to which *Orlando Furioso* remains, in C. P. Brand's words, "essentially undefined and uncategorized" (Brand 194). It is precisely as an uncompartmentalizable narrative that Ariosto's poem exhibits the closest affinities with *The Castle of Crossed Destinies*. Both texts, in rejecting an essentialist approach to human experience, produce fictional configurations which spurn the tyranny of atomistic individualism, favoring instead a dynamic, if precarious, balance of juxtapositions based on parallels and contrasts. *The Tale of the Ingrate and His Punishment* and *The Tale of the Alchemist Who Sold His Soul*, for instance, are linked by the two protagonists' megalomania and this basic correspondence gives rise to ancillary pairings and doublings of both characters and events. *The Waverer's Tale* and *Two Tales of Seeking and Losing*, for their part, offer an adversarial coupling where the former articulates the protagonist's inability to pursue consistently any one identifiable objective, and the latter dramatizes the predicament of mentalities hell-bent on monolithic quests.

Another recurrent motif in both *Orlando Furioso* and *The Castle of Crossed Destinies* is, of course, eros. As already argued in relation to *Our Ancestors*, the employment of amorous discourse as a structural and thematic leading thread is a highly ambiguous strategy, for the erratic nature of this topos inevitably frustrates the urge for resolution. Hence, what could potentially aspire to the status of a unifying principle turns out to be an elusively multiaccentual sign capable of initiating a proliferation of mercurial inconsistencies. Reynolds terms Ariosto's "range of erotic episodes" satisfyingly "comprehensive" (Ariosto, Part II, 11). However, the manipulations of eros offered by both Ariosto and Calvino could be seen as explosive fragmentations of a unitary *ars amatoria* into a phalanx of discordant phenomena: infidelity and faithfulness (*The Tale of the Ingrate and His Punishment* and *The Tale of the Doomed Bride*); monogamy and promiscuous intercourse (*The Tale of the Vampires' Kingdom*); primitive Dionysian lust (*The Tale of the Surviving Warrior*); obsessional longing (*The Tale of Roland Crazed with Love*); transvestism (*The Tale of the Forest's Revenge*); and, more generally, an interweaving of blissful voluptuousness and cruel exploitation. Ariosto's and Calvino's games, in positing structures of correspondence and recurrence, entice the reader into intrepid exertions to unravel the increasingly tangled skein of their tales, only to reveal that the moment a knot is untied, the whole narrative is likely to fall apart. Though a method may be detected in the apparent madness of both *Orlando Furioso* and *The Castle of Crossed Destinies*, the two texts' shared message is that any structural order is inexorably shrouded in anarchy, that any effort to shape narrative events toward harmonious ends may well end up engendering a monstrous body. Calvino's relationship with Ariosto will be revisited in the closing portion of this analysis.

Given Calvino's commitment to the parallel operations of literature and science (an aspect of his art discussed in the previous chapter and to be further explored in the next section), it is tempting to relate the confluence of binding and unbinding energies foregrounded by *The Castle of Crossed Destinies* to insights provided by contemporary science into the inextricability of order from chaos. Benjamin Woolley's observations on chaos theory are particularly relevant, in this regard: "chaos does not just produce order, it *has* order: there is a deep structure ... in the apparently random, chaotic behavior that characterizes all natural and some social phenomena. This structure takes the form of ... a 'strange attractor' ... a state toward which a system is drawn." Yet, this is no guarantee of incontrovertible stability insofar as "chaotic systems," while they "may be stable at the abstract level of the strange attractor," are nonetheless "highly unstable at the level we experience them directly" and indeed "fly off the handle at the slightest provocation. This is known as the 'butterfly effect'" (Woolley 88). This account of the ontological and epistemological ambivalence of chaos theory aptly sums up the unresolved tension highlighted by Calvino throughout *The Castle of Crossed Destinies* between the attraction of latent ordering structures and the acknowledgment of the ephemerality and propensity for self-disintegration of any ostensibly stable system.

Related to chaos theory, and no less relevant to Calvino's equivocal approach to structural stability, is catastrophe theory, given its focus on the abrupt and discontinuous changes which cause a system to move suddenly "from one state to another" (91). Calvino's unrelenting interest in the part played by unpredictable occurrences and swift changes of direction in the context of the creative process is echoed by the representation of the world advocated by catastrophe theory as a phenomenon of "ceaseless creation" (90). If chaos theory bears analogies with Calvino's grasp of the inseparability of order and anarchy, and catastrophe theory mirrors his concern with unexpected mutations, a third position, crisis theory, illuminates his conception of stability as an inevitably precarious state, a fleeting and always rescindable achievement. Crisis theory is concerned with "why systems that are on the point of crisis somehow manage to persist" and hence remain "stable, even self-sustaining" (94). Calvino, likewise, strives to identify the possibility of structural stability not in frozen, rigid and immutable formations but rather in a cosmological model based on the interaction of productive and entropic forces. Relatedly, Calvino emphasizes the coexistence of contrasting configurations of order, varyingly predicated on motionlessness or movement, and advocates the need to embrace diverse models of the cosmos simultaneously. His theoretical works thus posit the image of the crystal as a metaphor for the constancy of specific structures, and that of the flame as symbolic of the stability resulting from unremitting agitation. Those who feel instinctively drawn to the crystal as the epitome of reflective tranquillity should never neglect the value of the flame as an energizing companion, and those who, conversely, treasure the flame's effervescent dynamism ought not to ignore the quieter messages sent out by the crystal.

    The interpenetration and ultimate inseparability of contrasting worlds and world views is repeatedly stressed throughout *The Castle of Crossed Destinies*, especially in its descriptive techniques. The setting and cast of characters of *The Tavern of Crossed Destinies* are presented as far less meticulously groomed and aesthetically pleasing than those of *The Castle of Crossed Destinies*. This reflects Calvino's use of the more refined Bembo deck in the earlier text and the more pedestrian (though arguably more enigmatic) Marseilles deck in the later one. The adoption of different packs could also have abetted the transition from structure to structurality insofar as the high degree of abstraction which characterizes Bembo's miniatures makes the Visconti deck more amenable to a narrative method based primarily on the structural principles of expansion and interlocking. The greater solidity of the Marseilles pictures, with their minute details, discourages Calvino from prioritizing structural concerns, leading him instead to explore the associational powers of visionary description which each card invites. Nevertheless, in spite of this apparent divergence between the worlds of the two narratives, Calvino hints at the virtual interchangeability of their respective environments: the "castle" may have ceased to be a stately, aristocratic dwelling and actually "degenerated into an inn"; alternatively, a "tavern" may have "invaded ... the ancient, noble halls" (Calvino 1978, 4).

The collapse of neat dividing lines between seemingly conflicting universes highlighted by this example is perceived by Calvino as both tantalizing and frightening. As he observes in the *Note* attached to *The Castle of Crossed Destinies*, his own early attempts to evoke all the narrative situations potentially hosted by a pack of Tarot cards by mapping out a thoroughly exhaustive and all-encompassing structure resulted repeatedly in deep frustration or even downright mania: "I spent whole days taking apart and putting back together my puzzle ... I drew hundreds of patterns, in a square, a rhomboid, a star design.... The patterns became so complicated (they took on a third dimension, becoming cubes, polyhedrons) that I myself was lost in them" (120). The precariousness and openness of any structure based on permutational and combinatorial moves are confirmed by what some might see as Calvino's final inability to master the rules of the game: namely, his failure to produce the third intended narrative entitled *The Motel of Crossed Destinies*. In this story, comic strips would have served the same purpose served by the cards in the preceding ones, comics representing, for Calvino, the "contemporary equivalent" of the Tarot deck as a manifestation of the "collective unconscious" (121). It should be emphasized, however, that this unrealized task constitutes a failure only for those who genuinely believe in the attainability of totalizing structures. In fact, it represents something of a victory if it is assessed by reference to an unremitting desire for creative experimentation, which any sealed structure would necessarily atrophy — and thus a reflection of Calvino's yearning to face fresh challenges at every turn in his career rather than indulge in the torpid comforts of familiar and well-trodden terrain.

Calvino's dissatisfaction with the universalizing aspirations of structural thought is intimately connected with his sharp awareness of the inadequacies and limitations of verbal language. This is borne out by the opening words of the *Note* accompanying *The Castle of Crossed Destinies*: "this book is made first of pictures ... and secondly of written words. Through the sequence of the pictures stories are told, which the written word tries to reconstruct and interpret" (116). These preliminary observa-

Chapter 5—Structures and Their Explosion

tions underscore Calvino's ongoing concern with the ambiguity of the word, a concern which is insistently brought to the fore in *Six Memos* in conjunction with an emphasis on the centrality of visual images to Calvino's opus as unsurpassed inspirational forces. As the essay on Visibility stresses, the visual dimension should always be allowed to unleash its own intrinsic messages and the writer's function should consist fundamentally of a sustained attempt to identify which of these are most likely to cohere within an overarching pattern of meaning. *The Castle of Crossed Destinies* exemplifies this compositional strategy by underscoring the idea that the baffling and pluridirectional visual symbolism of the Tarot must be prioritized if disparate interpretative potentialities are to be released.

A. S. Cook and G. A. Hawk explicitly emphasize the visual powers of the Tarot and commend its use, particularly where the trumps (or Major Arcana) are concerned, "as doorways for visionary journeys" (Cook and Hawk 71). These experiences are based on imagining "that the picture on the trump covers the entire surface of a door, and that this door is going to open toward you," on calling "your power animal" and asking it "to accompany you through the open doorway," and finally on describing "what you see" (72). Like Calvino's tales, the illustrations of psychic voyages thus accomplished which *Shamanism and the Esoteric Tradition* supplies bear ample witness to the cards' ability to release storytelling skills in their readers, initiate complex narratives, suggest intriguing plots and, above all, trigger a phantasmagoria of surreal and grotesque images of endless metamorphosis. A journey inspired by the Major Arcanum of the *Priestess*, for example, evokes the landscape of a "night sky with millions of stars. A low hill with megalithic stones," gradually transmuting into "thin golden trumpets with attached banners, in a fan-like formation," and eventually into a "blue-green ocean seen from the sky" (74). In contemplating the *Hierophant* trump, as a further example, the visionary traveler sees "the Pope's head chang[ing] to a black crocodile" while "a multitude of figures run and dance around a truncated pyramid" (75). In a vein reminiscent of Calvino's *Invisible Cities*, the trump of the *Lovers*, for its part, conjures up the picture of "a brown-lavander flatland with many shallow pools. At intervals, the center of a pool will stir with large bubbles" until "a flat basin or valley surrounded by golden peaks" reveals itself (75–76). These are simply a few instances of the narrative prospects open before the dedicated reader of the Tarot—a reader who, as Cook and Hawk's instructions stress, is by no means a hyperrational critic but rather a subject willing to let the text work on her or his imaginative and perceptive faculties. Echoing Calvino's emphasis on the necessarily subjective and contingent significance of any one reading or tale, Cook and Hawk stress that a person's voyage through the Major Arcana will be "ultimately meaningful and valid only for that person" (82). What is vital is that the *story*telling dimension of the Tarot is no less central than its *fortune*telling function. After all, as Fenton points out, "even the most experienced readers are short of an idea from time to time" (Fenton 13) and it is precisely their narratorial and creative competences which enable them to overcome the impasse and produce viable interpretations. The reader, in other words, is not decoding a preexistent truth but rather producing a text out of the cards' submerged and multifarious narrative potentialities.

There can be little doubt that one of the elements that most fascinates Calvino in his experiments with the Tarot as a tale-making apparatus is the opaqueness of its origins. According to one available version of events, the Tarot's pictographic legacy is associated from its very inception with creative writing: "the Tarot trumps were probably invented in Northern Italy, possibly in Ferrara, around 1440 C.E., as illustrations to a cycle of poems or *Triumphs* by Petrarch. In 1956, Gertrude Moakley pointed out that the trumps tell the same story as the poems, and had the same name — *trionfi*" (Cook and Hawk 68–69). In the mid–fifteenth century, under the influence of the Neo-Platonist philosopher Marsilio Ficino and his reflections on magical knowledge, the Tarot came to be invested with astrological symbolism. If Cook and Hawk are somewhat tentative in retracing the origins of the cards, other critics and historians convey even more forcibly the mistiness of the speculations and hypotheses surrounding the Tarot's geographical, as well as temporal, point of emergence. Different scholars varyingly situate its cradle in China, Egypt and India. Some argue that the four suits of the Minor Arcana (which comprise the sixteen Court Cards and forty cards numbered one to ten in each of four suits) may have derived from the visual symbolism surrounding the figure of Vishnu. This deity is indeed often portrayed in conjunction with emblems akin to the Tarot's suits. As Fontana notes, these are "the disc, lotus, club and conch which symbolyze the divine powers of preservation (*karma yoga*), love (*bhakti yoga*), wisdom (*gnana yoga*) and inner realization (*raja yoga*)" (Fontana 168). What Calvino could not have failed to pick up, given his attraction to both real and imaginary explorations of the Orient by characters such as Polo, is that both the Minor and the Major Arcana are often thought to have been introduced into Western culture by Venetian traders returning from the East.

Chapter 5—Structures and Their Explosion

The Tarot as we know it today is most comprehensively described as an open system of interconnection of various symbolic discourses. Thus, the four suits displayed by the Minor Arcana, beside carrying an impressive range of symbolic connotations, can also be related to astrological, alchemic and magical principles:

Suit	Astrology	Alchemy	Magic	Symbolism
Cups (Hearts)	Water Signs (Cancer, Scorpio, Pisces)	Water (passivity) (introversion)	Undines	emotion intuition love possessions education the West
Staves (Clubs)	Fire Signs (Leo, Aries, Sagittarius)	Fire (activity) (extroversion)	Elves	energy initiative words choices travel the South
Swords (Spades)	Air Signs (Libra, Aquarius, Gemini)	Air (activity) (extroversion)	Sylphs	logic intellect action problems power the North
Coins (Diamonds)	Earth Signs (Taurus, Virgo, Capricorn)	Earth (passivity) (introversion)	Gnomes	practicality reliability money status production the East

Moreover, the Tarot displays important points of contact with one of the most complex esoteric systems, the Kabbalah. The most striking connections between the Tarot and the Kabbalah, as highlighted by the French occult author and magician Eliphas Lévi (born Alphonse Louis Constant, 1810–1875) consist of two numerical parallelisms. First, there are twenty-two Major Arcana as there are twenty-two letters in the Hebrew alphabet; and second, the Minor Arcana are divided according to four suits which could be said to correspond to the four Kabbalistic worlds: that is to say, the four stages through which God is held to have created the cosmos.

P. D. Ouspensky elaborates the relationship between the Tarot and the Kabbalah in terms of a geometrical configuration consisting of three interrelated elements: a triangle, a square and a point. The triangle is supposed to exemplify the noumenal world, the square the phenomenal world, and the point human consciousness as a dimension which partakes of both the noumenal and the phenomenal. The square is numerologically related to the ultimate tetragrammaton which is supposed to shape the whole cosmos, namely the four letters which in Hebrew spell the name of God (I.H.V.E.), and which correspond to the four basic elements. "I" refers to the "active principles" of "first cause, motion, energy," the "I"; "H" signifies the "passive elements" of "inertia, quietude," the "not-I"; "V" symbolizes the "balance of opposites"; and "E," finally, the "result of latent energy" (Ouspensky 6–8). The opposition between active and passive energies highlighted by this reading clearly echoes the astrological and alchemical interpretations presented above. In addition, the alchemic tradition advocates analogies between the four fundamental numbers and the four elements: the ace symbolizes Fire; the deuce, Water; the three-spot, Air; and the four-spot, Earth. However, the Tarot does not derive its numerical significance exclusively from the Kabbalah and alchemy. In fact, the cartomantic method proposes its own set of symbolic associations based on numbers: thus, aces correspond to beginnings, twos to relationships, threes to the beginning and ending of an experience, fours to stability and so on.

Calvino is sensitive to the Tarot's situation at the point of intersection of varied, indeed disparate, esoteric and ludic discourses. Although he claims that these traditions are only of marginal relevance to his project, primacy being accorded to subjective, individual readings of the cards "in the most simple and direct fashion" (Calvino 1978, 116), there can be little doubt that the latent vestiges of those traditions abiding in the novel's interstices are a source of intense, if liminal, fascination. Calvino adheres to many traditional interpretations, while alternating between the high symbolic mode and basic, literal decodings, emphasizing throughout each card's shifting import according to the role and location of the character using it as his or her narrative avatar. The text's keenness on foregrounding variable readings is triggered by a painstaking attention to the minutest iconic details, on the one hand, and broad allegorical meanings on the other. There is evidence, in this regard, for Calvino's debt to the gypsy method in his use of the physiognomic conventions associated with the Court cards. Accordingly, Kings generally stand for mature men, Queens for mature women, Knights for adult young men (or women in disguise) and Pages for very young (or immature) people of both sexes. The four suits, while encapsulating the various characters' associations with the symbolic properties outlined earlier, also point to contrasting somatic attributes: Cups tend to refer to blond and light-skinned characters, Staves to brown-haired and light-skinned ones, Swords to dark-haired and dark-skinned people, and Coins to very dark complexions. In Calvino's text, the *Knight of Cups* is "a pink and blond youth"; the *King of Coins* represents an "older personage ... with a mature and prosperous appearance" (7); the depiction of the *King of Swords* evokes a "bellicose past" (27), while the *Queen of Swords* conjures up the image of an enchantress with an "elusive smile" (28); the *Page of Clubs*, in turn, signifies a "youth ... slender, as coy as a girl" (29); the writer himself finds a symbolic counterpart in the *King of Clubs*, based on the visual resemblance between the implement held by this figure and a "pen" (95). Additionally, Calvino follows traditional interpretations of the four suits' symbolic connotations in associating Cups with "love" (21) and "wisdom" (26); Clubs with "a crossroads, a choice" (21) as well as with words (95); Swords with "power" (26); and Coins with a "hidden treasure" (21) and generally "riches" (26).

Throughout Calvino's writing, there is also evidence of his attraction toward quasi-alchemical metamorphoses, an interest fuelled by his reading of Ovid and grounded on the conviction that any form can be transmuted into quite a different form and a cogent grasp of reality therefore requires the dissolution of its putative density. Yet, Calvino is also, more specifically, drawn to alchemy's elemental mapping of different aspects of the creative temperament. Mythological and astrological connotations also come into play, in this matter. Mercury is an element which Calvino especially values, due to its figurative connection with the Olympian deity said to preside over the arts of communication, mediation and exchange, and often held to have invented the art of writing. Alchemically, mythologically and astrologically, Mercury exemplifies the qualities of lightness, agility, suppleness and adaptability which, as we have seen, Calvino warmly commends as necessary ingredients of the creative process. Nevertheless, *Six Memos*, in praising the variable spirit symbolized by Mercury, is concurrently aware of the metaphorical equation of the creative personality to the somber, reclusive and meditative proclivities typified by Saturn. Like the competent astrologist, reluctant to categorize humankind on the basis of twelve merely indicative typologies and eager instead to detect intricate patterns of influence — or indeed like the alchemist, unwilling to prioritize individual elements in favor of increasingly complex concoctions — Calvino is keener on highlighting the cumulative effects produced by the confluence of contrasting dispositions than in valorizing one at the expense of the others. He is attracted to Mercury's airborne dexterity and somewhat uninspired by Saturn's introverted and grave temperament but is eager to acknowledge the ultimate interdependence of the two drives they typify. Not content with simply challenging the Mercury/Saturn binary, Calvino proceeds to introduce a third deity (with its various mythical attributes) to whom he claims to be spontaneously drawn: Vulcan, a deity that does not dwell in the radiant glory of Olympus but moves solely in the subterranean shadows. Calvino's fascination with Mercury and Vulcan is of special relevance to the present analysis, for the two figures' agencies symbolize the two indissoluble and mutually completing poles of human existence as described by André Virel in *Histoire de notre image* (1965), a text which Calvino read in the process of exploring Tarot symbolism. Mercury, in this context, "represents *syntony*, or participation in the world around us" whereas Vulcan stands for "*focalization* or constructive concentration" (Calvino 1996, 53). Swift metamorphoses are conducive to the evaporation of the imaginative process unless they are registered by a focused mind; the products of concentrated labor, conversely, never come to fruition without an injection of energy from winged motility.

As far as numerical symbolism is concerned, *The Castle of Crossed Destinies* abounds with illustrations of the diverse potentialities implicit in any one numbered card depending on the context of its emergence. The *Two of Cups* is described as a likely marker of an "amorous encounter" (Calvino 1978, 9); the *Five of Cups* could be read as "the alchemistic secret the Devil revealed to Faust, or as a toast to seal their bargain ... or as a discourse upon the soul and upon the body" (17); the interpretation of the *Two of Coins* is a particularly fascinating example of Calvino's penchant not only for elaborating a highly personalized numerology but also for developing a whole, potentially inexhaustible narrative from his close contemplation of just *one* card — this time, specifically, in the direction of what could be seen as both an apotheosis and a parody of Saussurean and poststructuralist linguistics. The card is thus described as a "sign of exchange, of that exchange that is in every sign, from the first scrawl made in such a way as to be distinguished from the other scrawls of the first writer, ... the letter that must not be taken literally ... that transfers values that without a letter are valueless ... that twists to signify it is ready and waiting to signify significations" (96).

Calvino's interest in numerology is also evinced by the structural orchestration of *The Castle of Crossed Destinies*. Both *The Castle of Crossed Destinies* and *The Tavern of Crossed Destinies* consist of eight sections. In each text, the first part outlines the contexts and physical environments in which the narration is to take place. In the first, the remaining seven parts consist of six individual tales followed by the Other Tales — namely, as indicated, a web of alternative readings of the Tarots laid out by the preceding narrators. In the second, analogously, sections two to seven present stories based on a central character, and the eighth and final part offers a narrative interweaving of primarily Shakespearean themes and motifs. Given the Tarot's history of at least partial cross-fertilization with the tradition of numerical symbolism, it is worth noticing that the four key numbers thrown into relief by Calvino's structural constellations carry the following connotations: one, the number foregrounded by the card representing the individual teller, alludes to origins, birth and initiation; six, the number of individual tales, suggests the concept of a move forward, or the confrontation of a challenge — a concept appropriate to the nature of the individual tales as dramatizations of personal quests, tests and trials; seven, the overall number of stories in each text, complicates the message already conveyed by six, to indicate the notion of a cautious move forward requiring, above all, patience — a quality which Calvino's heroes patently lack; eight, the number of sections included in the two narratives, finally, refers to the gradual expansion of the present world: a fitting metaphor, therefore, for Calvino's accretional and ultimately boundless fictional structures.

In order to grasp the fundamental principles — if not, for obvious reasons, the virtually limitless figurative potentialities — held by the esoteric system pivotal to Calvino's novel, it seems necessary to engage in some analysis of the Major Arcana themselves: the underpinning of the Tarot's entire symbolic import. The paragraphs that follow look at the relevant cards in the order posited by their numerical designations.

Arcanum One: The Magician— Calvino fundamentally abides by popular interpretations of this card as a positive clue to fresh opportunities that is capable, however, of degenerating into the negative prospect of overconfidence. Hence, while pointing to a process of cosmic metamorphosis evoked in some decks by the figure's attempt to span the distance between Earth and the heavens, the *Magician* may also be conceived of as a shifty and mendacious trickster. Arcanum I partakes of the natures of the shaman and the clown, with their shared commitment to the possibility of prospects of regeneration surfacing out of chaos. The first trump's creative potentialities are highlighted by his association with the figure of the writer — as suggested, according to Calvino, by the "inkwell" (36) commonly used in the card as an accessory. Ultimately, the tale insinuates, there is no fundamental difference between the impostor and the artist for the *Magician*, like the writer, is a juggler that entertains the crowd by simply moving around a basic set of props and arranging them in variable patterns. In this respect, the *Magician* stands out as both the victim and the champion of *ars combinatoria*.

Arcanum Two: The High Priestess/The Popess— Traditionally associated with intuition and tough-mindedness, or lack thereof, this figure may signify a warning against the temptation to rely excessively on evidence supplied by visibility and presence: *"Listen only to the voice that is soundless ... Look only on that which is invisible,"* advises Ouspensky's *Priestess* (Ouspensky 20). At the same time, a connection is often perceived between the second trump and a latent feminine principle entailing an intuitive understanding of life's mysteries. Calvino collapses these two interpretations together, and indeed magnifies their occult allusions, by depicting the *Popess* as an enigmatic queen, a sorceress or the leader of a bloodthirsty female sect. Yet, this trump is also related to the Delphic Sybil's mantic powers, which offers scope for a reading of the card conducive to potentially more benevolent, if no less alarming, outcomes.

Arcanum Three: The Empress— Capable of standing for both productive energies (fertility, literal and metaphorical pregnancy) and dissatisfied stagnation, Calvino's *Empress* is both a handsome maiden and an aging woman with a bland mien. She thus combines the generative powers of a temperament inclined to perceive in all things the rhythms of a joyous and vibrant nature, the union of body and mind through procreation, and the fossilizing impetus of rigid familial and broadly structural conventions.

Arcanum Four: The Emperor— Calvino's usage of this trump, specifically in *The Tale of the Alchemist who Sold His Soul*, reinforces traditional interpretations of the *Emperor* as an archetypal incarnation of godlike male authority commanding timorous respect, while spotlighting a counter-reading in which ultimate power actually comes to signify the utter loss of power. (As we shall see, this theme is developed with studious care in the segment entitled "A King Listens" in the collection *Under the Jaguar Sun*, here discussed in Chapter 8.) After all, the Alchemist, having received an augur of omnipotence, ends up precipitating into an identity-erasing whirlpool of frenzied confusion. The ambivalence of the *Emperor* lies primarily in his symbolizing a notion of power which is so total and all-engulfing as to be unattainable by any one human agent. The power it thus symbolizes is comparable to the concept of authority encapsulated in the Lacanian concept of the Phallus as a signifier of ultimate control beyond the reach of any man or woman subjected to the deferring mechanisms of language and the Symbolic Order. The supreme law for which the *Emperor* stands is, like Lacan's "Name of the Father," a castrating force curtailing its subjects' chances of self-realization (Lacan 1977). It is also a warning against the temptation to even try to incarnate the ideal of unlimited mastery at the level of individual existence (hence, the trump's reverse reading as a signifier of powerlessness), since the that law may only be experienced as a forever regressing mirage.

Arcanum Five: The Hierophant/Pope— The words uttered by the figure represented on the fifth of the Major Arcana in Ouspensky's *The Symbolism of the Tarot* appear to encapsulate Calvino's ethos of absence and invisibility: "Aspire only after the impossible and the inaccessible. *Expect only that which shall not be*" (Ouspensky 40). In *The Castle of Crossed Destinies*, the *Pope* is quite stereotypically sketched as a severe and white-bearded ecclesiastical leader. In *The Tavern of Crossed Destinies*, however, he acquires a more specific identity: he is still endowed with the same basic somatic traits but also, more crucially, identified as the "interpreter of dreams Sigismund of Vindobona" (Calvino 1978, 98). The connection proposed by the text between the fifth trump and Sigmund Freud is, in a sense, implied by Ouspensky's association of the *Pope* with hidden domains (and hence, by implication, the unconscious). It is further sustained, with ironic undertones, by Fontana's portrayal of the card as symbolic of "male energy expressed as spiritual power, the feminine in the male" (Fontana 173), and by common readings of this same card as encompassing conflicting messages: traditionalism and eccentricity, wisdom and misinformation.

Arcanum Six: The Lovers/Love— Affection, meetings and partings, the notion of some impending choice, are all ideas conventionally associated with this trump. The card is also often held to hint iconographically at divergent aspects of femininity, such as the ones exemplified by the *High Priestess* and the *Empress*. Calvino is obviously eager to dramatize the vagaries of amorous experience in terms of continual and frequently painful choices, felicitous encounters and heart-rending separations. *Love* represents, above all, the wistful longing chronicled by an inevitably unfinished tale, an abortive project, a displaced goal — as well as an audacious attempt to transcend human paltriness and greed.

Arcanum Seven: The Chariot— Calvino often employs this card in fundamentally practical and instrumental ways to produce structural linkages in the areas of travel, action, the flight toward success or, in fact, total failure. Occasionally, he individualizes the rider: in *The Tale of Roland*, for instance, the chariot is led by a figure varyingly interpretable as a witch or an Eastern female leader. By and large, however, the seventh trump broadly refers to an imaginative endeavor to venture into the macrocosmic dimension which may easily degenerate into an egocentric, Icaresque and megalomaniac drive toward unattainable and eventually self-destructive objectives.

Arcanum Eight: Justice— Not surprisingly, this card tends to epitomize the principles of balance and fair play, and, in a reversed reading, disharmony and strife. In its positive role, the *Justice* trump is evocative of an ultimate equilibrium between internal and external levels of being, between the empirical and the occult. Nevertheless, it also holds radically unsettling potentialities as a power capable of stripping the human world of illusory dreams and thus leave us defenseless in the face of reality's brutal demands. Calvino, likewise, associates this trump with the quintessence of rational powers but warns that it is inextricable from madness, as typified by Roland's insanity and, more broadly, by the structural randomness of any story subjected to the capricious permutations of free-floating Tarot cards.

Arcanum Nine: The Hermit— In *The Castle of Crossed Destinies*, we encounter contrasting readings of this Arcanum as signifying productive reflectiveness and self-reliance, on the one hand, and a negative form of withdrawal accompanied by a rejection of the external world on the other. The characterization of the *Hermit* put forward in *The Tale of Astolpho*, for example, tallies with the ninth trump's association with self-discovery issuing from taxing experiences and deprivation, and with initiation rites aiming to unite the individual human mind with the cosmic mind by analogical association. Indeed, Calvino's *Hermit* is an ancient man capable of seeing the future and of reversing the flow of time. However, the *Hermit* is also, in keeping with the alternative interpretation of this card advocated by traditional cartomancy, a deranged and ostracized Lear-figure desperately wandering through the wilderness in search of his lost daughter.

Arcanum Ten: The Wheel— Calvino describes the tenth trump as one of the most challenging figures in the Tarot code as a whole. If anything, the writer's utilization of the *Wheel* serves to confound further this card's already puzzling connotations. Indeed, while broadly subscribing to popular readings which associate the *Wheel* with both positive and negative turning points, with medieval conceptions of the ephemerality of sublunary fame and with notions of Eternal Recurrence of Eastern orientation, Calvino also adds personal dimensions to the trump's customary interpretations. He seems to go along with the standard reading of the *Wheel* as a symbol of the progressively enriching impact of repetition and reiterated acts but also uses it to convey the idea that human life is always *in medias res* and that its trajectory — assuming it has one — is that of a curvilinear eternal journey. In *The Tale of the Alchemist*, the tenth Arcanum becomes a diabolical machine through which the whole world may be turned into gold. The animal transmutations portrayed in the card, for their part, are seen as premonitions of a return of the human species to the realms of minerals and plants, echoed, in *The Tale of the Vampires' Kingdom*, by the image of a chaotic swirl of bestial phantoms. *The Tale of Astolpho* develops the regression theme into an image of carnivalesque inversion, which in some ways sums up the topsy-turvy quality of the whole novel.

Arcanum Eleven: Strength — A traditional symbol of supreme control susceptible to deterioration into despotism and a tyrannical disposition toward both oneself and others, the eleventh trump as employed in *The Castle of Crossed Destinies* points to a range of alternative readings. Faithful to the principle that the only authentic strength is of a spiritual ilk, Calvino is concurrently aware that *Strength* epitomizes a boundless consciousness and may therefore degenerate into the mindless anarchy of a devastating earthquake unless it is restrained and tamed by sophisticated rituals and codes.

Arcanum Twelve: The Hanged Man — An image of serenity and radiance, as states which may only be attained through suffering and even the (temporary) loss of reason, the twelfth trump symbolizes the realization that the world can only be grasped through drastic inversions of perspective and viewpoint. Echoing the Phoenician sailor from T. S. Eliot's *The Waste Land*, the *Hanged Man* learns through self-annihilation, suspension and sacrifice how to juggle the contradictory imperatives posed by the necessity of adjusting to cosmic laws, on the one hand, and human drives on the other. The *Hanged Man* dramatizes a process of identity-construction based on the assimilation of non-being, on an understanding of that fringe of irreducible alterity which continually defies the image of bounded self-presence. Pathetic in his puny and trapped individuality, yet dauntless in his pursuit of meanings capable of transcending individual limitations, the figure depicted in this Arcanum encapsulates the central ambivalence of being: what Ouspensky describes as "the incommensurableness of the small and the great" in the human spirit (Ouspensky 58).

Arcanum Thirteen: Death— Throughout Calvino's novel, this trump represents a pivotal symbol of change, which may amount to a literal loss, to metaphorical lethargy and inertia, or even to a blessing in disguise: a rite of passage into the spiritual dimension. The significance of the thirteenth Arcanum as a symbol of potential regeneration serves to relativize the concept of physical disintegration and to highlight, concomitantly, the inextricability of constructive and destructive processes, of generation and decay.

Arcanum Fourteen: Temperance— A signifier of moderation and wholesome restraint which, however, may also stand for excess and overindulgence in its reversed reading, the fourteenth trump is varyingly employed by Calvino as a symbol of the peace that follows strenuous exertions, as an allegory of the psyche at its most creative, and as a synthesis of angelic strength and all-too-human weakness (typically exemplified by the figures of Ophelia and Cordelia in *Three Tales of Madness and Destruction*). The psychological interpretation of Arcanum Fourteen is reinforced by the suggestion that *Temperance* does not simply represent rational sobriety and conscious self-restraint but also, more interestingly, that affective dimension of the mind which comes to the foreground precisely when rationality and consciousness are suspended, the ego is relinquished and fresh energies are allowed to fill the vacuum it leaves in its wake.

Arcanum Fifteen: The Devil— Calvino's *Devil* is fundamentally the traditional champion of duplicitousness and mischief, as well as a protean vision blending male, female, human and bestial attributes with the power to unsettle the most inveterate binary oppositions. Arcanum Fifteen constitutes a drastic assault upon conventional distinctions between good and evil, truth and falsehood. Calvino's *Devil* is not so much a real incarnation of underworld mendacity as a hyperreal scapegoat upon which the daylight domain projects its own inherent fraudulence and hypocrisy: in other words, an ideological construct designed to efface the ghastly iniquity and untruthfulness of the world at large.

Arcanum Sixteen: The Tower— Chaos, devastation and confusion are the images which the *Tower* most readily conjures and indeed, Calvino equates it both with the mythical "Babel" (Calvino 1978, 26) and with the image of a city under siege, depicting with harrowing accuracy the dumping of dead bodies "from the bastions amid torrents of boiling oil" (34). Yet, this card also symbolizes a healthy purging of repressed emotions and the productive force that may emerge from utter chaos. The sixteenth trump should not be read merely as a prophecy of ineluctable doom but also as an invitation to embrace destruction as a necessary ingredient of existence and hence to cultivate a novel and more capacious conception of disorder. Anarchy and turmoil, relatedly, may symbolize the underpinnings of tyrannical dogmatism, of a totalitarian regime committed to the repression of creativity and independence. A critical awareness of the pervasiveness of chaos may help us oppose such a despotic doctrine and arrive at an enlightenment which does not result from wholly rational efforts but also, more importantly, from a nurturing of the irrational.

Arcanum Seventeen: The Star— This trump represents rebirth, a hopeful widening of conventional horizons and the imaginative side of nature: a nature, according to Ouspensky, that "dreams, improvises, creates worlds" (Ouspensky 38). Of course, as is always the case with Tarot cards, an opposed reading is concurrently available, whereby the *Star* symbolizes pessimism, self-doubt and hopelessness. In Calvino, Arcanum Seventeen is both a radiant source of energy symbolized by a gentle girl of star-like fairness and offering a glimpse of hope in the dark, and a harrowing visualization of insanity, remorse, damnation and defeat. Indeed, in *Three Tales of Madness and Destruction*, the *Star* stands simultaneously for the exiled Cordelia, reduced to sate her thirst by collecting rainwater from the "ditches" (Calvino 1978, 113), the raving Lady Macbeth as a naked somnambulist, and Ophelia on the verge of entering the stream destined to destroy her.

Arcanum Eighteen: The Moon— As a heavenly body, Calvino's Moon operates principally as a signifier of unfulfilling relationships and unrealized plans—a point anticipated in the discussion of Calvino's debt to Ariosto. Accordingly, it is ideated as the realm hosting people's unlived lives and inchoate ideas that have not managed to fully enter consciousness. The most touching depiction of the Moon's status as the receptacle of forever lost, squandered or missed chances comes in the segment devoted by Calvino to "Astolfo sulla Luna" ("Astolpho on the Moon") in *Orlando Furioso di Ludovico Ariosto raccontato da Italo Calvino* (*Ludovico Ariosto's Orlando Furioso recounted* [or *narrated*] *by Italo Calvino*), a text to be discussed in detail at the close of this chapter. The relevant passage is worth citing at this juncture for the sake of analytical cogency: "In the universe, nothing is ever lost. Where do things lost on Earth end up? On the Moon. In its white valleys reside evanescent fame, dishonest prayers, lovers' tears and sighs, time wasted by gamblers. And it is there, within sealed phials, that is kept the sanity of those who have lost it, wholly or in part" (Calvino 1995, 239). However, the *Moon* trump also carries more positive symbolic connotations as the emblem of a balanced relationship between feminine and masculine principles, *yin* and *yang*, the unconscious and consciousness, inside and outside, darkness and light. Calvino intensifies the *Moon*'s ambiguity, particularly in *The Tale of Roland*, where the relationship between the human planet and its silvery satellite is rendered highly problematic and the latter is hence portrayed at once as the Earth's prey and its captor. The duplicitousness of Arcanum Eighteen is underscored by Calvino's emphasis on the ambivalent images by recourse to which the Moon as such is traditionally depicted. On the one hand, it is associated — in a vein redolent of the celestial body's unsentimental portrayal in *Cosmicomics* and *Time and the Hunter*— with creatures and phenomena branded as unclean, such as the werewolf, the mosquito and the menstrual cycle. On the other hand, it is upheld as the quintessence of purity and grace. In *The Tale of Astolpho*, the *Moon* is implicitly celebrated as the receptacle of latent creativeness and, at the same time, as a powerful reminder of an irreducible margin of absence, nothingness and non-existence which radically unsettles any idealization of artistic productivity as an expression of fullness and gravity. Indeed, the *Moon* could be said to symbolize Calvino's aesthetic quest for Lightness, articulated in *Six Memos*, as a means of opposing the stultifying ponderousness of a life endured more than lived. The poet-magician met by Astolpho on the Moon asserts that the planet is indeed the spring from which the poetic imagination emanates. Since, at the same time, the character describes the Moon as an "empty horizon" (Calvino 1978, 37), he could be said to be voicing Calvino's own belief in the emergence of creativity from absence.

Arcanum Nineteen: The Sun— Calvino's use of this trump warns us against any monolithic, facile identification of the *Sun* with the forces of light, with triumphant self-confidence and unlimited success. That Arcanum Nineteen does not unproblematically coincide with illumination is emphasized by its utilization in *The Tale of Roland*, where the card is read as representing a flying "cupid" intent on snatching away the hapless hero's reason (30). Fontana likewise stresses the precariousness of any achievement or victory which the *Sun* may be taken to symbolize, by observing that all quests are ultimately inconclusive for the simple reason that "The sun rises each morning" (Fontana 178).

Arcanum Twenty: Judgment—The Castle of Crossed Destinies would appear to agree with popular interpretations of this card as symbolic of an epiphanic climax: an ultimate understanding of life's most refractory mysteries. Indeed, *The Tale of Astolpho* sees this card as indicative of an attempt to soar above human limitations by defying the laws of physics themselves, and *Two Tales of Seeking and Losing* explicitly relates Arcanum Twenty to the phenomenon of rebirth while also associating it with the image of a summon from heaven. The latter image mirrors the traditional reading of the card as pointing to a person's urge, once he or she has achieved a state of illumination, to endeavor also to raise the consciousnesses of his or her fellow humans.

Arcanum Twenty-One: The World—This trump is described by Calvino as the mightiest of the Tarot cards insofar as it emblematizes the sum total of possibilities and potentialities ever contemplated or contemplable. However, the World also represents, on a more mundane level, literal cities enduring siege in ancient wars. It also hints, somewhat puzzlingly, at erotic dalliance and at the apotheosis of grotesque mythological beings. Moreover, at the same time as the card may symbolize the heavenly realm of harmony and wholeness, it also stands for the underground domain of Death. It is clear, therefore, that the World does not unequivocally signify the power of totality, for its iconography displays diverse and even incompatible elements which make contrasting interpretations all equally viable.

Arcanum Zero: The Fool—The *Fool* is a figure willing, possibly out of impetuous childishness, possibly out of extreme boldness, to descend into the world's core, where "all possible orders" frenziedly intersect (Calvino 1978, 31). Like Lear's Fool, the character depicted by the zero trump can get away with voicing without shame or restraint the least palatable truths, protected by his so-called foolishness. Questioning what most other humans leave unexamined and urging them to follow suit much against their inclinations, the Fool symbolizes the specular image of sanctioned authority. At one level, the dominant powers feel uneasy in his presence; at a parallel level, they need the Fool as a negative force in contrast with which they may define and legitimize their own identity. For Calvino, as for Fontana, this double function is ultimately an effect of the Fool's unorthodox promotion of one of the most fundamentally contradictory aspects of humanity: "that part of ourselves that is wise enough to stand awestruck before the mystery of creation and bold enough to set off exploring" (Fontana 171).

    The universe inhabited by Calvino's aphasic narrators obviously transcends conventional spatial and temporal boundaries. The writer contemplates the possibility of elaborating a cognitive code capable of structuring and interpreting such an idiosyncratic world, of superimposing a systematic grid on its anarchic texture. Nevertheless, the narrative finally suggests that any attempt to embed chaos within the framework of an algebraic vision is inexorably contingent and provisional. On the thematic plane, the awareness that no narrative structure can operate as a reliable safety net is indicated by the dark, menacing images of fragmentation, flux, dismemberment, vampirism, madness, loss of identity, engulfment, torture, betrayal and, of course, death, which pervade *The Castle of Crossed Destinies* from cover to cover. If such bleak subject matter is marginalized and its structural orchestration is given priority instead, the emerging picture is no rosier: as JoAnn Cannon observes, "the structural model, stripped to its essence, is a system of purely relational and abstract units devoid of content" (Cannon 89) — in other words, something static or even unwholesomely stagnant. As indicated throughout the foregoing analysis, Calvino challenges the primacy of structure over subject matter through his infusion into the narrative construct of dynamic and destabilizing elements. Thus, if the text's basic pattern may seem repetitive and skeletal due to its manipulation of a limited repertoire of images and thematic motifs, the actual narration is a boundless feat of textual productivity, guaranteed by each teller's subjective handling of the tools at her or his disposal. *The Castle of Crossed Destinies* thrives on a paradoxical notion of difference as the product of sameness: as an infinite number of unique tales may be composed by recourse to identical building blocks, communicative and interpretative processes are concurrently unlimited, indefatigably stretched toward an invisible horizon of ever-shifting patterns and puzzles. The blank space around which the constellation of *The Tavern of Crossed Destinies* revolves epitomizes the text's penchant for endless creation, recreation and decreation. This absent center, in underscoring the open-endedness of any narrative venture, simultaneously inaugurates the possibility of unconfinable forms of expression. In this respect, the novel echoes Umberto Eco's contention that "the signifying message, at the point where it reaches its destination, is empty. But its emptiness ... is an openness to a signifying apparatus not yet illuminated by any of the codes I may choose to cause to converge over it" (Eco 362). Calvino's decision to

Chapter 5—Structures and Their Explosion 121

envisage the narrative's precarious point of arrival as a void points both to a recognition of the stultifying immobility of sealed and ostensibly replete structures and to a desire ceaselessly to release fresh expressive energies.

The Castle of Crossed Destinies shares a hearty appetite for mock-historical gestures with *Our Ancestors*, a fascination with non-verbal codes with *Invisible Cities* and *Under the Jaguar Sun* alike and a brave resolve to confront the severest repercussions of chaos with both *Mr. Palomar* and *If on a winter's night a traveler*. However, its closest companion piece is indubitably Calvino's retelling of Ariosto's *Orlando Furioso* (originally published in 1970)—a text touched upon in Chapter 2 and cited in the course of this chapter in conjunction with Arcanum Eighteen. The power that drew Calvino to this project is essentially the same force that led him to elect Ariostesque adventures as the core of *The Castle of Crossed Destinies*. What magnetized Calvino so very potently toward the Renaissance poem as to make him wish to embark on his own reconstruction of the titanic edifice was not only its prioritization of the fantastic dimension to arguably unprecedented degrees. More specifically, it was Ariosto's knack of releasing fantasy onto a vertiginous, darting and Byzantine cavalcade in such a fashion as to suggest that at its most genuine, the fantastic simply cannot help addressing and concretizing some intractable metaphysical issues haunting the human condition. Thus, the fantasy does not simply take us into parallel universes, though this is unquestionably one of its greatest assets: it also enjoins us to face up to the here-and-now from an unfamiliar perspective predicated upon a logic other than the one required by ordinary life—a logic capable of bringing into play objects, ideas and processes of free association unfettered by the blandness of the quotidian.

Calvino would never subscribe to the truistic assessment of fantasy as an ensemble of images disconnected from everyday reality. In fact, he believes that even in the context of the most bizarre fantastic construct, a connection between the fiction and the empirical domain subsists. This conviction proceeds from the writer's well-tested awareness that sensitivity to certain facets of prosaic concreteness is a prerequisite of the creative spirit's awakening. As Calvino intimates in the essay "Definitions of Territories: Fantasy," it is from a modicum of down-to-earthness that a fantasy-oriented author may develop a fruitfully pragmatic concern not with the "explanation" of peculiar or mysterious occurrences but rather with the "*order of things*" which an "extraordinary event produces in itself and around it; the pattern, the symmetry, the network of images deposited around it, as in the formation of a crystal" (Calvino 1987, 73)—in other words, with the structural dimension which for Calvino will always remain paramount even at times when he is most inclined to quiz and explode it. The recurrence of the image of the crystal is also noteworthy as an implicit connector between the world of *The Castle of Crossed Destinies* and the realm of the fantastic as epitomized by Ariosto's work. At the same time, Calvino never automatically assumes that the fantastic demands a reader's willingness to be so absorbed in the text's affective flow as to accept its veracity unquestioningly. This may be what modern fantasy has been expecting of readers, at least since the nineteenth century, but is patently not what a Renaissance author of fantasy-inflected literature would have anticipated. With specific reference to the writer here addressed, Calvino states: "Ariosto's readers were never faced with the problem of *believing*" (72).

A corollary of the hypotheses delineated in the foregoing paragraphs that impact directly on Calvino's retelling of *Orlando Furioso* is that fantasy is not meant by the writer to work as a cognitive instrument dependable unto itself. Rather, it is regarded as a key stage in an adventurous cognitive *process*: namely, the kind of metajourney embarked upon by artists and scientists alike when they recognize that for thought to move forward, it must be given free rein to venture beyond the orthodox logical associations invited (or indeed permitted) by empirical experience. Since such a process cannot be linked to obvious outcomes, it is, by definition, open-ended. Open-endedness is also one of the pivotal factors that renders *Orlando Furioso* so enticing to Calvino, and hence the aspect of the Renaissance poem he seeks to both foreground and reconceptualize most devotedly in his own version of the text. Calvino unobtrusively communicates this intention by selecting a number of Ariosto's narrative threads and constellating them thematically, yet also reminds us assiduously that such themes do not presume to summarize all of the events dramatized in *Orlando Furioso* or even begin to do justice to their inexhaustible potential for self-proliferation. The poem, he believes, could have been extended indefinitely — as pointedly attested to by the fact that Ariosto was engaged in lengthening, interweaving and multiplying its incidents till the day of his death.

Some pivotal structural attributes of Ariosto's poem clearly reverberate in the plotting and visual orchestration of *The Castle of Crossed Destinies*. These include the tendency to move alternately from one story to another by means of either fluid transitions (e.g., meetings and partings of characters involved in multiple yarns at different stages in the narra-

Chapter 5 — Structures and Their Explosion 123

tive) or more abrupt shifts (e.g., sudden interruptions of events accompanied by equally drastic changes in the cast). Calvino's attraction to Ariosto is not, however, motivated by the perception of purely structural affinities between the Renaissance author's vision and his own. In fact, Calvino is no less intensely drawn to Ariosto's openness to a virtually limitless literary and artistic tradition, plural traces of which inhabit *Orlando Furioso* with varying degrees of explicitness. Ariosto's commodious take on tradition, moreover, signals his parallel cultivation of a world view amenable to the possibility of a likewise unlimited reservoir of potential worlds and of hypothetical interlockings of temporal and spatial coordinates. In philosophical terms, Calvino also instinctively senses a deep-seated congeniality with Ariosto's emphasis on the flimsiness of human endeavor, and this is another important facet of the pseudo-epic that he strives to spotlight throughout his own alternate narration. The quest topos undoubtedly guides *Orlando Furioso* no less persistently than it informs earlier (and indeed subsequent) epics. Yet, the contingent objects to which Ariosto's knights indefatigably aspire are nothing as noble as the Holy Grail. In fact, they are palpably mundane objects of self-congratulatory, amorous or acquisitive concupiscence — in other words, highly iconoclastic and perhaps even slightly blasphemous variations on the type of epic goal enshrined in classic literature. At base, all of Ariosto's characters desire something but their yearnings are pursued in vain since the object of desire inexorably proves unattainable or inadequate. The related quest, therefore, is either unresolved or disappointing. In the process, not only do the characters fail to achieve anything worthwhile: they also, more ominously still, allow their minds to be led astray down labyrinthine corridors and murky eddies until any sense of purpose, responsibility or duty evaporates altogether from their blighted horizons.

Ariosto's iconoclastic proclivities often bring to mind Calvino's own irreverent use of canonical narrative formulae to suit his own, highly personal, creative vision. Thus, just as Ariosto does not hesitate to infuse an epic supposedly preoccupied with the grave mater of Christianity's defense against the infidel with pointedly fantastic and romantic elements, so Calvino — as we have seen — has no qualms in bending the rules of disparate forms, genres and even whole disciplines to his distinctive ends. Calvino is especially intrigued not only with Ariosto's displacement of traditional quest motifs but also with his ironical juxtaposition of two vastly divergent centers of narrative gravity within the poem's overall web. It is, accordingly, one of Calvino's chief objectives to throw this aspect of the

Renaissance poem into sharp relief. One of those pivots is perfectly consonant with the aesthetic and ethical requirements of the epic at its most conventional and serious insofar as it consists of the siege of Paris by the Saracens. The other center, conversely, could hardly be less orthodox a choice since it coincides with the magician Atlante's enchanted palace: an edifice no less daunting, sprangling and diffuse, in architectural terms, than the *Orlando Furioso* itself is in narrative and lyrical terms. The palace functions as a kind of black hole eager to swallow all of the main personae, one by one, and to trap them within protean spatial illusions. What Calvino seeks to highlight, in his approach to the magical construct within the adapted version of the poem, is its significance not merely as a convenient receptacle for all manner of fairytalish complications but also as a metaphorically dispassionate commentary on human foolishness. The building indeed operates as a microcosmic model of the world in its entirety as the ephemeral stage on which people pointlessly pursue their paltry, yet tenaciously elusive, goals. The unreality of the visions evoked by Atlante finds a direct parallel in the vapidity of human ambitions, since the images themselves are designed to capture what each individual captive fantasizes about and yearns for from the depths of his or her damning solipsism. The sought-for objects, in this scenario, are posited as purely subjective and evanescent concoctions whose value is wholly contingent on personal longings and imaginings.

In assessing the cumulative significance of Calvino's retelling of *Orlando Furioso*, it must also be noted that the modern text does not simply reactivate the chivalric tradition embedded in Ariosto's own work (in a more or less inverted or subverted fashion)—a tradition, incidentally, that was already felt to carry an antiquarian patina in Ariosto's own time. In fact, it also harks back, albeit obliquely, to a whole galaxy of mythological interpretations of early medieval history spawned not exclusively by poetic genius but also — and often to greater effect — by troubadours. These tales, even when they appear to take the Crusades as their pivotal theme, actually bring together the martial, magical and amorous exploits of countless other epochs and cultures — including Greco-Roman and Arthurian milieux — in cyclical and serial formats that foreshadow far more recent dramatic constructs. As Calvino notes, the scale of such narratives thus comes to constitute a distillation of "all times and all wars" (Calvino 1995, 12). The legacy of this tradition is still alive today in several art forms rooted in folklore, and particularly in performances based on the coalescence of narration and song or on the allegorical deployment of puppets.

Chapter 5—Structures and Their Explosion

What is ultimately most refreshing about Calvino's retelling of *Orlando Furioso* from the analytical standpoint of someone who does not regard himself solely, or indeed primarily, as a critic but also as a fan, a student, a disciple and a creative writer in his own right is that he never relinquishes his personal imaginative powers, speculative curiosity and, most crucially, utterly unsentimental, yet compassionate, sense of irony.

Calvino thereby delivers some genuinely inspired poetic flourishes that illuminate both his stance toward Ariosto's writings and, no less vitally, the fabric of his own special imagination. It is in celebrating the Renaissance author's flair for integrating magisterially the frisson of rapid action and the quieter pleasure of deliberate ambulation through time and space that Calvino expresses in memorable notes his own ability to harmonize dynamic vitality and slow-paced contemplation. In so doing, he implicitly demonstrates the applicability to himself and his own works of he words he uses to sum up Ariosto's uncanny appeal: "Ariosto appears to be a transparent, cheerful and unproblematic poet, yet remains mysterious ... he appears primarily concerned with hiding himself" (30). The concept of the invisible author addressed in Chapter 1 resonates again in these reflections. Furthermore, the very mood perceived by Calvino to pervade Ariosto's inconclusive resolution of his life's work also characterizes the culmination of *Orlando Furioso*'s latter-day avatar in the guise of *The Castle of Crossed Destinies*. Like the character of the Saracen Rodomonte, who "encapsulates the poem's prismatic spirit, sonorous exuberance, melancholy, inexhaustible reservoir of energy," *Orlando Furioso* and *The Castle of Crossed Destinies* alike leave the scene with delicately morose restraint, "winding down in a slow spiral toward the dark Acheron of silence" (301).

Chapter 6

Science and Play: *Mr. Palomar* and *Numbers in the Dark*

The passion for geometrical arrangements, arithmetical operations, symmetries, parallelisms and correspondences plays a pivotal part in Calvino's artistic career from its early stages. *The Cloven Viscount* is sustained throughout by a keen, even slightly perverse, attraction to the concept of symmetry. Formal schemata of scientific derivation operate as the animating principle at the core of *Cosmicomics* and *Time and the Hunter*, and are subsequently adapted to fit the specific requirements of architectural and iconographic visions in *Invisible Cities* and *The Castle of Crossed Destinies* respectively. In *Mr. Palomar*, originally published in 1983, Calvino's mathematical sensibility reaches unprecedented heights. As indicated in relation to *The Castle of Crossed Destinies*, the writer's utilization of mathematical and geometrical structures is not intended to subject experience to ironclad rules but rather to underscore the limitations of any putatively all-encompassing system.

Beno Weiss, among other commentators, has interpreted Calvino's penchant for "systems, scientific principles, combinatorial games" rather than "human qualities" as symptomatic of a self-distancing, depersonalizing and unemotional tendency to dismiss character depth and plot complexity. The result, the critic argues, is that the writer "seems to be intentionally lacking in pathos, the quality of art which stimulates our emotions: pity, tenderness, sorrow, joy, love, affection" (Weiss 204). It could be argued, however, that it is precisely when Calvino's scientific experiments gain thematic and structural preeminence that the writer's existential preoccupations are most uncompromisingly foregrounded. Calvino's keenness on geometric grids is only cold, detached, and dehumanizing by narrowly conceived liberal humanist standards. It is far from passionless, however, when it is recognized as the indicator of a brave, stoical and repeatedly frustrated struggle to understand and to come to terms with reality's imponderable absences. Nowhere is this existentialist proclivity more beautifully and painfully recorded than in *Mr. Palomar*.

Calvino's hero may appear stereotypical, emblematic, a mere narratological function made wholly subservient to the practice of logical rationalization. But one only needs to consider the titanic obsessiveness with which Palomar pursues his analytical task, his possession by a decoding demon that compels him to intercept signals beyond any code, to realize that the novel, far from lacking pathos, is filled with pathos to the very brim. "A nervous man ... in a frenzied and congested world" (Calvino 1994, 4), Palomar "does not love himself" (106), is "absent-minded, introverted" and unable to take "pleasure" in any object he observes, for in prioritizing criteria of "selection" and "exclusion," he "soon realizes he is spoiling everything" (101). He is also, at least partially, "egocentric" and "megalomaniac" (11), yet "depressive, self-wounding" (12) and, above all, impatient, fretful, and pathetically shortsighted despite, paradoxically, his being named after the world's most famous observatory. Palomar's emotional burden consists of posing riddles that shift and multiply endlessly, the protagonist's anguish growing proportionally to his inquisitiveness. His ordeal stems from a heightened awareness of the world's intricacy, exacerbated by the realization that the segmentation of any complex whole only yields further involutions in each of the segments, and that any attempt to establish a sense of unity or cohesiveness among the individual components through the identification of relations and analogies will reveal not predictable but rather random connections. Accidental patterns may recur but this realization yields scarce solace for the cycle of recurrence itself remains inscrutable.

The book is divided into three sections, namely, "Mr. Palomar's Vacation," "Mr. Palomar in the City" and "The Silences of Mr. Palomar," and to each of these corresponds a thematic and rhetorical emphasis on three intercomplementary facets of experience: the visual, the broadly cultural and the existential. The third category addresses most explicitly the issue of the individual self's relationship with the cosmos. This structural partitioning does not amount to a prescriptive schema intended to impose a rational grid upon otherwise elusive or even inchoate sensations. Had this been the case, the book would feasibly have yielded intellectual appeal but held little in store for the senses to feast upon—which is precisely what it does, in spadefuls in fact. Hence, it proves endlessly rewarding even for the least scientifically disposed of readers. Relatedly, while the protagonist often seems just about to precipitate into an abyss of undiluted solipsism, he is always held in check by an unquenchable thirst for experience enabling him not merely to venture but actually to maraud outside the cage of the self. Palomar's narrative function is well captured in Seamus Heaney's felicitously titled review of *Mr. Palomar*, "The Sensual Philosopher," as "a lens employed by his author in order to inspect the phenomena of the world" that is also "apt to turn into a mirror which reflects the hesitations and self-corrections" of the character's analytical mentality. Thus, the text delivers "a graduated sequence of descriptions and speculations in which the protagonist confronts the problem of discovering his place in the world and of watching those discoveries dissolve under his habitual intellectual scrutiny" (Heaney).

Through the neurotic Palomar, Calvino articulates most explicitly his mistrust of classic analytical procedures — something which, as discussed in the preceding chapter, also characterizes the structural orchestration of the Tarot narratives. Palomar operates on the premise that the "world's complexity" may be mastered "by reducing it to the simplest mechanism," only to discover, alas, that every endeavor to fashion a model of irreducible simplicity only serves to posit further complications, for any individual fragment becomes dulled and confounded by overlapping elements that eventually cause the "general pattern" to break down into segments that "rise and vanish" (Calvino 1994, 6). Longing for a "single, absolute principle" or, at least, for "a certain number of distinct principles, lines of force that intersect" (13), what Calvino's hero actually meets is a world of "phantoms" (14). Palomar's fundamental curse is that he feels "obliged never to stop working" (20): he insists at all times on being "quite aware of what he is doing" and, so as "to avoid vague sensations, he establishes for his every action a limited and precise object" (3). But how does one separate one single wave, say, from the constant ebb and flow of the vast sea to which it belongs? How does one "fix the boundaries" (5) of the zone under scrutiny when this is surrounded by unrelenting movement and agitation, reshaped and crushed continually by neighboring fields of energy?

These sorts of questions are no less pressing if located in an ethical perspective. The segment "The naked bosom," for instance, invites diverse ways of seeing, or regimes of visuality, pregnant with ethical implications. If Palomar, in catching sight of a topless female sunbather, "looks away at the horizon of the sea," he is immediately conscious of displaying "a refusal to see" which implicitly reinforces the prejudice that "declares illicit any sight of the breast" (8). If, alternatively, he walks past the woman keeping "his eyes fixed straight ahead," he feels embarrassed by his "having the bosom completely absorbed by the landscape," as this amounts to a "flattening of the human person to the level of things." If he allows himself to direct a "darting glance" toward the bosom, he then senses that he is perpetuating an ethos of "sexomaniac puritanism." Finally, he decides to "linger on the breast" (9–10). Needless to say, by now the sunbather has had enough of Palomar's perambulations in her vicinity, and "goes off, shrugging in irritation, as if she were avoiding the tiresome insistence of a satyr" (10).

Hence, the pathos evoked by Palomar's adventures is that of the absurd, of *ennui*, of the grotesque, even — as the ending suggests — of the macabre. After all, the final hypothesis on which Palomar exerts himself, having already become a sort of "anonymous and incorporeal dot" (106), consists of acting "as if he were dead" as, hopefully, the only means of exonerating himself from relentlessly "having to wonder what the world has in store for him" (108). Even at this extreme juncture, what the character encounters is a chain of insoluble analytical conundrums, resulting in an image of vertiginous recession of the real into an eddy of invisibility: "if time has no end, it can be described, instant by instant ... and each instant, when described, expands so that its end can no longer be seen" (112–113). This assumption would seem to suggest that if one were to describe every instant of one's life, letting each expand toward the edge of invisibility, death could somehow be kept at bay. It is precisely while contemplating this surreal conjecture that Calvino's archanalyzer "dies" (113).

Clearly, the emotions explored by the novel may not be in line with conventional expectations harbored by classic humanism. No doubt, they are generally activated by mental impulses, aesthetic and symbolic codes and disembodied signs — namely, abstract concepts — rather than by the stirring pulsations of flesh and blood. Nevertheless, in foregrounding Palomar's deductive mania as an exercise that places feelings on the plane of brainwork, Calvino also, no less vitally, draws attention to the infinitely elaborate and largely untapped languages of the physical senses, thus anticipating the central preoccupations lying behind *Under the Jaguar Sun*. The three segments comprised by "Palomar does the shopping" clearly exemplify Calvino's desire to explore the cornucopian richness of interweaving sensory and sensual discourses. Thus, in the segment "Two pounds of goose-fat," the sight of this humble culinary ingredient sparks off erotic fantasies, whereby "from a mountain of goose-fat a female figure surfaces" (61). Like the three tales which constitute *Under the Jaguar Sun*, this vignette relies substantially on the principle of synesthesia: the "beauty-spots of black truffle" that adorn the "gelatine sheaths" resemble "the notes of a score" (62), and Palomar waits anxiously "to hear the vibration of an orchestra of flavors" (63). The evocative richness of the forgotten languages of the senses, additionally, is sharply contrasted with the faceless and depersonalized customers. At the same time, the sense of sight, traditionally allotted the highest rank in the sensorium, is undermined by Palomar's keen awareness of the eye's disembodying and objectifying proclivities — its manic urge to turn everything it skims into something of a "museum exhibit" (63). This idea is pursued in the segment "The cheese museum," where Palomar is torn between a latent desire to yield to the sensuous atmosphere of the Parisian cheese shop, and an obsessively taxonomic urge to transform the shop into an utterly decarnalized compendium itemizing punctiliously the "names," "meanings," "histories" and "psychologies" of diverse types of cheese (65).

Like the tale devoted to the sense of taste in *Under the Jaguar Sun*, the segment "Marble and blood," finally, draws attention to the sophistication of culinary expertise as both a precise science and an atavistic form of "sacrificial learning" (68), thus preempting conventional tendencies to associate the discourses of gustation and olfaction with the domain of primitive and unrefined experience. What most pains Palomar, in his struggle to unravel diverse sensory registers, is the complexity of their "morphology," the stunning abundance of "synonyms, idiomatic usages, connotations and nuances of meaning" displayed by their vocabulary (66) and, above all, the realization that any attempt to produce a precise record of flavors or smells will be crippled by the incidence of vague "memories" (63). The elusiveness of all sensory traces epitomizes the penetration of any form of presence by absent remainders. Palomar's experiences, in particular, articulate Calvino's ongoing concern with the coexistence of absence and presence, invisibility and visibility, by intimating that the observable is at all time traversed by the imperceptible. As noted by Paul Fournel, a member of the experimental literary-scientific group Oulipo, Calvino's "pedagogy of observation and reflection" requires the reader to "learn to keenly observe and never be satisfied with what he has seen" (Fournel 87).

Palomar's rationalistic games are not, ultimately, a means of framing reality within the confines of schematic configurations but rather contribute to quiz the validity of abstract systems which, despite their endeavors to transcend the vagaries of the physical world, are ill-equipped to erase its baffling pockets of invisibility. By refusing to engage in conventional depictions of psychological depth, Calvino may be suggesting that depth simply does not obtain, either for his pathetic hero or for any of us, or else that if depth exists, its substance is that of a vacuum. Indeed, things most deserve our attention, Palomar insinuates, when they imperceptibly evade us, when they inhabit the threshold between the visible and the invisible, when their existence, as emphasized by the segment "The moon in the afternoon," cannot be taken for granted. The real is, quite often, plainly inaccessible, the sole factor which all forms seem to share being ultimately "darkness" (Calvino 1994, 12). Darkness does not univocally symbolize the annihilation of being, for it also signals, more creatively, the tentative emergence of presence from a substratum of absence. Palomar is incapable of surrendering totally to this final and potentially prosperous emptiness, seeking as he does to fill each breach in the landscape, in the sea, in the firmament, with a modicum of empirically verifiable knowledge. At the same time, the world's surfaces are so rich, varied and polysemantic in themselves as to discourage the search for what may lie underneath. In the segment "From the terrace," for instance, Palomar offers a eulogy of the surface as the potentially most genuine manifestation of the urban environment. The city's outermost layers present a map so wide and various that they prove more than sufficient to impregnate the brain "with information and meanings" (50), causing its attemps at logical rumination to be inevitably counterpointed by concealed perspectives, edges and folds. Palomar's Rome is redolent of Polo's fifty-five Venices: "trapped between the subterranean hordes of rats and the grievous flight of the pigeons, the ancient city allows itself to be corroded from below and from above" (47). Sadly, although Palomar is willing to acknowledge the surface's richness, his analytical mentality still eggs him on to seek what the surface may conceal. Ensnared in the pursuit of this structuralist Grail, he is bound to panic whenever he is forced to acknowledge that surfaces themselves are incalculably complex.

The concept of inexhaustibility is arguably central to the whole narrative, its enduring segnificance secured by its twofold and contradictory import. On the one hand, inexhaustibility points to a boundless panorama of coexisting, if disparate and indeed incompatible, options, which constantly throws into relief the inseparability of any site of solidity from lacunary and spectral regions. On the other hand, inexhaustibility represents the governing impulse beyond Palomar's stubborn determination to venture into the heart of things: the uncertainty and instability of the world's boundaries and the absence of intelligible meanings within the gaps that pockmark his territory are what fuel and renew ad infinitum his appetite for completion and plenitude. Paradoxically, while Palomar may be reluctant to accept the world's inexhaustibility in one sense of the term — infinity, measurelessness — he concurrently ensconces a distressingly innocent faith in his own inexhaustibility as an unflinching and inexhaustible, albeit exhausting, commitment to analytical verification. The pathos of Palomar's adventures, in this regard, may lie precisely with the pitifully disproportionate levels of energy which he channels into various efforts to define both the sensory and the cogitative qualities of his lucubrations.

A further paradox evinced by the character's experiences derives from his rhetorical proclivities. Indeed, his language is often highly poetical and somewhat at odds with both his analytical/structural objectives and with the views, outlined at the beginning of this chapter, that brand his speculative experiments as coldly intellectual. Pursuing this argument, it could be maintained that Palomar is defeated, at the end of virtually all of his painstaking mentations, not by the world but rather by his own linguistic and affective make-up. The world itself, after all, is riddled with absences, blind spots and incongruities of which it is neither proud nor ashamed. It is Palomar, in fact, that feels uncomfortable in the face of the world's aporias and relentlessly embarks on attempts to iron them out. When he waxes lyrical, his images revolve primarily around evocations of uncertainty and dissolution: scenarios which the world accommodates at each moment of its explosive and implosive existence, and which Calvino's hero vainly struggles to redesign. This aspect of the novel is especially important because it foregrounds the analytical temperament's deconstructive disposition. Palomar yearns for presence and cogency, yet is repeatedly confronted by omissions and inconsistencies. The temptation to blame the world for its evasiveness is powerful but, ultimately, it is hardly deniable that the world never explicitly invites the protagonist to make sense of its indefiniteness. It is Palomar that takes it upon himself to dam the unbounded and, in the process, ironically ends up confirming the world's fluidity through an increasingly imaginative register. "The invasion of the starlings," for instance, uses the image of the migratory birds travelling through the Roman skies in late autumn to construct a picture of the universe as an "empty immensity ... traversed by very rapid and light presences." The cosmos in its entirety, by analogy with the ancient city, becomes a space without balance, a space of unpredictably converging, diverging, advancing, expanding, whirling shapes, which conjures up the possibility of "threats of catastrophe everywhere," any "illusion of regularity" being proverbially "treacherous" (57).

No less unsettling, throughout the novel, is Calvino's emphasis on the gulf that separates the perceiver from the perceived. In the segment "The sword of the sun," for instance, as Palomar swims in the direction of the sword-shaped reflection which the sun casts on the sea toward evening, he realizes that "at every stroke of his," the shining sword "retreats and never allows him to overtake it" (10). The natural world at large descends into the realm of absence, confronting him with the most terrifying nightmares of them all: the suggestion that "nothing of what he sees exists in nature" (14). Nature, of course, does exist as an effect of subjective perceptions. What afflicts Palomar is the realization that, in this tragicomedy of warped individualism, there is no way of demonstrating that the world would not disappear in the absence of any one individual perceiver.

In certain respects, *Mr. Palomar* could be read almost as a parody of the principle of Exactitude, as formulated in *Six Memos for the Next Millennium*. This aesthetic ideal, Calvino proposes, should encompass a clearly defined plan for the work to be undertaken, communicated through crisp, pithy and memorable visual images, and a language as accurate as possible in its selection of words and expressions meant to convey the subtle nuances of imagination and thought. If *Mr. Palomar* does not overtly satirize the pursuit of exactitude, it certainly documents its degeneration into an obsessionally futile quest. Palomar is distressed by the haphazard character of ordinary mental procedures, the automatism with which conclusions are drawn, the evaporation of sensory experiences into a cloud of fading images, their distinctiveness blunted by unreflective language usage. Palomar, like Calvino himself, senses unease in the face of the amorphousness that he notices in life. The crucial difference between the writer and the character—and, plausibly, the cause of the latter's unrelieved frustration—is that Palomar cannot help identifying precision and clarity with neatly definable structures of thought, whereas Calvino believes that they may well ensue from a cultivation of the vague and the indefinite. A meticulous attention to detail, an accurate grasp of the composition of an image, may emerge in the context of a celebration of uncertainty and imprecision.

Thus, while Palomar equates precision of thought to purity of both presentation and content, Calvino warns us against the tendency to divorce the opaque from the crystalline. Exactitude is indeed often inextricable from vagueness since the search for the indefinite inevitably entails loving attention to all that is multiple, diverse and overflowing with innumerable particles. The artist willing to accept the inseparability of imprecision and accuracy will ultimately let the multiple be multiple, the teeming rejoice in its profusion, aware that he may only, at best, record this fluidity. Palomar, conversely, though he unwittingly produces a sometimes sublime, sometimes farcical poetry of indefiniteness from the vortex of his minute observations, remains committed to a logic of disassociation of each particle from the others. He cannot resign himself to a cosmos of uncompromising diversity and in the effort to comprehend it, he actually strays further and further away from the light of understanding.

Part of Palomar's predicament may originate in his confusion of the infinite and the indefinite. The former, Calvino intimates, issues from humanity's instinctive tendency to fantasize about a world in which pleasure is unending. The latter results from a recognition that the human mind simply cannot conceive of such a limitless realm — and is, in fact, intimately terrified of its possibility — and must therefore make do with the indefinite (the unspecific, the indeterminate) even though this only provides a paltry approximation to the genuine boundlessness of the infinite per se. Palomar often comes across as plainly unaware that his quest for the absolute, the infinite, is actually a relative series of encounters with the indefinite: hence, his inability to admit to the contingency of any one scientific solution. Palomar would probably have been happier or, more to the point, less unhappy, had he come to terms with the partiality of all putatively total solutions and focused instead on the circumstantial particularity of each observable phenomenon. He does, nevertheless, occasionally catch a glimpse of a universe of undefinable qualities. The observation of a lawn wherein "harmful" and "good" grasses (27) become inextricably intertwined, for example, calls to his mind the image of a double-edged world, "finite but countless" (29).

Moreover, the pivotal enigma dramatized by the novel is succinctly summed up by the paradoxical image, offered in the essay from *Six Memos* devoted to Visibility, of an infinite mass hosting a plethora of further infinite quantities. The essay on Multiplicity, in turn, situates Palomar's myopic apprehension of the relationship between the infinite and the indefinite in the context of a speculative temperament strikingly reminiscent of the character's own personality. Palomar, like the type of the obsessive writer, is at all times intent on increasing the range of details unleashed by his observations to the point that his accounts thereof become potentially infinite. The matter at his disposal insanely spirals out of control, expanding in countless directions toward increasingly remote horizons in a vain effort to encompass the whole cosmos. At the same time, in cultivating singlemindedly his penchant for classification, exact labelling and mathematical accuracy, the protagonist is sooner or later caught in an unresolved conflict between rational precision and delirious distortion as the elemental building blocks of any cognitive exercise, for the structures he devises ceaselessly alter, become entangled, disintegrate before his very eyes or else grow progressively thicker from within. Driven by a deep dissatisfaction with the arbitrariness of the real, Palomar is compelled to subject himself to strict rules and procedures even if he is subliminally conscious of their own utter arbitrariness. Furthermore, whereas his passion for systematic categorization may appear mechanical and contrived, his musings bear witness to virtually unbounded creative faculties. As Palomar fantasizes about absolute and incontrovertible taxonomic principles, he cannot ultimately stifle his imaginative proclivities — cannot help, say, visualizing the relationship between a "planet" and "its satellites" as "air-bubbles rising from the gills of a round fish of the depths, luminescent and striped" (37).

In his relentless pursuit of alternative forms of stability, Calvino's hero frequently toys with the possibility of anthropomorphizing non-human phenomena in an effort, arguably, to bring the indistinct into some kind of familiar focus. Yet, this strategy does not deliver a humanistic ideation of the world, capable of confirming the superiority of human experience. In fact, it calls that presumed preeminence radically into question. The effects of anthropomorphism are uncertainly, if at all, satisfying or illuminating. For example, what do forms of communication among animals teach us about language? Palomar may quantify the blackbirds' whistle according to a human nomenclature but he cannot ascertain whether or not the birds are engaged in some sort of conversation. Nor can he establish whether messages are contained in the whistles or rather in the silences, intervals and pauses that separate any two utterances. Palomar's humanization of the animal realm does not help him explain the human world — let alone assert the latter's dominance — for it only, at best, highlights the grim travesty of a symbolic language wherein "no one can understand anyone" (22) and each individual sends out messages which he or she misrecognizes as essential to him or her while, in fact, they belong to no one.

The segment "The loves of the tortoises" intimates that animal eroticism, anthropomorphize it as we may, remains a mystery, as does the question of whether or not its pleasures may exceed anything which human sexuality is capable of comprehending. Perhaps the tortoises enjoy a more "intense mental life" than humans, who are trapped in the mechanical operations of "the computer of feelings" (18–19). At other times, to pursue the mechanical metaphor further, Palomar's anthropomorphizing process pivots on the perception of analogies between human beings and other animals based on their shared commonality with non-organic apparatuses. If humans conduct their erotic rituals in a computerized fashion, there are evident vestiges of robotism in the structure of non-human beasts, too. In the cases of both humans and non-humans, moreover, there are intimations of wasted efforts on nature's part: the "gecko" and the "giraffe" are memorably invoked to corroborate this proposition.

If the humanization of non-human animals does not deliver any guarantee of anthropocentric excellence, it often becomes an indirect, defamiliarizing means of posing poignant questions about humanity's own nightmares. "What is sleep like," wonders Palomar after hours spent observing the gecko, "for someone who has eyes without eyelids?" (55). What is it like, the segment on "The albino gorilla" asks, to be "the sole exemplar in the world of a form not chosen, not loved" (73)? The scaly creatures in the reptilarium offer a dismal panorama of "forms without style and without plan" (77) that harrowingly recall the stagnant motionlessness of all life "torn from a natural continuum that might also never have existed" (78), compelling Palomar to ponder the illegibility of the temporal dimension. These and legion other questions raised by the part entitled "Palomar at the zoo" ultimately point to unresolved tensions between the real and the virtual, and hence to the necessity of situating any form of realization in a context of unfulfilled potentialities.

Unpalatable and demoralizing as the version of selfhood articulated by *Mr. Palomar* may seem to a humanistically oriented reader, it is nonetheless vital to realize that the collapse of the barrier between subject and object envisaged by the protagonist constitutes a potentially emancipating move. Indeed, it posits subjectivity as a permutational game of half-glimpsed visions, half-lived experiences, half-hearted appropriations of a seamless and largely indifferent flow of information. If the reiteration of the "half" prefix may come across as a harrowing reminder of the schizoid existence endured by the cloven Viscount Medardo, it is also worth remembering that for Calvino, it is from within the fluctuating boundaries of an incomplete, mutable, and partially absent self that creative energy may flow. Much as Palomar may struggle to assert his separateness from the physical items he is so eager to understand, it is tempting to detect, in his decoding and narrative procedures, traces of the chameleon personality theorized by John Keats (and echoed by Calvino in the closing lines of *Six Memos*). Indeed, how truly distinct is Palomar from the wave, the blackbird, the giraffe, the lawn, a pound of goose-fat?

While the individual character's identity dissolves in this plethora of involuntary identifications, the cosmic web of abstract concepts around which Palomar's cogitations tend to revolve are inserted in a relatively trivial grid of everyday actions. Even as the novel engages with grand narratives about space, time, consciousness, existence, responsibility and free will, to name but a few of Calvino's recurrent preoccupations, the protagonist's quotidian routine is assumed as the skeletal framework wherein, as Christina Benussi points out, "Palomar observes the microphysical constellation of desires and pulsions, rituals devoid of myths, and his own phenomenological drive toward disappearance" (Benussi 147). On the one hand, the postmodernist side of Palomar's temperament occasionally encourages him to abandon the quest for an extra-textual order and be contented with sojourning on the mobile threshold of fiction: what if sensory experiences could simply be narrated? What if they were merely stories, after all? On the other hand, his attempts to exorcize the deciphering mania almost invariably result in heightened analytical obsessiveness, as borne out by his desire to record any one experience not only in relation to his chosen viewpoint but also in relation to all the variables entailed by the potential adoption of countless other perspectives. Palomar is patently incapable of entertaining the possibility of "decentration" commended by Jean Piaget and other genetic psychologists as the ability to surmount the tendency to focus on a limited aspect of the phenomenon under scrutiny and strive instead to grasp configurations of related, if frequently conflicting and ubiquitous, factors (Piaget and Inhelder). Like Parsifal in *The Castle of Crossed Destinies*, Palomar is forced to realize that an incremental grasp of the void, of the construction of existence around absence, is eventually bound to reveal the Tao of one's own nothingness. According to Benussi, "the expansion of each instant of time and life" takes Palomar "to the inertia of death" (148).

However, if Palomar's death is interpretable as Calvino's final, tragic comment on the specious aspirations of analytical thought, it could also, less cynically, be read as a metaphor for the rejection of pathologically deductive modalities. Palomar's death may represent simultaneously a dirge dedicated to the demise of any masterful, yet ineluctably self-defeating, approach to knowledge, and a paean to the emergence of alternative powers: powers based, above all, on the supplanting of an assertive and vigilant gaze by a flickering and self-eliding glance, ironically sustained by unstable and endlessly renegotiable hypotheses. Faced with contrasting versions of scientific knowledge, Palomar cannot abandon what Edward de Bono terms "the jig-saw approach" (de Bono 38), namely, the methodology that prioritizes the minute detail, that aims at studying a system by isolating its tiniest components. Yet, argues de Bono, "a detailed examination of the components will not, by itself, be very helpful any more than a detailed examination of a building stone will give a picture of the architecture of Venice. The organization of the system is as important, or more important, than the actual components." In advocating the greater usefulness of system-based, rather than component-oriented, methodologies, de Bono is also aware that the "result" of working with broad structures "may be a myth, but then," he adds, closely mirroring Calvino's own position, "science consists of proceeding from one myth to a better one" (39). What Palomar does not adequately address is the interpenetration of science and myth foregrounded by the above citation. Indeed, analytical rigor and storytelling, for Calvino's hero, are utterly incompatible: a somber paradox, if we consider that Palomar's descriptive exercises are far less of the order of scientific exercises than they are of the order of imaginatively conjectural tales.

Even when Calvino does not construct an actual plot around his protagonist's objects of observation, his vignettes contain enough vivid details and inspiring clues to trigger the narrativizing drive in the reader. Furthermore, what Palomar does not seem to realize is that the products of his reflections are precisely myths, symbolic and inevitably biased translations of the world into belief-systems. The mythical character of Palomar's cerebrations is not, however, the only relativizing factor in his putatively scientific autopsies of sensory data. Another stumbling block in the way toward unequivocal knowledge is memory. Even though Palomar longs for a mnemonic model capable of absorbing incoming information and recording data without the inputs being in the least modified or tampered with by the receiving apparatus, his mind — like all human minds, presumably — works quite differently. The brain, however analytically disposed, cannot simply record the effects of a sensory excitation as a discrete occurrence, let alone locate it in an impregnable niche, thereby insulating it from previous and future events. In fact, when new data enter Palomar's mind, much as he may wish to anchor them to a definite spot, they instantly start flowing, or even racing, toward already existing data (mem-

Chapter 6—Science and Play 139

ories, fantasies, expectations), sculpting deeper and deeper furrows into the mental landscape. Philip K. Dick's writings indirectly offer a terse diagnosis of Palomar's affliction with reference to the image of the phenomenal world as the deceptive veil of Maya by arguing that new knowledge is unlikely to swipe the slate clean, for "were we to penetrate it ... this strange veil-like dream would reinstate itself retroactively, in terms of our perceptions and in terms of our memories" (Dick 207).

The human apparatus, *Mr. Palomar* suggests, cannot register any type of information accurately or objectively, since it will always, consciously or unconsciously, tend to modify that information on the basis of prior incidents and future projections, any empirical knowledge it may thereby glean very possibly consisting of increasingly intricate frameworks of accumulation and exchange. Able only to perceive what experience has taught him to perceive, to think only what he is programmed to think, Calvino's hero is locked into a pattern which appears to preclude the formulation of authentically new concepts. What Palomar desperately needs, in de Bono's evocative phrase, is a "de-patterning device" (de Bono 48). This is not to say that he is plainly unimaginative and solely capable of routinized thinking. His predicament is far more problematic than that: Palomar's imagination *is* tremendously fertile, yet he does not know, or will not acnowledge it. Hence, if the analytical trajectory of his reflections is impinged upon by unquantifiable fantasies or memories (as in the aforementioned segment "The cheese museum," for instance), and his functionally controlling structures are accordingly de-patterned by non-functional and dysfunctional associations, he does not feel released to the promise of creative reinvention of the perceptible but rather befuddled beyond the limits of sanity.

Why, the novel implicitly asks, is any endeavor to investigate the hidden attributes of existing forms always hauling us back to a recognition that they simply exist, that the exploration of putative presence cannot provide access to the origins of presence? Why can't absence be transferred into the realm of presence? Why are solutions reasonable only after they have been reached? And why are they reached so seldom and so belatedly? The analytical observer's world is the planet of the always-already, no less markedly than the Moon is the sphere of the never-never. He sees only the things he presupposes and is presupposed to see, is able to detect presence only in what an impersonal symbolic system has already sanctioned as existent, and is hence incapable of any alternative mode of being — madness and suicidal grief representing the only viable alternatives. Palomar's experience draws Calvino's misgivings about structuralist world views to a somewhat unsurpassable extreme. It would not be wholly apposite, however, to argue that via Palomar, Calvino is proposing to discredit rational processes of speculation and creation in their entirety. In fact, the writer may be advocating the necessity of the de-patterning move commended by de Bono as a "lateral" type of thinking, which is "*provocative* rather than descriptive or analytical" (52). Just as it would be fallacious to entertain the possibility of de-patterning methods of perception without first accepting that human brains function within a universe of patterns, so it would be misleading to assume that Calvino's interrogation of the concept of structure amounts to the annihilation of structure altogether. While it challenges rationalism through its zealous rehabilitation of the intrinsically non-verbal languages of the sensorium, *Mr. Palomar* simultaneously stresses the reliance of these very languages on complex systems of significations and sprawling webs of metaphors.

Throughout *Mr. Palomar*, Calvino approaches the functionings of the imagination as analogous to those of an apparatus designed to work out a large, possibly indefinite, number of plausibilities. Nevertheless, the writer is skeptical of scientific models of the mind harnessed to the purposes of analysis and, therefore, this kind of mechanized imagination comes to be embroiled with unpredictable ludic permutations. The creative mind chooses the images that are relevant to a contingent objective, or simply those that strike it as most thought-provoking, aesthetically appealing or funny. Hence, we are presented with unpredictable syntheses of an incalculable number of available images that insistently underscore the limitations of any logical dissection of the possible. This theme is further developed in the collection of fables, tales and dialogues *Numbers in the Dark*, originally published in 1992, where it is proposed that the power of analysis is conventionally expected to make life more manageable by breaking complex situations down to their minutest components and details. The hope sustained by a methodic itemization of the real is that although a complex state of affairs cannot be explored, let alone understood, as a whole, it may become intelligible once its individual parts have been singled out and separated from one another. Yet, Calvino's texts repeatedly stress that analysis may turn out to make reality only more complex and unyielding. This is no more obviously (and frustratingly) the case than when the human mind itself is assumed as the primary object of analysis. In trying to make sense of the mind's complexity, one may begin by dividing it into its constituent parts with the intention of investigating them one at a time. Alas, each part proves as complicated as the initial whole, because no single element can be properly grasped independently of its connections with countless others. However, the analytical method — such is its stubbornness — will not be automatically defeated by the recognition of inextricable connections: if its next and sole option is to accept that individual facets of the mind are always interrelated, it may still argue that the various pieces combine on the basis of a limited, albeit enormous, set of available rules, codes and conventions. We may not be in a position to detail the mind down to its individual segments, this approach would maintain, but we may still be able to fix the principles according to which its elements interact with one another.

To back up this idea, Calvino's metaphor of the chessboard can be brought into play: the billions of particles that make up the human mind could be compared to the thirty-two pieces on the chessboard, and the interactions among mental fragments to the moves available for the components of the game of chess. In both cases, things happen only as a result of certain pieces performing certain moves in accordance with given possibilities of combination. The difficulty highlighted by Calvino, at this juncture, is that even this neat map of the human mind as a chessboard does not exhaust all the options implicit in our mental lives. No individual subject is ever going to live long enough to experience all the possible moves and plays of which the mind is potentially capable — and believing that there are rules for those moves and plays offers inadequate consolation — any more than any one isolated brain could presume to provide an accurate report of a single second of cosmic transformation. This idea is pursued in the story "Nothing and Not Much" with humorously distressing lucidity: "to tell everything that happened in the first second of the history of the universe, I should have to put together an account so long that the whole subsequent duration of the universe with its millions of centuries past and future would not be enough" (Calvino 1996a, 266).

A more successful model could consist, Calvino recurringly suggests, of an analogy between the human mind and a computer system. Computers count on two fingers, after all, and can therefore digest complexity virtually instantly: how well-equipped is the mind to achieve comparably astonishing results? And, conversely, to what extent are computers furnished with a temperament likely to enable them to reproduce all mental faculties? These issues are addressed explicitly in "The Burning of the Abominable House," a short story written in response to the question, raised by IBM in 1973, of whether a narrative could be produced by using a computer. (As shown in Chapter 7, *If on a winter's night a traveler* develops a germane idea by locating mechanized productivity in the broader contexts of readerly and writerly creativeness, authorship, originality and plagiarism.) The tale's protagonist, a computer expert, sets out to orchestrate his murder plot by trying to establish the number of alternative ways in which his computer could process and combine a given set of data: characters, their personalities and proclivities, their possible reasons for committing the crime, the weapons which could have been employed. "Following this method," the narrator boasts, "allows me to rewrite my flow-chart: to establish a system of exclusions that will enable the computer to discard billions of incongruous combinations, to reduce the number of plausible concatenations, to approach a selection of the solution which will present itself as true." Although technology enables the writer to work out a large number of feasible combinations and permutations of physical, psychological and logistical factors, it is not ultimately capable of transforming the creative process into a purely mathematical exercise. Echoing Benjamin Woolley's assertion that "to ascribe the computer as a medium with powers to 'discover' the imaginary realm would be as absurd as ascribing the typewriter with the power to discover the world of literature" (Woolley 249), Calvino's author cannot help identifying with his four characters in spite of himself, imagining their faces, bodies and gestures, wondering about their hidden motives, and fantasizing about complex stage sets jammed with graphic images and physical detail: "Half I'm concentrating on constructing algebraic models where factors and functions are anonymous and interchangeable, thus dismissing the faces and gestures of those four phantoms from my thoughts; and half I am identifying with the characters, evoking the scenes in a mental film packed with fades and metamorphoses" (Calvino 1996a, 161).

Ultimately, argues Calvino in *Six Memos*, the analytical disposition offers not elucidations but dizzying complications, in a *reductio ad absurdum* of the deductive process: the liking for "geometrical" shapes, in particular, may rapidly degenerate into "a devouring and destructive obsession" conducive to a vertiginous attraction to "the detail of the detail of the detail" (Calvino 1996, 68–69). The schizoid attitude exemplified by the writer/narrator in "The Burning of the Abominable House" would seem to point to the final impossibility of equating the human mind to a computer, and vice versa. The mind is fundamentally incapable, in this context, of either recording incoming information with a degree of impassive non-interference that will leave the information unaltered or of processing it exclusively in terms of programmed instructions. In fact, any fresh data entering the brain tend to flow into already existing troughs, depressions and channels, deepening, lengthening or widening them, as the case may be.

At the same time as it aptly complements the analytical ordeal chronicled by *Mr. Palomar*, *Numbers in the Dark* also echoes the cosmicomic tales discussed in Chapter 3. The aforementioned "Nothing and Not Much," for example, offers a narrative of unfulfilled desire set in the unthinkable time zone which follows — according to the preface — the emergence of the universe from the void. This tale, published by the *Washington Post* in the last year of Calvino's life, encapsulates some of the writer's central insights into the relationship between presence and absence, the visible and the invisible, thereby illuminating one of this study's chief concerns. "Nothing and Not Much" argues that existence is not, essentially, an attribute of reality but rather an effect of virtuality, of speculative experiments with the sheer possibility of existence: "it's only if you begin to exist in the virtual sense ... that sooner or later you may find yourself existing in reality" (Calvino 1996a, 266). The primordial realization that existence may well amount to an accident engenders a longing almost to erase the memory of life's origin in a void without substance, dimensions, duration. This desire is triggered, fundamentally, by an acute feeling of "precariousness" (267) triggered by the subliminal apprehension that the nothingness from which the world has emanated is an ever-present phantasmatic reality to which it might feasibly return with the same staggering rapidity with which it materialized in the first place. If presence is the frail and forever premature offspring of absence, there is every reason to suspect that the translation of non-being into being may be reversed without notice, that existence may be proceeding blindly toward self-attenuation and, finally, self-erasure, drawn by an "abnegatory abulia" (268).

Calvino's poetics of absence is once again, as it was in the three novels comprised by *Our Ancestors*, inseparable from the vagaries of amorous discourse. Eager to impress Nugkta, Qfwfq starts off by exploiting to the maximum the joys of the recently formed universe, only to find that his enthusiastic responses to the bounty of creation leaves his beloved utterly cold. He then shifts to a more practical mode and decides to bank on "solidity" but only meets, one more time, her scornful indifference. It is at this point that the protagonist begins to understand that for Nugkta, the sole and undiluted attraction is total emptiness. It is at this same juncture that the narrative supplies what, had Calvino been a less protean or more dogmatic writer, could have been described as his manifesto. Indeed, via a much more somber voice than the one which characterizes Qfwfq in either *Cosmicomics* or *Time and the Hunter*, the writer suggests that absence holds a potential for "absoluteness" (269) that dwarfs the properties of completeness and fullness vaunted by presence into pale imitations of being.

Calvino does not propound the desirability of a utopian regression to an imaginary void of undifferentiation — assuming that such an option were even remotely tenable — but rather a courageous acceptance of the ephemerality and paltriness of what is present to us as *a* world or *the* world. The emergence of the present universe from absence does not make it a climactic realization of completeness. In fact, it operates as a constant reminder of the dependence of presence upon absence: the unrealized, the unrepresentable, the atopic for it is only in "the absences, the silences, the gaps" that the narrator can ultimately descry any weight. Despite the grave tone of Qfwfq's reflections in this late cosmicomic story, however, Calvino does not regard the present world's foibles as capable solely of generating unrelieved frustration. In fact, they may spark alternative affects and drives, including a generous and sympathetic disposition toward the world inspired by a frank recognition of its status as "a poor thing scratched together on the edge of nothingness" (271). Our imperfect world offers oblique glimmers of the void as the realm of all the potential manifestations of being of which the actual cosmos is only an infinitesimal fragment. We cannot envisage nothingness, the infinite and submerged hypertexts of absence per se. Yet, without some intimation, however oneiric or virtual, of absolute potentiality, we would not be able to ideate, fantasize or ultimately create anything at all. Hence, this pygmy world of ours, as a transitory simulation of presence everywhere riddled with blanks and fractures, comes into its own as a contingent illustration of what may be engendered from nothing as "the little that is and might very well not be, or be even smaller" (272) — in other words, as the *not much* without which the *nothing* would remain forever beyond our reach.

In the tale "Implosion," the descent into the recesses of non-meaning and non-being comes to constitute an ironical celebration of subjectivity as a "dark deletion" (262) of itself, a site marked by an erasure and hence only readable by virtue of its obliteration. The story echoes Jean Baudrillard's contention that "We can no longer imagine other universes.... Classic SF was one of expanding universes ... [today we witness] a period of implosion, after centuries of explosion and expansion. When a system reaches its limits, its own saturation point, a reversal begins to take place" (Baudrillard 310). Pitting himself against the champions of explosion as the ultimate emblem of energy, adventurousness, the conquering thrust, "passions, poetry and the ego" (Calvino 1996a, 262), the narrator opts for a fate of self-undoing: "the choice is made: I shall implode ... collapse inside the abyss of myself, towards my buried centre, infinitely" (261). Nowhere is Calvino's emphasis on the fullness of nothingness, the invisibility of presence, the overreaching compass of absence, more explicit than in "Implosion." Tracing the momentous trajectory of the dying star toward the final "collapse when everything, even light itself, falls inwards never to emerge again," the story praises implosion as the symbol of "a new freedom"—a state coinciding with the annihilation of time and space—and of the humbling solidity of the void: "'Black holes' is a derogatory nickname ... nothing could be fuller and heavier and denser and more compact" (262). Encapsulating a central idea expounded in this chapter and, hopefully, throughout this study as a whole, "Implosion" argues that it is only through a grasp of the inseparability of being and non-being that we may ultimately gain access "to a space-time where the implicit and the unexpressed don't lose their energy" and encounter "the presence of a body of enormous mass that nevertheless remains invisible" (263).

Chapter 7

The Universal Library:
If on a winter's night a traveler

In an interview featuring in the daily newspaper *La Repubblica* on the eve of the publication of *If on a winter's night a traveler*, Calvino describes the book as an "encyclopedia of the novel" (Calvino 1979, 11): namely, a catalogue of narrative possibilities and of as many attitudes to the world. In the course of the same interview, Calvino expresses his desire to write a book which would only consist of an *incipit*, and thus maintain throughout the openness and limitless potential inherent in the beginning. *If on a winter's night a traveler* (originally published in 1979) comprises the inaugural chapters of ten novels of diverse genres, styles and cultural origins, conceived from scratch by Calvino, yet uncannily redolent of real novels one seems to have read, chronicling the transition from each book to the next as experienced by the protagonist, a nameless "Reader." This narrative journey is necessitated by the fact that for one reason or another, the Reader is prevented from pursuing any one of the ten stories beyond its *incipit*. As his aggravation escalates with each frustrated attempt to simply enjoy a good read, the Reader's search for subsequent chapters of the ten aborted narratives grows progressively frantic and hopeless. Meanwhile, his quest becomes more and more intimately embroiled, in both intellectual and sexual terms, with the parallel quest undertaken by a female reader named Ludmilla (a.k.a. the "Other Reader").

Calvino's polyphonic text addresses with unmatched narrative energy the transformational qualities of the fictional text, of the reading experience and of the history of literature itself. The novel emphasizes that what we come to name reality is the product of intersubjective narratives and that the continuous process of converting the world into stories is often invisible. It in only by subscribing to an epistemology of progress that we may harbor the belief that we are going somewhere and that such a somewhere will be revealed to us. Calvino, in fact, challenges the myths of advancement and epiphanic visibility by stressing that not all stories — if any — have a satisfying end. Hence, the text offers a mobile encyclopedia of forever deferred combinations and permutations, mirroring Calvino's conviction, put forward in *Six Memos for the Next Millennium*, that not only books but also "Each life" amounts to "an encyclopedia, a library, an inventory of objects" (Calvino 1996, 124). If *Invisible Cities* dramatizes the notion of urban space as mutable, as a text made of labyrinthine routes through uncharted spaces, *If on a winter's night a traveler* articulates textual space as comparable to a boundless city capable of exceeding anything that might be imagined about it. The two novels, taken in tandem, thus elaborate the interpenetration of textual, textural and architectural functions. The metaphorical city mapped out in *If on a winter's night a traveler* evinces the elusive plan of a library where the books one needs most urgently are invariably missing or overdue, misplaced or uncatalogued. It is an emporium of unconsumable goods. A dominantly surreal atmosphere translates all empirical experiences into a web of disconnected, or only obscurely interrelated, clues. The novel's map, by analogy with the virtual geographies discussed in Chapter 4, hence displays a disconcerting juxtaposition of competing patterns and constellations, delivering a harlequinade of tumultuously clashing images and drives in a paradoxical harmony born of cacophony.

While Calvino's old passion for systematization is made evident, in *If on a winter's night a traveler*, by his attempt to produce an encyclopedia of stylistic and generic modalities, what gains the upper hand right from the start is an opposite pull toward digression, multiperspectivalism and incompleteness. The text reminds us, no less insistently than *Mr. Palomar*, that there are always elements which an ostensibly all-encompassing structure simply will not accommodate. These elements are as active, unstable and hence productive of meaning as the ones that can be reliably situated within the boundaries of the narrative construct. This seems to be the message conveyed by the narrator in the segment titled "Looks down in the gathering shadow." As he loses repeatedly the thread of his narration and wanders off into a maze of digressions, the character explains that what he wishes the reader to sense is that he is not simply telling the story that reaches the page but rather endeavoring to allude to a swirling plethora of other narratives gravitating around the main tale, or else sprouting out of its kernel in a process of potentially endless germination. The space envisioned by this narrator is so thoroughly saturated with conjectural narratives that each and every one of its countless points evinces the same exuberant proliferation of narratable materials. Any structure, however complex and apparently exhaustive, is always made relative by a plethora of rejected solutions, and any individual narrative is therefore implicitly defined by a vast tapestry of other possible stories.

Accordingly, the ten narrative situations presented in *If on a winter's night a traveler* are not distinct entries in a supposedly taxonomic treatment of the novel form but rather waves in a flux that continually fade into one another. The novel's world is one of incessant creation and incessant death. As the character known as the "seventh reader" observes, in traditional romantic fiction, these two facets of experience are kept conveniently separate to supply, in the end, a satisfactory closure: "the hero and the heroine married, or else they died. The ultimate meaning to which all stories refer has two faces: the continuity of life, the inevitability of death" (Calvino 1993, 253). In Calvino's Janus-like novel, however, the two faces coexist. The courtship plot that runs parallel to the reading plot does end with marriage; yet, the final words provide no compensatory rounding off of the fictional experience: "Just a moment—I've almost finished *If on a winter's night a traveler* by Italo Calvino" (254). Not only has the reader *almost* but not *quite* finished the novel (and given what has happened so far, there are reasons to suspect he may *never* finish it) but it is also patent that there can be no end to a novel about the endless pleasure of reading. The book thus highlights at the same time the continuity of life and the inevitability of death. The latter is imposed by the fact that all books have to end, somehow. The former is guaranteed by the possibility of going on indefinitely reading stories that have no final full stop, as the book's physical end does not unproblematically coincide with its conceptual or aesthetic closure. In fact, as stated in the essay "Literature as Projection of Desire," the "model" favoured by the writer is one of "permanent revolution" (Calvino 1987, 59).

Fundamentally, *If on a winter's night a traveler* calls the authority of the classificatory mentality drastically into question by proposing that even though its ten fictional scenes are presented as possible interconnected entries in an overarching encyclopedic structure, each of them actually consists of a mini-encyclopedia in its own right. This is because *If on a winter's night a traveler*—like virtually any text in Calvino's ethos—"is not a book, but a library" and is hence predicated on the assumption that "Literature is not composed simply of books but of libraries, systems in which the various epochs and traditions arrange their 'canonical' texts and their 'apocryphal' ones.... The ideal library that I would like to see is one that gravitates toward the outside, toward the 'apocryphal' books, in the etymological sense of the word: that is, 'hidden' books ... still to be rediscovered or invented" (60–61). This definition of the apocryphal text is endorsed, in the novel, by the character of Silas Flannery, an Irish author afflicted by writer's block and by his books' misappropriation by plagiarists and unscrupulous translators: "writing always means hiding something in such a way that it then is discovered" (Calvino 1993, 188). The interpenetration of concealment and revelation, absence and presence, foregrounded by Calvino's fictional author is one of the most salient features of *If on a winter's night a traveler* itself as a composite portrait not only of textuality but also of human relationships as intertextual patterns of combination and permutation — mobile tapestries in which singular experiences relentlessly spawn the strands of a fluid yarn. A single isolated occurrence of seemingly peripheral significance, such as the accidental meeting of two individuals, may bring forth an intricate tapestry of occurrences, situations and characters whence an unquantifiable range of narratives will inexorably emanate. In Calvino's universe, moreover, even the most marginal confluence is capable of opening up fantastical and dreamlike scenarios worthy of Lautréamont's famous description of surrealism as "the chance encounter, on a dissecting table, of a sewing-machine and an umbrella."

If on a winter's night a traveler, in exploding the encyclopedia's taxonomic thrust, concurrently mocks the pretensions of all sorts of organizing systems — e.g., inventories, catalogues, directories, databases, archives, museums, photo albums and collections. What these systems share is a desire to keep the world's baffling diversity at bay by reducing it to rigidly arranged selections of items intended to stand, metonymically, for the whole from which they have been extracted. *If on a winter's night a traveler* intimates that the passion for order evinced by systems of this kind could never be appeased by any human-made construct. In fact, the more human beings commit themselves to the cultivation of such apparatuses in order to assert their superiority over the environment and other species, the more they risk relinquishing their very humanity. Walter Benjamin pursues a cognate argument in *Reflections* by proposing that the collector paradigmatically incarnates the ordering itch as a fantasy of disengagement from practical concerns. Therefore, an activity that is presumed to enthrone and celebrate humankind's organizing flair ironically turns out to be a kind of escape into a vapid utopia: "The collector dreams that he is not only in a distant or past world but also, at the same time, in a better one in which, although men are as unprovided with what they need as in the everyday world, things are free of the drudgery of being useful" (Benjamin 1978, 55). In the essay "Unpacking My Library," Benjamin comments further on the collector's curious predicament by highlighting the speciousness of any notion of order afforded by the collecting mania: "for what else is this collection but a disorder to which habit has accommodated itself to such an extent that it can appear as order? ... any order is a balancing act of extreme precariousness." If "the order of the catalogue" constitutes "a counterpart to the confusion of the library," it is nevertheless the case that no functional system of classification may live up to the collector's decidedly anti-utilitarian, spellbinding relation to his or her possessions: "for a true collector the whole background of an item adds up to a magic encyclopedia" (Benjamin 1985, 60).

The ontological and teleological ambitions of the encyclopedic project stem from the attempt to give a center and a limit to the sprawling web of language, yet also reveal that any centered structure is ultimately narrative, rhetorical, and hence liable to constant displacement. Eugenio Donato argues, in this regard, that "the Encyclopedia-Library is a lay version of the medieval metaphor of the Book of Nature. Implicit in that metaphor is the assumption that the world can be completely textualized and, vice versa, that any element of the world can be treated as a textual element" (Donato 223) In deconstructing the encyclopedia's totalizing ambitions, Calvino concomitantly debilitates the pretensions of any structure designed to contain the act of reading — such as libraries and attendant forms of programmatic classification — as arbitrary, selective and fundamentally artificial. The emphasis placed by *If on a winter's night a traveler* at every turn on any one individual book's implicit connections with innumerable other books (read and unread, to-be-read or unreadable, written, writable, never-to-be-written) suggests that the strict categorization of books within systems amounts to a tyrannical limitation of the reader's imagination. As Alberto Manguel stresses, on this point, one of the reader's main responsibilities is precisely "to *rescue* the book from the category to which it has been condemned" (Manguel 199). The world of boundless shelves and inventories depicted by Calvino is also, however, an eerie and destabilizing realm of parallel lives, reminiscent of J. L. Borges' "Library of Babel." In this short story, the library is an unmappable universe of both actual and imaginary entities, including histories of the future, accounts of treatises that nobody ever wrote, autobiographies of archangels, and catalogues of catalogues generally amounting to mumbo-jumbo (Borges 1970). More surreal still is the intimation that this one particular library is only a fragment of an unthinkably large system of libraries and that an "almost infinite collection of books is periodically repeated throughout a bookish eternity" (Manguel 199).

Throughout *If on a winter's night a traveler*, the critique of all-encompassing systems is paralleled by an interrogation of the conventions of classic realism. The pursuit of meticulously detailed descriptive techniques, in particular, does not unproblematically communicate a comfortable impression of the fullness of reality. In fact, it betrays an urge to fill every conceivable gap so intense as to suggest that its trigger can only be a latent and troubled awareness of lack. Hence, any feeling of solidity harbors daunting reminders of the "vertigo of dissolution" (Calvino 1993, 35). Ludmilla's response to the *incipit* of the novel titled "Outside the town of Malbork" reinforces the feeling of lack inherent in exacting realism by suggesting that the celebration of presence does not exhaust reality. In fact, it stimulates a longing to approach the absence by which any text is inevitably traversed, whether or not it is willing to admit it. Relatedly, Ludmilla yearns for a kind of minimalist text in which objects are not incontrovertibly concrete and do not, therefore, communicate a palpable sense of presence but rather host an irreducible element of mystery and absence. The segment titled "On the carpet of leaves illuminated by the moon" similarly alerts us to the importance of those elements of absence and invisibility that always surround and somewhat define the present object of reading: some "essential" element inevitably lingers beyond the "written sentence" (198), since the amount of words which a text leaves out is always much larger than the amount of words it manages to accommodate within its compass.

Constructing an existence in which one is constantly surrounded by books, in the form of unsteady piles resembling the rocks of a weather-beaten landscape, of dusty and overpopulated shelves, of individually valued specimens, or of anonymous items scattered across nameless libraries, is a way of treasuring the entire ensemble of books one has read, wished to read, neglected to read. Yet, it is also a means of honoring the ghostly archive of voices, scents and textures which no one personal memory is capable of housing. It is, in a sense, irrelevant how many of those books are real, how many virtual, how many have been consumed in practice, how many in the imagination. Just as any real volume may end up gathering dust, forgotten and unperused, so any hypothetical tome may develop a peculiar substantiality in the mind of the reader who longs for its existence. In *If on a winter's night a traveler*, moreover, this desire extends from the mind to the body through the conception of any book as a pointedly corporeal entity.

Calvino is well aware, in emphasizing the material dimension of textuality, that books do not truly belong to anybody. The volume one may cherish as a personal possession is, after all, only a minute manifestation of a narrative bearing that title, and possibly that author's name, that is actually dispersed across innumerable sites. However, the copy one might own has an irreducible individuality: that of a body like no others. Trivial as this example may seem, the body of a book going through the hands of a reader inclined to break its spine, write into its margins, pig-ear its pages, is substantially different from the anatomy of a book—possibly telling the same story—whose reader would regard these habits as unpardonably violatory. The awareness of the corporeal aspects of textuality prompts a simple question: what *makes* reading? The first chapter of *If on a winter's night a traveler* offers a series of at least tentative answers. First of all, reading is inseparable from one's physical environment and one's relationships with others, for it requires the attainment of a fine balance between private and public dimensions, on the one hand, and of mind and body, on the other hand. Thus, while he is intent on finding a pocket of relative privacy amid constant noise and bustling activity, the Reader concurrently has to negotiate his relation to the book not merely in intellectual but also in physical terms. The writer urges him to adopt a convenient posture in order to ensure maximum comfort, yet reminds him that when it comes to the act of reading, this is almost certainly an impossible feat.

Second, reading provides the bodily substratum for a cerebral play with expectations, a means of fantasizing about potential outcomes, available even to the thoroughly disillusioned creature that no longer pursues any dreams of fulfillment and is simply content to dodge the worst-case scenario. A third facet of reading, connected with the one just mentioned, concerns its primarily virtual status. Indeed, if reading is a game of conjectures and guesses, this is fundamentally due to the fact that any contingently accomplished act—e.g., the purchase of a volume, the foreplay consisting of exploring its dust jacket, even the text's actual perusal—is always surrounded by a plethora of unrealized, and indeed unrealizable, events. Reading is steeped in a hypothetical universe of unfulfilled potentialities, which Calvino depicts in all its bodiliness as the dense "barricade" (5) of books one has not read—for any one of many possible reasons enumerated by the narrator with parodically inflated subdivisional gusto.

At the same time as it supplies an entertaining satire of the fantasy entertained by any ravenous reader, namely, the exhaustion of the readable, Calvino's portrayal of the incalculable array of unconsumed books that surround the chosen book on all sides as so many "embattled troops" (6) also exposes the act of selection as arbitrary and somewhat pathetic. Furthermore, the Reader, in operating his choice, does not assert his autonomy but rather becomes a passive, vulnerable spectacle. The purchased book is akin to the lucky hound rescued by his owner from the municipal pound, leaving behind hordes of less fortunate fellows capable of inducing a strong sense of guilt in the Reader with their morose side-glances. Ultimately, Chapter One emphasizes, reading is about communing with an object. What books tell us, in the act of reading, is experienced as tangible but not merely in the sense of our being able to participate in their — or their authors'—worlds by means of pathetic fallacy or sympathetic imagination. In fact, the perception of concreteness in a book's content is coextensive with the awareness of the materiality of the book-as-object, of themes and imagery being as physically embedded within the book's covers as its typographic characters are. Content is palpable because the book itself is. As Manguel points out, books do not solely "declare themselves through their titles, their authors, their places in a catalogue or on a bookshelf, the illustrations on their jackets" but also "through their size," their "cover" and their "shape" (Manguel 125). The narrator of *If on a winter's night a traveler* likewise reminds the Reader of the text's bodiliness as a feature of bookish existence inseparable from its status as a commodity, "an object fresh from the factory" (Calvino 1993, 6). No less crucially, *If on a winter's night a traveler* also suggests that the ability or willingness on a reader's part to retain memories of particular books and of their readings is inextricable from his or her physical dialogue with books as material entities. An especially intriguing dramatization of the idea of the book-as-object is supplied by the experimental art form devised by Irnerio, the Non-Reader. Asked what he could possibly *do* with a book, given his proverbial resistance to reading, Irnerio states: "It's not for reading. It's for making. I make things with books. I make objects. Yes, artworks: statues, pictures ... I give them forms, I carve them" (144). In a sense, Irnerio's sculptures literally materialize Calvino's ongoing emphasis on the text's transformability, intimating that the ultimate value of any book lies with its potential status as an objet trouvé.

Each of the ten incipits is an invitation to the reader to reflect on any individual book's penchant for metamorphosis and displacement: in framing the embryonic tales by reference to established stylistic and generic conventions and simultaneously reframing them to display their interconnections with other styles and genres, the writer hints both at the possibility of new structures coming into existence and at the possibility of existing structures being seen in a fresh perspective. Irnerio's manipulation of books as raw materials for artistic experimentation magnifies these dialectical operations. In his patently corporeal dislocations of textuality, the new should be understood not as something fundamentally different from the old but rather as something curiously out of focus in relation to what already exists. This out-of-focus condition blurs the boundaries of both the original book and of the artwork derived from it so that both parties turn out to be new and old at one and the same time. Irnerio's experience also points to the book's omnipresence, its ability to continually reinstate itself by means of a hermeneutic vampirism which turns everything into something about which a book could be written. Convinced that Irnerio's contribution to modern art is highly significant, critics are devoting entire volumes to his works which, of course, he uses to make other works. These, in turn, will soon be placed by critics in yet more books — "and so on" (145).

If on a winter's night a traveler thus outlines the following phenomena of unstoppable metamorphosis: (a) of one narrative into another narrative; (b) of the conceptual text into the physical book; (c) of the book into a three-dimensional structure amenable to reinscription by the written word and yet capable of transcending it, ad infinitum. In all these processes, meaning lies neither with the original entity nor with its offspring for both are equally dependent upon, and playfully violated by, the transformative act. Any meaning, therefore, may only be situated in the invisible fold produced by each form turning into and over an alternative form, in the dimensionless gap that articulates relentlessly the possibility of new relationships. The invisible fold ushers in an ironical idea of novelty where the new neither divorces itself from the old nor endeavors to parrot it slavishly. In fact, it surfaces as an in-between figure, ideally capable of generating new patterns of meaning. As argued earlier, although Calvino does not cite empirically existing books but actually invents ten potential ones, the reader may feel he or she has encountered these stories before. Any meaning derived from the ten *incipits*, therefore, rests neither with their originality nor with their relation to authoritative predecessors but rather with the third figure (so to speak) of a ridge where the new feels strangely recognizable and the old, by implication, is brought into play. Irnerio, by analogy, implies that the sheer "energy" (146) of the books he manipulates may only be expressed through their transformation into sculptures. The meaning of either a book or a sculpture is therefore not wholly self-generating and autonomous: the sculpture would not signify were it not for the book or books it is constructed from, while the book, for its part, may signify little, if anything, independently of its openness to creative processes of reconstitution and reframing. Again, meaning lies in the unseen site of the fold from which both the old and the new may be set off in fresh directions.

Irnerio's art stresses that the book is an object, or better a body, and that we cannot help, therefore, relating to it in terms of mass, shape, volume, size, amplitude, at times drawn by substantiality, at others by diminutive dimensions. The shapes and sizes of the books we commune with, moreover, remind us of our own bodiliness in the act of reading. It is worth recalling, in this regard, that the weight and largeness of the majority of tomes in the early phases of the modern history of reading often led to the invention of cunning contraptions designed to help the reader negotiate that elephantine bulk. As Manguel points out, "In order to be able to read a book comfortably, readers invented ingenious improvements on the lectern and the desk.... A fourteenth-century engraving shows a scholar in a book-lined library writing at an elevated, octagonal desk-cum-lectern that allows him to work on one side, then swivel the desk and read the books laid ready for him on the seven other sides." Another canny contrivance worthy of consideration is the eighteenth-century English device known as the "cockfighting chair" and designed purposely for library users: "The reader sat astride it," Manguel explains, "facing the desk at the back of the chair while leaning on the broad armrests for support and comfort" (Manguel 131). No less imaginative are Agostino Ramelli's sixteenth-century rotary reading desk and similar devices resembling a fairground wheel, hosting a different volume on each seat, as it were. What is most illuminating about these mechanisms, however extravagant they may appear to the contemporary reader who finds even the hardback somewhat unwieldy or might even prefer the electronic version of a book to the actual object, is the emphasis they place on the eminently physical character of the act of reading. Calvino offers his own alternative (and characteristically barmy) reflections on the possible development of a history of reading appliances, and speculates that our ancestors could have feasibly read "on horseback" with the aid of a device attached to the animal's head as the equivalent of a lectern (Calvino 1993, 3). Flamboyantly corroborating Manguel's proposition that the book's body clearly demands specific "postures of the reader's body that in turn require reading-places appropriate to those postures" (Manguel 151), Calvino's narrator surmises: "You can even stand on your hands, head down, in the yoga position. With the book upside down, naturally" (Calvino 1993, 3).

Furthermore, if reading is a bodily activity, writing is no less material. Indeed, writing is capable, in the logic of *If on a winter's night a traveler*, of reconstituting the physical body in its own image. The physical dimension of the writing process might indeed conjure up an image of the self consisting exclusively of "ink and periods and commas" (186). Additionally, Calvino's emphasis on the physical dimension of writing could be attributed to the author's desire to fantasize about the value of language as something more solid than an arbitrary symbolic system — an urge to pursue a reality that he knows not to be viable and yet, arguably for this very reason, remains deeply alluring. In this regard, Calvino's work captures the conundrum tersely described by M. W. Redfield: "The materiality of the letter consists in the necessary though impossible possibility that a sign may not be a sign" (Redfield 150). *If on a winter's night a traveler* articulates the notion of the textual body most powerfully by recourse to the image of the novel itself as a complex organic structure of gradually emerging patterns and interconnections among apparently discrete narrative blocks. As a corollary, the individual narrative attributes of each block are ultimately less significant than shared, intertextual factors. In addition, the text highlights manifold interconnections among different fictional realms by means of transworld migrations of characters and places. So, the characters in the *incipits* titled "Outside the town of Malbork" and "Leaning from the steep slope" share the same names, and Kauderer features again in "Without fear of wind or vertigo"; Jan's widow in "Outside the town of Malbork" brings back to mind the Jan murdered in "If on a winter's night a traveler"; the Nouvelle Titania of "Looks down in the gathering shadow" appears as New Titania in "Without fear of wind or vertigo"; the character of Amaranta, prominent in "Around an empty grave," features again in "What story down there awaits its end?," this time merely as a name on a page torn from a book. This last example is particularly enlightening as it draws attention to the status of the characters in the novel as a whole as purely verbal fabrications, combinable and recombinable just as typographic characters are.

The novel's polysemic structure, while capitalizing on difference and variety, concurrently relies on basic principles of recurrence. The triangulation of erotic relationships is one of the elementary frameworks to which the ten *incipits* insistently return. These can be schematically rendered as follows:

"If on a winter's night a traveler":
traveler/Madame Marne/her husband
"Outside the town of Malbork":
Gritzvi/Ponko/Zwida-Brigd
"Leaning from the steep slope":
narrator/Miss Zwida/inmate
"Without fear of wind or vertigo":
narrator/Irina/Valerian
"Looks down in the gathering shadow":
Ruedi/Jojo/Bernadette
"In a network of lines that enlace":
narrator/Marjorie/mysterious telephone caller
"In a network of lines that intersect":
narrator/Lorna/Efidia
"On the carpet of leaves illuminated by the moon":
narrator/Mr. Okeda/Madame Miyagi-Makiko
"Around an empty grave":
Nacho/Faustino/Amaranta
"What story down there awaits its end?":
narrator/Franziska/Section D men

The framing narrative does not fail to supply its own sexual triangles, as the Reader/Other Reader relationship is repeatedly challenged by the emergence of third parties: most notably, Irnerio, Flannery and Ermes Marana.

Another recurrent idea deployed throughout *If on a winter's night a traveler* is the tension between the dread of dissolution, typified by the vertiginous perspectives opened up by kaleidoscopes, labyrinths, Chinese boxes and halls of mirrors, and an ecstatic celebration of flux as the only way of participating in intersubjective structures of signification. The protagonist of "In a network of lines that intersect," for instance, comes to the conclusion that any semblance of order one may glean from a chaotic universe is inevitably a fleeting constellation, and draws pleasure from this realization. Whenever he looks into a kaleidoscope, he avers, he feels that at the same time as the "heterogeneous fragments of colors and lines assemble to compose regular figures," his brain instinctively senses the "procedure to be followed: even if it is only the peremptory and ephemeral revelation of a rigorous construction that comes to pieces at the slightest tap of a fingernail" (Calvino 1993, 157). Kaleidoscomania affords a sense of liberation from the imperative of order which may amount to a form of indirect control. Indeed, Calvino's character relies on his complex optical devices to keep an incalculable number of enemies and conspiracies at bay. It also, however, points to a dangerous disassociation from the world: the same character eventually becomes trapped in the halls of mirrors he has so carefully contrived. According to Erkki Huhtamo, the kaleidoscomaniac may become so mesmerized by what he or she sees inside the tube as to lose any sense of reality: a phenomenon, he argues, currently revived by "immersive, peep-show like experiences in the form of the virtual reality craze" (Huhtamo 300). The kaleidoscopic text as articulated by Calvino in *If on a winter's night a traveler* reminds us that order and disorder are inextricable. Concomitantly, Calvino emphasizes that the body of the book, like the ever-changing patterns yielded by the kaleidoscope, is ultimately a galaxy of mutable signifiers that bear witness to the genesis not of univocal meanings but of unpredictable textual permutations.

One of Calvino's most pivotal concerns throughout the text consists of the articulation of a symbolic connection between reading and sexual desire. On one level, it is the eminently private character of the reading experience that makes it akin to the erotic one. It seems worth recalling, however, that the association of reading with privacy, silence, even secrecy, is a relatively modern phenomenon. As Manguel notes, "reading out loud was the norm from the beginnings of the written word" and there is little doubt that in the ancient libraries, scholars "must have worked in the midst of a rumbling din" (Manguel 43). Silent reading was mistrusted, in the conviction that it "allowed for day-dreaming, for the danger of accidie" and, no less problematically, that "a book that can be read privately ... is no longer subject to immediate clarification or guidance, condemnation or censorship" (51). Indeed, public reading "gives the versatile text a respectable identity, a sense of unity in time and an existence in space that it seldom has in the capricious hands of a solitary reader" (123). The negative connotations carried by silent reading as something latently illicit can surreptitiously creep even into religious iconography, as indicated by Antonello da Messina's famous *Saint Jerome in His Study*. As noted in Phaidon's acclaimed *Art Book*, this painting invites the viewer to assume a pointedly voyeuristic position: "Stealing a look through the open window of St Jerome's study, the viewer sees the saint absorbed in reading. Only the lion on the right pauses in his tracks to acknowledge the outside world" (Butler, Van Cleave and Stirling 15). *If on a winter's night a traveler* validates the idea that silent, private reading unleashes highly subjective and capricious impressions, while facilitating an especially intimate partnership between the reader and the book saturated with emotive undertones. The notion of intimacy is endowed with overtly sexual undertones by the fact that private reading often takes place in bed. The properties of privacy and invisibility to the outside world held by reading in bed are symbolically linked to the idea that anything happening within the nocturnal cocoon belongs to the domain of deeply intimate, even forbidden pleasures.

For the Reader and the Other Reader, bed and book alike are a means of establishing a dialogue, of digging channels of mutual exploration. They read each other via the novels they both cherish, and via the senses, in the "unrecognizable tangle" formed by their bodies beneath the "rumpled sheet" (Calvino 1993, 149). Yet, any understanding or satisfaction thus achieved are inevitably riddled with doubts. The Reader cannot help wondering whether Ludmilla is in fact reading him as he truly is or rather as an assortment of "fragments" extrapolated from his body and then translated into a phantasmic companion "known to her alone," an "apocryphal visitor" (151). By analogy, there is no reliable way of ascertaining whether the readers/lovers actually share comparable sensations and thoughts in their respective readings of fiction, or whether they inhabit parallel universes, destined to coexist but never to coalesce. As Peter Washington observes in his introduction to the Everyman's edition of *If on a winter's night a traveler*, in the context of the relationship portrayed by Calvino, the book is "both a refuge and a barrier, a symbol of communication and a sign of our absolute solitude" (Calvino 1993, xxiv). Calvino's ironical voice taunts the Reader by inquiring whether he would like to enter the Other Reader's "shell" (143) by worming his way into the volumes with which she quotidianly interacts, in full knowledge that such a move is quite unaccomplishable. In the novel, both the reading of the book and the reading of the body yield a narrative of cracked plenitude, a story that "skips, repeats itself, goes backward, insists, ramifies in simultaneous and divergent messages" (151). Books and bodies enable intersubjective communication by offering not comforting presences but rather the disconcerting voice of a "silent nobody made of ink and typographical spacing" (143) which anyone can appropriate because, ultimately, it is nobody's unequivocal possession.

According to Jürgen Habermas, the novel's sustained analogies between reading and eroticism are confirmed by the fact that it is precisely when Calvino takes "the anonymity of the fabricated reader away from him" by placing him "under Ludmilla's influence" that "the dynamics of the action ... fills in the empty place of the singular 'you' more and more with flesh and blood" (Habermas 221). Sexual desire and the promise of amorous union are thus posited as a means of buttressing an otherwise flimsy identity and, by extension, of furnishing the individual with protective or defensive mechanisms. This is borne out by the scene in which the hoary scholar Uzzi-Tuzii claims that any book is above all a gateway to a dusky otherworld of silence and death, and the Reader and Ludmilla respond by erecting a bodily barrier against these bleak premonitions of dissolution. Seeking refuge in a recluse nook of the room, the two characters hug each other tightly, as though struggling to counteract the dead language of books with their own living language — unfixable and unrecordable by words as it is. An important difference, however, distinguishes the Reader's reactions from Ludmilla's. The Reader is inclined to resist Uzzi-Tuzii's dark omens by recourse to a literal coalition of bodies, which implicitly rests on a separation between sexuality and textuality: in his case, the spectral book envisaged by the old professor is a threat to be counteracted through amorous solidarity.

The Other Reader, for her part, is reluctant to differentiate between reading and eros, and therefore trusts the regenerative power of reading — even the reading of the abysmal beyond — as a form of physical *jouissance* in its own right. The Reader needs to cling to what physically exists, though aware that much of what he deems existent is merely a product of his imagination, whereas the Other Reader emphasizes that the non-existent is the repository of all creativity. While she agrees with Uzzi-Tuzii about the idea of reading being a confrontation with absence, Ludmilla is averse to see this state simply as a forlorn, wordless and lifeless realm, and keen instead on stressing the imaginative potentialities of absence, of what is "not present because it does not yet exist" (Calvino 1993, 70) — and, by implication, could or might come into being. The segment headed "Without fear of wind or vertigo" supplies an analogous image of erotic attachment as a defence against the void — a reality its narrator posits as ubiquitous — and concurrently portrays it as an act of submission to its engulfing power. In embracing Irina to alleviate a dizzy spell, the narrator experiences simultaneously the reassuring prospect of erotic union and a contagious transmission of vertigo: "in a distress that lasts an instant, I seem to be feeling what she feels." Metafictionally, the story, too, is infected by the spreading of vertigo in the guise of a haunting realization that "beneath every word there is nothingness" (80).

Calvino's equation of the act of reading to a sexual encounter is explicitly made evident by his tendency to poke fun at the type of reader who subordinates the pleasure of the text to the dire convolutions of textual analysis. Addressing the Reader after the latter's first exposure to an incomplete novel, the narrator sarcastically pretends to be acknowledging his critical skills by admiring his ability to identify recurrent motifs and effortlessly grasp all nuances of even the obscurest authorial intent. The Reader's bathetic humiliation comes with the realization that what he might have thought of as a "stylistic subtlety ... is simply a printer's mistake" (24). The ability to lose oneself in the text, which in itself is an intensely erotic experience, is radically contrasted with the act of possessing or raping the narrative. Significantly, in this respect, the frustration of a further attempt to read a novel (this time occasioned by the Shandean appearance of two blank sheets) occurs concomitantly with the sensuous experience derived from the use of a paper knife — an activity requiring a knack of "penetrating among the pages from below" and "opening a vertical cut in a flowing succession of slashes" (40). The reader's disappointment, in this case, may stem from the sexually proprietorial quality of his relationship with the book, evinced by the phallocentric register employed in the passage. In this matter, Calvino subscribes to Roland Barthes' idea that "the pleasure of the text is not the pleasure of the corporeal striptease of the narrative," which would amount to an "Oedipal pleasure" proceeding from the equation of the text to an "absent, hidden or hypostatised father" (Barthes 1990a, 10). The text's sexual appeal, like the labyrinth's challenge, cannot be met by a show of brute force: in fact, it calls for considerable subtlety. The act of consummation must be arrived at gradually if it is to be fully enjoyed: hence, the "circling" of a volume and the act of "reading around" it (Calvino 1993, 8) prior to engaging in its actual perusal are vital components of the acquisition of a fresh book.

The comparison between sexuality and textuality implies that in the sexual act, the body is made into an object of methodical decoding based on the whole network of sensory communication. Like the act of reading — and writing, for that matter — lovemaking revolves on the ability to combine and recombine a given number of multifaceted components. Many of these are neither "visible" nor "present" and yet are inscribed in "visible and present" situations (150), just as many of the fragments that go into the making of a book are meaningless in themselves but acquire value through their relation to other fragments with which they are combined. As hinted at earlier, it is always possible to isolate and abstract (fetishistically or otherwise) fragments of one's partner's identity to construct a phantasmatic companion, just as the reading of a book pivots on the subjective narrativization, or fulfillment, of purely virtual narrative states. What both reading and lovemaking most intimately share is an ability to foster the illusion that a direction may be recognized in their unfolding, and at the same time reveal that no climax guarantees either closure or resolution, since the putative moment of fruition is inexorably antagonized by an opposite force working squarely against it.

In presenting writing as a function of the reader's creative contribution to the text through the actualization of an otherwise purely potential narrative, Calvino prompts us to ponder what specific kinds of reading are deemed capable of generating a text. His characters, in this regard, exemplify two contrasting attitudes to reading. On the one hand, they follow breathlessly events and plot intrigues at such a staggering rate that the story is inexorably hurtled beyond any reasonable closure. On the other hand, they carefully scrutinize the text in order to unravel its meanings with such methodical precision and so deliberate a pace as to make the book's last page feel endlessly postponed, unattainable. In both cases, the idea of a definite ending is radically questioned. While the Reader and the Other Reader accelerate down the fast lane, racing toward full consumption of the novels which have afforded them only an antipastory nibble, several of the characters they encounter in the ten *incipits* painstakingly linger on minutiae, as though both time and space were somewhat irrelevant to them. For the narrator of "Leaning from the steep slope," every infinitesimal aspect of his environment appears to be "charged with meaning" (52). Trapped in a circuit of solipsistic decoding wherein he is hellbent on extracting from the interstices of language any clues to what fate might hold for him and him alone, the character has no inkling of what is really going on in the surrounding universe, as though he were the unchallenged character of a one-part play. Thus, when Miss Zwida asks him to buy her a "grapnel" and "twelve meters" of rope, on the pretext that she wishes to draw these objects, he cannot grasp any connection between this strange request and the lady's association with the local prison (and one of its inmates), and entertains instead a neurotically convoluted series of interpretations of the grapnel's figurative relevance to his personal lot as symbolic of an "exhortation to attach" himself, as well as a cautionary reminder of the prospects of "laceration and suffering" (60) inevitably attendant on such an act. The central character in "On the carpet of leaves illuminated by the moon," for his part, evinces a Palomaresque addiction to infinitesimal details, sustained by the desire to dissect every portion of the real into its atomic components. This is characteristically evinced by his mind-boggling analysis of the motion of each leaf falling from a ginkgo tree within the gentle shower of myriad leaves dancing through the air before landing of the lawn below.

The novel as a whole, however, repeatedly frustrates this decoding obsessiveness, this pathological passion for the isolated detail based on the assumption that the world exists for the sole benefit of the self-centered observer. In fact, it creates a narrative tapestry wherein the apparent presence of individual elements is repeatedly obfuscated by their embedding in a cloudy continuum of absent traces. As a trope, absence also impacts on Calvino's ideal author as a depersonalized and self-effacing "graphic energy" (167). This idea is amplified by the suggestion that books may be both written and read by means of suitably programmed computers. Calvino's interrogation of authorship is most overtly conveyed by his treatment of the authorial persona as a spectral entity — a strategy sustained, as Kathryn Hume suggests, by the play with "variations of ghosts throughout his novel" (Hume 125). As already mentioned, the Reader broods over the possibility that Ludmilla may have created a phantasmic partner by extrapolating fragments of his own body from their context. He also speculates about the ghostly nature of Uzzi-Tuzii's identity, conveyed by his becoming increasingly so ethereal as to vanish altogether into the cracks "greedy for dust" (Calvino 1993, 68). At the same time, the Reader subliminally resents the person to whom the Other Reader is invisibly bound by her books, whom he ideates as a voiceless phantom. Marana, too, envies the silent creature supposedly able to communicate with Ludmilla via books as a "ghost with a thousand faces and faceless" (154). Flannery, in turn, contemplates every day the woman reader on the terrace across the valley, increasingly enthralled by the invisible workings of her brain until he is turned into one of her inner "ghosts" (165). For this author, the process of writing in its entirety is predicated on an intangible dialogue with legion phantasms insofar as any book should, he believes, be about "what does not exist and cannot exist except when written" and convey its "absence" through existing forms by obliquely drawing attention to the latter's own inherent "incompleteness" (167).

Calvino's radical debunking of individual genius is most starkly epitomized by the character of Marana, the paradigmatic ghost writer. His forgeries and mystifying recreations of authors, characters and plots redesign the very concept of literary history. Habermas views Marana's operations as emblematic forms of deconstruction at work: "Marana/Derrida systematically produces uncertainties about the identity of works, authors, and generative contexts. ... there are no originals, only their traces, no texts, only readings, no fictional world *in contrast to* reality" (Habermas 219). It should be noted, however, that Marana is not a genuine deconstructionist. He dreams of a literary universe consisting exclusively of apocryphal, counterfeited and plagiarized texts, which could be plausibly regarded as a radical assault on logocentrism and the metaphysics of presence. However, it is also clear that although his actions patently underscore the irrelevance of any concept of origin, they are nevertheless teleologically driven to the extent that he is spurred on all along by a personal feud centered on his obsession with Ludmilla. Moreover, his desire to infiltrate the traces of nothingness in her private intercourse with books, itself a potentially deconstructive move, turns out to be a means of asserting not simply the absence of the author as a guarantee of meaning but also, more crucially, his own eccentric presence.

It is not so much in its characterization of the arch-mystifier as in its treatment of the idea and the practice of translation with which Marana is associated that *If on a winter's night a traveler* strikes deconstructive chords. Translation, arguably, is the area to which Calvino's novel attributes the most riotous penchant for permutation. Indeed, it takes to unparalleled limits the idea, advocated by Benjamin in the essay "The Task of the Translator," that translation should aim at reproducing not merely "information" but also, more importantly, "the unfathomable, the mysterious, the poetic'" and that, concomitantly, this goal may be achieved only if the translator "is also a poet" (Benjamin 1985, 70). The acts of systematic displacement and dismemberment to which Marana subjects the texts he is putatively translating present translation as a quite literal metamorphosis, requiring imaginative interventions on the translator's part. Spatial dislocations of textual material are accompanied by equally radical recombinations of the identities of authors and characters. Marana's theory of translation is obviously unsympathetic to the practice of compiling lexical taxonomies to be deftly handled by the competent professional. This method may suit the encyclopedically oriented translator but is clearly at odds with Calvino's anti-taxonomic ethos. For the translator of Marana's ilk, texts are regarded as "spare parts" (Calvino 1993, 112). When it is all a matter of constructing and reconstructing the machine of language, writing becomes a predominantly automatic act and the writing agent accordingly turns into something of a combinatorial apparatus. In translating a text, we are confronted with a magnified image of what happens whenever we read any text at all: namely, the conversion of a constellation of signs into another. As the epitome of unrelentingly mutating textual productivity, translation incarnates the quintessence of the act of creative reading itself as a process through which meaning "is gleaned but never made explicit, because in the particular alchemy of this kind of reading the meaning is immediately transformed into another equivalent text" (Manguel 266).

Calvino's polyphonic novel advocates that no text, however infallible its messages may be deemed, can escape the destiny of incremental transposition from words into other words into yet more words. This state of affairs is pushed to surreal limits in the following practice: new books can be produced by extracting the formula of a popular writer's fiction, by deploying it in texts written in a language other than that writer's and advertised as translations of his work, and by subsequently translating these texts into the cannibalized author's own language. The outcome of this demonic ruse is that the pseudo-translations become critically indiscernible from authentic products penned by the actual writer. It is inane to assume that the reader of any text — translated or otherwise — could mentally reconstruct a text as originally intended by its author: the reader's own actualization of the text simply displaces, though provisionally and inconclusively, the author's creation. Translation magnifies the implications of this process of incessant dislocation by problematizing the status of the so-called original text at the basis of the translated item. For one thing, the presumed superiority of the original is shrouded in ambiguity. If the original were indeed unassailable, then it would not be translatable. Of course, nothing is translatable, if by translation we mean the word-by-word transcription of one language into another, but the fact remains that people go on translating books, making money out of this activity, and enabling others to enjoy stories which would not otherwise be available to them — in whatever form.

Those who praise a translation according to the measure of its fidelity to an original seek to affirm that original's superiority by presenting it as the repository of absolute values that should not in any way be tampered with. Yet, they also hint, albeit elliptically, to the original's vulnerability to distortion and abuse. It could even be argued that the champions of fidelity labor under the illusion that a correct translation may divest the original text of its inherent fragility, that it may fix the text once and for all, thereby implicitly admitting to the original's dependence on its displaced counterparts. The original's chances of survival, moreover, would be slim, were it not for its translation's ability to mark its "stage of continued life" (Benjamin 1985, 71). The phenomenon of translation as dramatized in Calvino's novel jeopardizes not only the original's putative distinctiveness but also, no less significantly, the notion that different languages are mutually exclusive representations of specific national and ideological territories by exposing the permeability of all languages and the eminently material effects of one language on any other. Translators, in the logic of *If on a winter's night a traveler*, can never take their languages for granted, for those languages are continually and powerfully affected by other languages, and indeed enhanced and deepened by their intercourse with foreign idioms. What might have seemed literal in the original is rendered explicitly rhetorical in the translated text, as the relationship between the sign and its referent is drastically denaturalized: "While content and language form a certain unity in the original, like a fruit and its skin," Benjamin picturesquely maintains, "the language of the translation envelops its content like a royal robe with ample folds." The systems of reference of both the object language and the target language are accordingly undermined: "translation is ... a somewhat provisional way of coming to terms with the foreignness of languages" (75).

In asking the reader to meditate on aspects of the fiction-making process which we are normally encouraged to take for granted, the first *incipit*—"If on a winter's night a traveler"—emphasizes that the reader is simultaneously reading a story and reading about the act of reading a story. The narrator, by analogy, is both telling a story and telling us about writing. The narrative's metafictional character is stressed from the start through the establishment of a series of correspondences between the physical features of the tale's environment, the material attributes of writing and the corporeal shape of the text. The night's darkness is coterminous with the blackness of ink, for example, and the impenetrability of the situation described is akin to the physical density of the printer's lead. The opening paragraph does not simply convey the atmosphere of the ensuing action: it also engineers an audacious conflation of narrative and narration, whereby smoke and steam dim not only the old railway station in which the story commences but also the leaves of the tome itself. Similar devices are employed in the *incipit* headed "Outside the town of Malbork," where the Reader's entrance into the physical space of the story is enveloped in an effluvium of "frying" in order to emphasize that in this book, every sentence is supposed to feel solid, tangible (Calvino 1993, 33). The segment "Without fear of wind or vertigo" likewise underlines the inseparability of the page-world from the world evoked by the narrative as "military vehicles cross the square and the page" at once and the ensuing sentences teem with "names of generals and deputies" (82).

The first *incipit* also reinforces the interpenetration of story and storytelling, reading and decoding, by alerting us to the fact that what we are perusing is a cluster of signs slowly converging to form a specific picture of a particular time and place. The inseparability of the interpretative process from the reader's diachronic progression through the text's linear body is consistently sustained. Near the end of the second page of "If on a winter's night a traveler," for instance, readers are reminded that they have thus far perused approximately two pages, and that while by now the situation should have become clearer, the strings of words still unfold tentatively and vaguely. The narrator warns that this is probably a crafty ruse intended to draw readers slowly and almost surreptitiously into the yarn. This cautionary remark, as other similar guidelines proffered by the narrator throughout the first *incipit*, may suggest that Calvino is deliberately overcoding his text on the assumption that the type of reader he is dealing with is pitiably subcritical. It can hardly be denied that this patronizing narrator is quite simply telling the reader what and how to read. It would be preposterous, however, automatically to infer from this that Calvino himself has no faith in the reader's creative faculties and that he has entrusted a narrator of his own making with the responsibility for steering the reader's responses. In fact, Calvino's narrative procedures could be regarded as an obliquely ironical — at times even sardonic — way of pouring scorn on the conventional image of the omniscient author rather than a way of reinstating authorial centrality by orchestrating the fiction on the basis of an expert's lesson in deciphering.

First, it is quite obvious that the narrator is not the author of the story, as the former repeatedly draws attention to his separateness from the latter. Second, there is no way of demonstrating that the author in question may be unproblematically named Calvino. If Calvino is, presumably, the name on the cover of a book titled *If on a winter' night a traveler*, it remains debatable, at the level of the novel's plot, whether the first *incipit* could be justifiably attributed to a fictional author of that name simply because it shares its title with the book as a whole. Indeed, the Reader and Ludmilla are led to believe, at one point, that the author of the first unfinished novel is some Tazio Bazakbal — until they are disabused of this belief and drawn into the imaginary textual universe initially of Cimmerian and subsequently of Cimbrian letters. Third, the narrator is far from all-knowing, let alone all-powerful. He is explicitly posited as a textual function no more solid than a "stark pronoun" (14), a mere grammatical shifter: a person named "I" (11) about whom the reader does not know anything else. Moreover, the narrator's impotence, uncertainty and frustration are repeatedly emphasized: the victim of misleading clues, he is an "outsider" condemned to gaze enviously upon "the life of an ordinary evening in an ordinary little city" (16). His alienated status brings to mind the germane condition endured by the eternal traveler depicted in *Invisible Cities*, particularly in conjunction with the city of Diomira. In spite of his attempts to direct readers and monitor their responses, the narrator is no more than a puppet in the hands of an invisible, utterly indifferent author. Unable to fathom the latter's intentions, he can only interpret his circumstances by educing random leads from the very text in which he is embedded and from the dense layers of words through which he hopes to move, unheeded by strangers and by possible foes. A basic affinity between the narrator and the reader is thereby alluded to insofar as both parties fumble in a twilight zone of nebulous options.

The narrator reinforces this metaphorical resemblance by seeking something of an accomplice in the reader and by pointing out that his lack of control over the story's unfolding is a fate shared by the reader as they plough together through the textual outcome of authorial intentions they cannot presume to fathom. Yet, the relative powerlessness of narrator and reader alike does not guarantee the absent author's omniscience since the author's own grip on the narrative is patently slight. He cannot contemplate the story from a transcendental viewpoint of detached mastery, due to the lure of self-identification with the narrator. Thus, while the reader is drawn to the figure of the narrator as an agency worth identifying with simply because of its designation as "I," the author adopts the narrator's "I" as a textual space into which he might legitimately insert a shard of his own being while retaining a modicum of privacy and detachment. Reader and author are thus ironically drawn together onto a common plane of relational subjectivity. Furthermore, the reason for the general mistiness of information that characterizes the first *incipit*, the narrator opines, may well be that the author has not yet established what kind of story the reader fancies or expects. It would be arduous to argue, in this context, that Calvino is promulgating an author-centered configuration of textuality insofar as his author cannot unproblematically flaunt any autonomous powers of his own.

It should be noted, at this juncture, that there is no consensus among critics over the issue of Calvino's treatment of narrative authority. JoAnn

Cannon, for example, maintains that Calvino struggles to dominate the reader, albeit indirectly, and eventually fails to do so: "The author's attempt to inscribe the activity of reading into his text ultimately reveals his desire to domesticate the dialogue between text and reader which is beyond the writer's control. But this strategy is unsuccessful: rather than bringing the text back within the author's sphere, it merely underlines the degree to which the text cannot be controlled or closed by the author. For if Calvino can inscribe a reader-protagonist into his writing, he cannot control the empirical reader and the potential meanings created in that reader's dialogue with the text" (Cannon 108–109). Even though the writer might be striving to frame the decoding activity in accordance with a preestablished template, he is ultimately incapable of arresting the play of interpretation. As we move through the text from one *incipit* to the next, from one book-hunting adventure involving the Reader and the Other Reader to the next, this failure on the author's part feels more and more deliberate — that is to say, a means of exploding the myth of authorial control *from within* the text itself.

Habermas, for his part, argues that Calvino ends up controlling the reader, possibly against his intentions. Nevertheless, he also acknowledges the open-endedness of the reading operation and, by implication, the precariousness of any author's power. It would seem that for Habermas, Calvino is simultaneously determined to retain control over the world of reading — in spite of having accorded the reader and the book leading roles — and eager to eclipse the perimeters of the author's and the reader's territories: "Calvino *tells* a story whose scenes are literally played out in the world of the book," the German philosopher maintains. "But in the end he still remains the only director of this world and gazes down from above upon his male reader and his female reader." Habermas then quotes a few key lines from the book's finale and hazards the following tentative interpretation of their import: "'Now you are man and wife, Reader and Reader. A great double bed receives your parallel readings.' Ludmilla closes her book and asks ... 'Turn off your light, too. Aren't you tired of reading?' A last, vain attempt to *blur* the transition from one world into the other?" (Habermas 222–223). Habermas presumably describes the attempt as vain because he takes the novel's ending to foreground neither the interpenetration nor the interchangeability of the world of books and the everyday world but rather their incompatibility. Indeed, he argues that Ludmilla's final words indicate that she "is let go into everyday life" and that the "contact with the extraordinary remains limited to an interim" (223).

Yet, it could be argued that the novel's closing words do confuse the boundary between the fictional and the quotidian realms by underscoring their shared destiny, by reminding us that both reading and living are rooted in the contemplation of closure as a forever receding mirage. As anticipated earlier in this discussion, it is by spotlighting the fact that the Reader has almost, not yet, finished the novel he is reading, that Calvino's text most potently reminds us that the book's physical end simply cannot be made to coincide with either its conceptual or its aesthetic closure. To this extent, it throws into relief the infiltration of any realized act by unperformed and indeed unmanageable acts. As Stéphane Mallarmé observes in a letter to Paul Verlaine of 1869, we may only prove that a book "does exist" through "finished portions" which indirectly bear witness to what one "wasn't able to accomplish" (cited in Manguel, 307).

Metaphorically speaking, the world depicted by *If on a winter's night a traveler* is one in which crowds of people congregate quotidianly around a hypothetical venue held to house the ultimate book — something like a Book's Temple, so to speak — as though in anticipation of an epiphany, only to find that what lies ahead of them is not an icon of godly plenitude but rather a peculiarly dismembered body. By the time works enter the public domain, argues the character of Arkadian Porphyrich, Director General of the State Police Archives of the fictional state of Ircania, they have been subjected to the sanitizing manipulations of so many eager censors as to represent no more than "mutilated" and "edulcorated" versions of their originals — in other words, the originals themselves have now become practically "unrecognizable" (Calvino 1993, 232). To pursue the metaphor invoked above, it could further be argued that Calvino's personae are by and large unable to register the inanity of the object they are so intent on venerating, and hence continue expressing their faith with the mythomaniac insistence of thoroughly indoctrinated pilgrims through respectful silence, polite whispers or ecstatic cheering. These disparate reactions emphasize that "reading is solitude" (143), a path traversed by a lonely figure and leading toward landscapes of haunting emptiness, since any text, given the variability of interpretation, could be said to portray a setting without a story, a layered construct without a kernel. The narrator of "Around an empty grave" exemplifies this state of affairs when he describes the experience of moving through a sequence of locations that should logically lead him further and further toward an inner spatial core but, in fact, incrementally push him toward the external world. (Faria's predicament in "The Count of Monte Cristo," here examined in Chapter 3, springs to mind.)

Chapter 7—The Universal Library

Benjamin subscribes to the idea of reading as an eminently solitary activity: "the reader of a novel ... is isolated, more so than any other reader," he remarks in the essay "The Storyteller." Yet, the critic is keen to add, it is precisely from this sense of isolation that the reader's own creative energies ensue as a corollary of his or her desire to incorporate, indeed feed on, the text: "in this solitude of his, the reader of a novel seizes upon his material more jealously than anyone else. He is ready to make it completely his own, to devour it, as it were" (Benjamin 1985, 100). Calvino underscores each and every reader's loneliness and, at the same time, his or her longing to appropriate the text as a private possession in the penultimate chapter of the novel. Here, the seven readers gathered in the library, in proffering their personal definitions of the ideal book, are virtually oblivious to the opinions of any of the others. What may at first look like a conversation turns out to be an interweaving of seven monologues. Indeed, even when a character claims to agree with another character's intervention, he or she is merely using the latter as a cue to expound a totally separate discourse. Any illusion of a reading community is riven by atomizing individualism. One participant praises the kind of book that cannot be perused "for more than a few lines," while another seeks the "nugget" hidden at the book's core, and another still expects every fresh encounter with the same volume to give him or her the impression that he or she is perusing an unfamiliar text. Then there is the reader that is intrigued with the ultimate narrative of which all other stories appear to "carry an echo," alongside the reader that most treasures the "promise of reading," and, climactically, the one who only truly values the worlds that stretch beyond the book's dénouement (Calvino 1993, 248–250). In spite of the individualistic tenor of the chapter as a whole, these different positions share an emphasis on the impossibility of demarcating the book's limits: it is by no means clear where the book begins or ends, where its message may lie, or indeed where it stands in the overall map of the readable. Though anxious to specify the attributes of the optimal book, therefore, no reader may abate the futility of his or her mission, for any act of worship of the ultimate model is rendered vain by the realization that reading does not lead to knowledge but rather to the amplification of the desire to read.

Humbled and frustrated in their quest for answers on the thematic level, readers may still fuel their yearning for truth by seeking structurally satisfying organizations of ideas. What Calvino's novel offers, in this regard, is both a pattern of interrelations within which discrete entities may be identified, and an unstable whirl of singular forms nesting together one moment and floating apart the next. The stories alluded to by the ten *incipits* and the parallel plots developed in the numbered chapters with each they alternate come across as obviously interdependent, yet not welded together in a univocal way. In a sense, they could be picked up and interchanged with one another at any point: they are juxtaposed more than they are interwoven. By recourse to a visual analogy, it could be suggested that *If on a winter's night a traveler* combines, within the boundaries of its canvas, stylistic and chromatic uniformity and baffling variations of theme and technique, the raw energy of sweeping slashes of wild color and delicate effects of fluttering indeterminacy, as though to imply that subtle modulations may be achieved through the application of pure paint straight out of the tube. As the desire to read merges almost indistinguishably with erotic desire, this paradoxical coexistence of monochromatic and polychromatic proclivities manifests itself as a search for disparate and individualized identities which, at the same time, irresistibly tend to acquire one and the same face, body, voice — those of the *Other* Reader. The term Other does not simply designate the character of Ludmilla, at this point, but also, more broadly, an unspecified and unlocalizable object of desire combining the most enticing features of the ideal book and the ideal partner.

The instability of the author-function both reflects and magnifies the tension between personalizing and depersonalizing drives, for the creation of distinctive voices entails, inexorably, a process of self-effacement, while the pursuit of wholeness, for its part, is only ever conducive to a scenario of apocryphal displacement. Thus, if the text's polychromatic facet conjures up plural identities and subject positions for both its characters and its readers, the monochromatic element draws all difference toward the void of non-identity. Writers willing to obliterate themselves may intentionally embrace this fate as the very fountainhead of creativity. The *incipit* titled "What story down there awaits its end?" pushes this strategy of minimalist reduction of the real to Kafkaesque extremes. Its narrator, intent on mentally deleting all political and economic structures, all vestiges of both the built environment and the natural world, finds that the blank slate he has been creating, in an act of imaginary protest, has become the norm, in the aberrant logic of a totalitarian government eager to start from scratch. A bottomless abyss opens beneath his feet, seemingly stretching for all eternity — and beyond. This story thus allegorizes the sustained process of authorial self-erasure commended by Calvino via the character of Flannery. However, it concurrently emphasizes the need to confront the void produced by this incremental procedure not as total negation but rather as the receptacle of alternate and discordant imaginative potentialities. Calvino consistently reminds us that the world is not an organic whole but a jumbled assortment of quirky details, and that this makes the process of seeing the world inevitably strenuous. By and large, we project our gaze into the distance for what is actually at hand. We are restrained by the lure of stationary meaning, while the ultimate object of our desire dances in and out of the shadows cast by our own clouded vision. A complete surrender to the lure of nothingness will only yield yet more nothingness, whereas an understanding of the void as the precondition of inventiveness may provide scope for an ingenious juggling of presence and absence.

Chapter 8

Empire of the Senses:
Under the Jaguar Sun

Under the Jaguar Sun (first published posthumously in 1986) explicitly epitomizes Calvino's commitment to the writing exercise as a way of engineering the encounter of abstraction and intangibility, the mental and the corporeal, through textual constellations increasingly devoted to brevity and to the open-endedness of work in progress. As the writer himself states, he believes that his "books which are made up of brief texts are never concluded. Each one represents a direction of work" in which he aims "to probe deeply" (cited in Fournel 88). Time and again, Calvino channels his imaginative energies into the attempt to translate a fantasy or mental image into the substance of a story: a construct with which the reader may engage not only intellectually but also physically. In *Under the Jaguar Sun*, the senses and the mythologies to which they are germane supply the leading thread for such a process of translation. The unfinished collection comprises three novellas: "Under the Jaguar Sun," "A King Listens" and "The Name, the Nose," where the senses of taste, hearing and smell are explored. Calvino explains his choice of this particular theme thus: "Modern man perceives certain things but fails to intercept others: olfaction is atrophied, taste is limited to a restricted range of sensations. And as far as our sight is concerned, given our habit of reading and interpreting fabricated images, it no longer has the ability to distinguish details, traces, signs, the way the tribal man no doubt was able to" (cited in Nascimbeni 3). In an article for the *New York Review of Books* published a year earlier, the writer comments specifically on some of the difficulties experienced in the process of writing *Under the Jaguar Sun*: "Writing it, I have the problem that my sense of smell is not very sharp. I lack really keen hearing, I am not a gourmet, my sense of touch is unrefined, and I am nearsighted. For each one of the five senses, I have to make an effort in order to master a range of sensations and nuances. I don't know if I shall succeed, but my efforts ... are not merely aimed at making a book but also at changing myself, the goal of all human endeavor" (Calvino 1983, 39).

In his attempt to unravel and enhance the languages of the senses, Calvino is implicitly also striving to rewrite the *history* of the senses, a track record of almost uniform omission. The contention, as old as ancient Greek philosophy, that the senses are both central to human life and a fallible source of information has traditionally placed their languages and histories on a puzzling threshold of indecidability. It is this very ambiguity, arguably, that has recurrently justified the subordination of the sensorium to the mind, in the belief that while the latter discloses ideas, the former may only disclose things. If this has generally led to the marginalization of the senses from both philosophy and the social sciences, it is also worth observing that not all of the five senses have been equally neglected. In fact, the sensory hierarchies fabricated by legion theoreticians throughout the history of Western thought have, by and large, tended to accord sight a privileged status. Prioritized by Plato as an index of human excellence, the sense of sight is further equated by Aristotle with the metaphysical concept of illumination. With the advent of the Enlightenment, the desensualization of knowledge promulgated by Descartes again grants sight a superior role in the sensory hierarchy: the eye celebrated by Cartesian rationalism, moreover, is a fundamentally disembodied icon of unitary, perspectivalist perception, ratifying the correct processing of images within the sealed chamber of the mind. Christianity, for its part, has conventionally associated sensory experience with the path to damnation, as succinctly typified by the eating of the forbidden fruit. However, Christian mythology has also argued that the senses may serve a legitimate purpose as long as they are not regarded as ends in themselves but rather as means to a loftier end, and hence proposed hierarchical distinctions between those senses that may be used to the glory of God and those that are, conversely, most likely to lead to abuse and hence sin. Sight and hearing belong to the former category: the manifestation of God's Logos and its translation into flesh figure the genesis of the universe in terms of the joint agency of visual and auditory effects. Smell, taste and touch, to various degrees, epitomize the danger of sensory abuse, be it in the form of gluttony or lust. The preposterousness of these repressive strategies becomes blatant when one observes, with Anthony Synnott, that "We are social beings, and we communicate in and with and through the senses. Long before we are rational beings, humans are sensing beings. Life without the senses does not make sense" (Synnott 128).

Calvino, in dedicating his collection to a rehabilitation of the sensorium, drastically questions the tradition of pervasive neglect documented by the foregoing selection of representative voices. Nevertheless, he is also acutely aware of the fact that any alternative history is bound to be as inconclusive, faltering, hesitant and traversed by perplexities as all canonical versions of history will always be. This is partly attributable to the recognition that the senses inhabit a borderline zone between presence and absence. The presences evoked by the senses are also, ineluctably, marked by irreducible absences for in giving us access to reality's olfactory, tactile, gustatory, acoustic and visual facets, they never deliver reality as such but rather fleeting impressions, effects and interpretations of reality. Conversely, it could be argued that any sensory experience introduces an element of material presence into the decarnalized structures of symbolic systems of signification. However, if this partial solidity offers the basis for a celebration of the life of the senses, its inscription in a structure of decorporealized signs points to the inextricability of life from vexing reminders of dissolution and degeneration. Indeed, as Christina Benussi observes, if *Under the Jaguar Sun* deals with "the ego's journey through the primary sources of empirical knowledge," it is also the case that what is "dominant is a sense of decay and corruption ... impotence and death" (Benussi 150). It should be stressed, in this regard, that central to Calvino's articulation of a mythology of the senses is the unfulfillable nature of desire as a force that renders any quest endless and futile. At the same time, the dynamics of desire highlight the tenacious coalescence of life drives and death drives. Intimations of loss and of the inevitable interpenetration of presence and absence pervade the three tales as ways of foregrounding the forever unfinished status of all cognitive enterprises based on the pursuit of sensory traces and stimuli that are concurrently physical and immaterial, corporeal and linguistically mediated. This theme will be returned to in the portions of this analysis devoted to the three tales' distinctive climaxes.

Concomitantly, to say that *Under the Jaguar Sun* aims at rehabilitating the neglected languages of the senses is not tantamount to saying that the text dismisses the powers of the word altogether. Words do matter and substantially so: this is persuasively demonstrated for example, by the imaginative force carried by the names of dishes and scents enumerated in "Under the Jaguar Sun" and "The Name, the Nose," respectively. What Calvino emphasizes, however, is that the magnetism of words should be consistently related to the sensory experiences they evoke or provoke — to the absent body which abstract systems of symbolization and communication strive to repress but cannot ultimately dispense with. The text reminds us that it is utterly pointless to presume that the senses' symbolic inscription can be transcended since the senses are both material, corporeal and animal mechanisms, and apparatuses subsumed to abstract ideological frameworks. It is worth noting, in this regard, that Calvino's initial heading for the piece eventually titled "Sotto il Sole Giaguaro," i.e., "Under the Jaguar Sun," was "*Sapore, Sapere*"—"To Taste, to Know." This provisional designation patently underscores the complicity of physical sensation with conceptual procedures. Furthermore, the story as presently available reinforces the interpenetration of sensory and cognitive processes by suggesting that the gustatory experience is not simply conducive to the knowledge of what one is tasting but also, in turn, bound to be intensified by that knowledge. There is a two-way movement between corporeal and mental experiences whereby the former may induce the latter, while the latter may heighten the former. The gastronomical voyage mapped out by Calvino thus encompasses the physical dimension as the sheer *jouissance* springing from letting myriad flavors flow, via tongue, teeth and palate, through the whole body; the scientific dimension as a detached awareness of the material entities that pass through that body; and the reflective dimension as the knowledge of how such materials may be harnessed to a climactic enhancement of the tasting event. Bodily and mental planes of existence are symbiotically locked together: absent from each other, they are nevertheless only present at all to the extent that they are capable of mediating each other.

It is tempting to view *Under the Jaguar Sun* as an exemplification of the principle of Lightness as described by Calvino in *Six Memos for the Next Millennium*. The text's emphasis on the inextricability of any cognitive process from the ephemeral traces of sensory experience and its attendant etherealization of the sensible could plausibly result from Calvino's endeavor to attenuate the stifling ponderousness of conventional language usage, especially in the narrative realm, and hence counteract the dangers of stagnation, opaqueness and incremental ossification that threaten all human life and certainly do not spare the act of writing. In the languages of the senses, Lightness is primarily typified by a pervasive atmosphere of transience: though sensations may produce enduring memories, the sensory perception itself pivots on a contingent contact with flimsy sounds, tastes and smells that simply cannot be monumentalized as weighty presences. Olfactory traces inevitably dissipate once they are extrapolated from their particular contexts; gustation itself is consigned to the realm of absence if it is contemplated outside the boundaries of specific alimentary circumstances; sounds, for their part, dissolve into spectral echoes wherein empirically measurable waves and acoustic hallucinations merge indistinguishably.

The marginal intangibility of sensory experience suggests a universe in which invisibility is no less instrumental to our ideation of the body than concreteness and solidity are, thus echoing the existential perspective delineated in *Our Ancestors*. Relatedly, the life of the sensorium supplies a correlative for a "poetry of the invisible" that is also, importantly, a poetry of "infinite unexpected possibilities" (Calvino 1996, 9) — a version of textuality in which Lightness, far from constituting an escapist flight into a world of fantastical irresponsibility, actually requires rigor, tenacity and a scrupulous understanding of the tribulations of embodied existence. Calvino's cultivation of a poetics of Lightness is often conveyed, in *Under the Jaguar Sun*, by his emphasis not only on the specific traits of each of the senses but also on synesthetic interrelations, as if to convey the image of a fluid, Lucretian, or perhaps Ovidian body of endless transformations, substitutions and exchanges. Thus, in "The Name, the Nose," synesthetic effects are evoked by the equation of flawed olfaction with the possession of "deaf nostrils" and by the portrayal of old-fashioned perfumes as the artful producers of myriad "harmonies, assonances, dissonances, counterpoints, modulations, cadenzas" (Calvino 2009a, 67). "Under the Jaguar Sun," in turn, refers to the "notes," "modulations" and "chords" of taste relying on the orchestral "receptivity of all the senses" (5), while in "A King Listens," hearing is presented as the point of convergence of all other forms of perception. It is also worth noting that the vocabulary and imagery employed in each story repeatedly parallel the characteristics of the sense under investigation, as if to take the weight away from language by underscoring its connivance with the weightlessness of sensory experience itself. So, for example, "The Name, the Nose" depends vitally on the image of *evaporating* memories, "Under the Jaguar Sun" on that of a *devouring* chasm, and "A King Listens" on that of the *voice* of the city.

It should here be noted that the virtual inexhaustibility of the languages of the sensorium is also celebrated, with a characteristically Calvinesque admixture of melancholy and joy, in the earlier collection of short stories titled *Marcovaldo or the Seasons in the City*, originally published in 1963. An instinctively arcadian, bucolic or even downright rustic soul, the protagonist feels ill-at-ease in the big city. As a result, his senses are utterly oblivious to the cancerous proliferation of "billboards, traffic lights, shop windows, neon signs, posters" with which the urban spectacle constantly bombards him — so much so that those images "might have been running over the desert sands." By contrast, all manner of natural phenomena absorb his entire sensorium at the first available opportunity, regaling an exquisitely nuanced spectrum of impressions and reflections: "he would never miss a leaf yellowing on a branch, a feather trapped by a roof-tile; ... a horsefly on a horse's back, ... a wormhole in a plank, or fig-peel squashed on the sidewalk" (Calvino 1997a, 1). By focusing on a mechanized and alienating environment riven by rampant consumerism, emotional atomization and anomie, and its impact on the candid Marcovaldo, Calvino exposes the dismal fate met by the senses when the equilibrium between human beings and nature is disrupted and any prospects of restoring it appear more and more vapidly utopian as each day goes by.

"Under the Jaguar Sun," the novella devoted primarily to the sense of taste, posits gustation as a mediating discourse designed to compensate for, and possibly redress, the inadequacies of symbolic language and its marginalization of the body. As argued in the preceding paragraphs, however, Calvino does not view the narrative articulation of the senses as a means of advocating a utopian regression to a pre-linguistic universe. In fact, he is acutely aware of the inevitable inscription of both the sensorium and its idioms into a markedly abstract system. Thus, the language of taste is highly coded indeed: the tourist guide Salustiano, for example, though reluctant to go into specific details, is eager to stress that his ancestors' sacred cuisine must have involved "rules" for their "food couldn't be consumed without a special ceremony" (Calvino 2009a, 20). Kathryn Hume concurs that "culinary description is a highly specialized and surprisingly difficult art" (Hume 17). The central trope on which the story revolves is encapsulated in the tension between mixing and taming. The eating rituals with which the narrator and his partner, Olivia, become gradually acquainted represent a potent cultural challenge to the Western obsession with the harmonization and reconciliation of conflicting values and viewpoints: namely, a colonizing project designed to produce safely anodyne results. What "Under the Jaguar Sun" proposes, in fact, is an unsettling juxtaposition of contrasts wherein sublime harmony is born of dissonance. As Salustiano points out, ancient Mexican cuisine bears witness to this distinctive cultural preference insofar as it "had to celebrate the harmony of the elements achieved through sacrifice — a terrible harmony, flaming, incandescent" (Calvino 2009a, 20).

The admixture of discordant flavors underlines two further motifs which, as indicated throughout this study, are seldom absent from Calvino's work: metamorphosis and flux. In the universe of taste, everything — from the human characters, through the animal and vegetable realms, to architecture — is caught in the same spiral of fluid transformation, in a relentless whirl of melting and flowing processes, and hence defined by a drastic rupture of conventional barriers between self and other. This negation of rigidly compartmentalizing structures is simultaneously perceived as a threat to individuality, typified by the subject's engulfment by the random energies of primeval chaos, and as an ecstatic, indeed orgasmic experience. As the protagonist and his beloved eat, their "teeth" begin "to move slowly, with equal rhythm," and their eyes are transfixed onto "each other's with the intensity of serpents' — serpents concentrated in the ecstasy of swallowing each other in turn," at the same time as they are jointly "swallowed by the serpent that digests us all ... in the universal cannibalism that leaves its imprint on every amorous relationship" (29). The extract just quoted posits an overt analogy between gustation and sexuality. Nevertheless, what is tasted, ingested and digested in the process is not merely the body of the loved one. In fact, culinary practices are also a means — possibly the only available means — through which Olivia and her partner may come to understand an unfamiliar culture via the metonym of food. The image of the two sitting up in bed during breakfast "in the *chacmool* pose" (27) explicitly suggests that the language of taste is not only an imaginative substitute for an otherwise routinized eroticism but also a way of merging with the visited culture in its most esoteric and primordial manifestations.

For the nuns of the "Convent of Santa Catalina," before its transformation into the bar/hotel "Las Novicias" (3), the ingenious handling of culinary codes is held to have provided an imaginative substitute for the voicing of repressed yearnings that would otherwise have found no form of expression whatsoever and hence for the sublimated articulation of the "fantasies ... of sophisticated women who needed absolutes, whose reading told of ecstasies and transfigurations, martyrs and tortures, women with conflicting calls in their blood, genealogies in which the descendants of the conquistadores mingled with those of Indian princesses or slaves" (6). The activity of mixing, for which cooking operates as a pivotal metaphor, thus also symbolizes the reality of a multicultural and multiracial society, in which many of the binary oppositions beloved of Western thought collapse or else are exposed as pathetic lies. This motif is again picked up in the course of Salustiano's enigmatic description of human immolation, where the conventional dichotomy between winner and loser is problematized, if not downright ridiculed. The so-called sacrificial victim is actually enthroned as the privileged party deserving of ceremonious treatment, whereas the supposedly dominant executioner is placed in the subordinate position of a mere instrument in the satisfaction of the gods' appetite. The hybrid character of Mexican cuisine, moreover, is paralleled by central features of the local architecture as an art "impelled by the same drive toward the extreme" that also governs the practice of "curing" the "hundred or more native varieties of hot peppers" to create "a flaming ecstasy" (7).

Throughout "Under the Jaguar Sun," changes and fluctuations in the sexual relationship between the narrator and Olivia are paralleled by the gradual development of their knowledge of, and attitudes to, local cuisine and, via food, by an incremental understanding of each other. Psychoanalytical theory of a Freudian orientation has been especially attracted to the association of sexuality with eating, regarding oral drives conducive to the introjection of objects of all sorts on the child's part as a symbolic equivalent of the urge to incorporate the object of libidinal desire. Arguably, this infantile tendency survives in later life through forms of eroticism that involve the deriving of pleasure from oral activity: possibly as a substitute or replacement for an unsatisfactory negotiation, and hence a stunted enjoyment, of post–Oedipal sexuality. On the metacannibalistic level, Olivia's partner is disappointingly "insipid" (25), and erotic fulfillment is correspondingly displaced onto the level of gastronomic consumption. Hume, too, remarks on the significance of "images of engulfment as oral fantasies" and opines that "adult sexual problems are relieved," in Calvino's tale, "following the ingestion of a dish called 'plump girls pinched with butter'" (Hume 21)—a sexually suggestive recipe name indeed if ever there was one.

The absence of intimacy and verbal communication is thus partly compensated for by a return to atavistic forms of physical gratification. It is noteworthy, however, that the primordial pleasures of the oral stage remain shrouded in mystery as sensations that may only be guessed at and imaginatively relived not as realities but as phantasmatic vestiges of an invisible and inaccessible past. Indeed, the protagonists' exploration of Mexican culture and cuisine, of themselves and, eventually, of each other, exhibits the traits of a riddle throughout the unfolding of the story. The initial dilemma is posited by the enigmatic image of the "extraordinary love" binding an abbess and her confessor: a passion that "in its spiritual sense sublimated but did not erase the physical emotion." Olivia and her partner feel "intimidated" by the paradox of a love based on erotic displacement, yet not on the utter repression of bodily sensations, and it is this unsettling feeling — so alien to their cultural background — that first guides them, "walking like somnambulists," to the inner sanctum of the "dining-room" (Calvino 2009a, 4). What the two characters gradually discover is that the language of food, experienced as a subtly varied range of tastes "gained through secret and subtle complicity," is exactly what enabled that paradoxical passion, "perfectly chaste and at the same time infinitely carnal," to take form and flourish. The same medium, they gradually realize, may become the means of healing their own flawed relationship. In Olivia's case, the relationship with food oscillates between a state of absorption so intense as to verge on solipsism and an anxious longing to share gustatory experiences with the narrator. Aware that eating and the dining-table are increasingly replacing sex and the bed, the narrator comments: "The desire her whole person expressed was that of communicating to me what she was tasting: communicating with me through flavors, or communicating with flavors through a double set of taste buds, hers and mine" (9). Yet, communication is at first impaired by lack of reciprocity, as the narrator occupies a purely secondary place in the liaison and therefore feels that he may only contemplate Olivia's own relationship with food from a respectful distance.

As suggested earlier, the ingestion of food also operates as a metaphor for the figurative incorporation of a radically alien, mysterious and even mystifying culture. This process requires participation in and involvement with the Other, something which both home-packaged versions of distant cultures — e.g., in the guise of seductively (and speciously) foreign gastronomic venues in Western metropolises — and organized tourist rituals of the kind contained in standard package holidays grotesquely distort. The need to resist the colonizing temptation to interpret an unfamiliar culture according to normative parameters of familiarity is made especially vital, in Calvino's tale, by its emphasis on the "cyclic, tragic concept of time" entailed by "the calendars of the ancient Mexican civilizations" (13), which would appear totally meaningless to blinkered Western eyes. A willing suspension of narrowly defined ethical and moral standards is also required, implies "Under the Jaguar Sun," if the ancient practice of human sacrifice is to be understood as something other than barbaric bloodshed. According to Silvana Borutti, Olivia's curiosity about cannibalism is of fundamental significance in the narrative's unfolding, as it intimates that "comprised in a way of eating there is a way of thinking" (Borutti 14–15). As noted, central to the unfamiliar (and defamiliarizing) philosophy with which the protagonists are confronted is a radical reversal of Western antilogical assumptions about notions of victory and defeat inherent in the Aztecs' sacrificial rites. Furthermore, as it becomes evident that the sacrificed bodies were neither incinerated nor wholly consumed by birds of prey but actually turned into "divine food" (Calvino 2009a, 19) for the Aztec priests' ceremonial meal, another Western taboo is drastically questioned. If the ritual cooking of sacrificial victims comes to represent the supreme devotional act, it also turns out to be the case that the employment of powerful seasoning was meant not to conceal the taste of human flesh but rather to "enhance that flavor, to give it a worthy background, to honor it." Olivia interprets the ancient practices as an honest, open recognition of cannibalistic drives, of which an eminently spicy cuisine is the latter-day heir, and hence a corrective of Western hypocrisy and its latently anthropophagous tendencies: the drives of putatively civilized people whom she unsentimentally describes as "we who tear one another apart, pretending not to know it" (22).

It is from a somewhat epiphanic vision of the crude inadequacy of Western binary thinking and of the arbitrariness of the ethical tenets on which it depends that the narrator gains a fresh perspective on his own personal understanding of sexuality, eroticism and the gustatory sensations so closely associated with both. Finally aware that the fundamental flaw at the core of his relationship with Olivia lies with his passivity and attendant conviction that she is the consumer and he is the food, the narrator realizes that in fact, anyone is simultaneously an agent and a patient, a potential wielder of the sacred knife and a potential recipient of its lethal cut. Therefore, in order to become appealing to her taste buds, he must be prepared to devour Olivia in turn, since "The most appetizingly flavored human flesh belongs to the eater of human flesh" (26). Hume's comments effectively sum up the world view articulated by Calvino with this novella: "Whether aimed at the bourgeoisie or at Western culture or capitalism, one can indeed say that we pretend not to devour others, when really we are just afraid to face and acknowledge our predations. Indeed, the anticolonialist would argue, as Calvino himself does ... that the European conquistadores shed far more blood than did the Aztecs in their sanguinary rites" (Hume 29–30). Throughout the tale, Calvino's writing exhibits a steadily growing attraction to the amalgamation of sexual desire and cultural production in their manifold aspects with gastronomy as a metamorphic activity based on the principles of *ars combinatoria* at its most creative. Laura Esquivel's *Like Water For Hot Chocolate* (1989), incidentally, provides an articulation of analogous motifs, by literally equating each of the characters' erotic tribulations to so many traditional Mexican dishes, whose ingredients and methods of preparation are minutely outlined at the start of each chapter of the novel.

In the tale "A King Listens," the sense of hearing is utilized as a vehicle for the exploration of the interrelated dynamics of power and desire. The monarch is apparently omnipotent: he does not even need to leave the throne to satisfy his corporeal needs or to enjoy sexual intercourse. Yet, he is rendered utterly powerless by his unrelieved isolation and paranoid fears of conspiracy and mutiny. His seclusion only serves to fuel his manic conviction that, sooner or later, he will be brutally toppled from power. To keep the threat of insurrection at bay by nipping the slightest hint at unrest in the bud, the king listens unrelentingly to the faintest of noises vibrating through the halls and corridors of his palace, appearing to imbue every single stone and fissure and, in his pathological hunt for meaning, comes to attribute no less significance to silences than to sounds as though these, too, were furtive omens of disaster. Paradoxically, the king's decoding instinct, though supposed to supply the ruler with highly refined surviving tools, degenerates into a curse. Immobilized in the most secluded areas of his "palace-ear" (Calvino 2009a, 38), he thus falls prey to increasingly obsessive consternation. As Cynthia Ozick points out, "the ear is all petrified anxiety; to listen acutely is to be powerless, even if you sit on a throne ... the ear turns out to be the most imagining organ, because it is the most accomplished at deciphering" (Ozick 7). The conundrum of powerful disempowerment in which the king is locked is bound up with his warped relation to desire: although the narrator keeps reassuring him that none of his wishes will ever remain unfulfilled, these wishes are only pale shadows of a deeper, primeval desire which, in fact, is by definition insatiable. As indicated in more detail later, the ending of the story testifies to the unfulfillable nature of an all-absorbing desire which no contingent of guards, spies, attendants or courtesans could ever have it in their power to satisfy.

The image of the palace as a "clock" (Calvino 2009a, 37) adumbrates the possibility of a sense of stability, or at least continuity, resulting from the acknowledgment of repetitive patterns. However, the potentially soothing effect of rhythmic reiteration epitomized by the image of the palace as a "weft of regular sounds, always the same, like the heart's beat" (43) is undermined by the opposite perception of repetition as an unfathomable threat: the more regular the quotidian sounds appear to be, the more menacing they become. Like the beating of the heart, the cyclic alternation of day and night, the seasonal patterns and the revolutions of the planets, repetitive phenomena of all sorts may be a source of comfort in a world pulled adrift by the random tides of chance and contingency. Yet, repetition is also associated with mechanical recurrence, with the blind, unfeeling and grotesquely comical performance of routinized acts and, to this extent, threatens to transform human beings themselves into clownish automata. Moreover, the notion of repetition is inextricable, as Gilles Deleuze persuasively argues, from that of difference — indeed, Calvino's monarch, in registering repetition, concurrently struggles to detect clues to possible deviations from the status quo. If repetition promises constancy, its intercourse with difference and with the latter's dislocating proclivities introduces an element of uncertainty, discontinuity, slippage. Far from guaranteeing stability, then, repetition turns out to constitute "by nature transgression or exception, always revealing a singularity opposed to the particulars subsumed under laws, a universal opposed to the generalities which give rise to laws" (Deleuze, 5). Petrified into an extension of his lifeless throne, all activity reduced to the tormented fantasies of his all-perceiving, yet necessarily misrecognizing ear, the king epitomizes routinized humanity. His passivity is made especially poignant by his compulsive subjection to a conspiracy theory of existence that suggests, echoing *If on a winter's night a traveler*, that what is ultimately paramount is not the actual existence of a secret plot, plan or seditious machination, but rather the human need, or indeed ability, to construct one.

The king is kept alive precisely by his flair for imagining potential intrigues as the only outlet, in his condition of frozen confinement, for whatever imaginative energies he may possess. He depends, for his very survival, on the belief that "spies are stationed behind every drapery, curtain, arras," that "the court teems with enemies" (Calvino 2009a, 38). The main difficulty the monarch encounters, in his stubborn determination to read any text at his acoustic disposal as a fundamentally conspiratorial one, is that he is unable to distinguish between motivated and unmotivated signs, intentional messages and accidental noises. Whatever meaning may be extracted from the plethora of auditory signals that surround him at all times is a product of sheer speculation. Like the narrator of "Leaning from the steep slope" in *If on a winter's night a traveler*, "A King Listens" encodes textuality as the contingent effect of a pathological deciphering drive, based on the fretful search for relational constellations that may be lurking behind individual scraps of both sense and nonsense.

In this respect, the monarch's situation recalls Roland Barthes' distinction between "hearing" as "a physiological phenomenon" and "listening" as "a psychological act." The former can be assessed with reference to "acoustics" and "the physiology of the ear." The latter is a much more complex event insofar as it operates at a variety of levels and cannot, therefore, be evaluated merely in terms of an "object" or "goal." Listening revolves on a sustained endeavor to harness the ear to the act of "*deciphering*": in this context, the auditory apparatus is enjoined not simply to register sounds but, more importantly, to "intercept" particular "*signs*" (Barthes 1985, 247). In other words, listening is inseparable from the human urge to pursue varyingly sophisticated hermeneutic activities. Unsurprisingly, though situated at the center of the palace-ear, the king regards his location as deeply estranging, alienating, and ultimately monstrous. He thus stands out as an aporetic entity: he is axial to, yet absent from, the activities that constitute the structure whose very pivot he is supposed to embody. In this respect, he personifies the deconstructive concept of the absent center as theorized by Jacques Derrida to describe the ambiguous notion of a focal locus that is simultaneously representative of a whole complex structure of continuous permutations and yet exempt from movement and change. This point is posited as the special site around which the structure revolves and, at the same time, conceived of—by definition—as fixed and immobilized. It is questionable, Derrida proposes, that a point that fails to participate in what is most distinctive about the system it purports to control—namely, its knack of metamorphosis and play—could actually sustain its putatively privileged status (Derrida 1978.) Calvino's monarch is, apparently, the nerve center from which all authority emanates. He incarnates all the energies that animate the structure over which he presides and yet, while the structure itself moves around relentlessly, alters, explodes and implodes, the king himself is cut off from such activities. Fossilized in his auricular chamber, he is patently unrepresentative of the world he is reputed to epitomize.

The king's powerlessness is also conveyed in the guise of a challenge to the myth of the Body Politic, whereby the ruler is supposed to unite, within one sacred shape, the natural individual body and the collective metaphysical body of the nation. Calvino's king, by contrast, is "bodiless" (Calvino 2009a, 53). His mastery is accordingly precarious: the king may be at his least powerful precisely when everything in his environment seems most firmly under control. His dispossession is signalled by the fact that his receptivity to all manner of sounds reaching him from the outside makes him incapable of articulating any sounds of his own. Indeed, his voice constitutes not so much a personal attribute as the whole city's intertextual heteroglossia, vocal patchwork, polyphony: hearing all and seeing nothing, the king epitomizes the idea of the *subject spoken by language*. In the story's climactic moments, the monarch hears a woman's song which, for the first time perhaps, entices him to take interest in something other than the maintenance of power by rupturing the "nightmare" of his long "insomnia" (52). Yet, this is also the first occasion on which the king has to confront explicitly the daunting possibility of a desire of his remaining unfulfilled. Surrounded by an endless and largely meaningless drone, he becomes gradually aware that what ought to be *his* voice may, in fact, be appropriated by anybody, even his worst enemy. The disembodying effects of language, magnified to pathological extremes by the ruthless pursuit of absolute power, have robbed him of any viable means of self-expression. Unable to find his own authentic voice and hence to produce the song which alone would enable him to establish a dialogue with the invisible woman, the king is locked in a fateful circuit of sensory deprivation that ultimately questions not only the perception but also the very existence of reality: any attempt to escape from the "cage is destined to fail: it is futile to seek yourself in a world that does not belong to you, that perhaps does not exist" (58–59).

In spite of its vital role in the unfolding of civilization, olfaction has been the most insistently neglected of all the senses, mainly due to its inextricable association with bodily functions and the idea of physical proximity. In "The Name, the Nose," Calvino mourns the lost language of smell through an elegiac celebration of the submerged world of the *parfumeries*, "Epigraphs in an undecipherable language" bound to lose their entire meaning the moment their prismatic "olfactory alphabet" and "precious lexicon" are allowed to sink into oblivion and scents themselves become "speechless, inarticulate, illegible" (68). Smell, confirms Synnott, is the "least researched of the senses," which is eloquently demonstrated by the "lack of a specialized vocabulary of olfaction" and of any adequate "scientific classification system" of its physiological and affective components (Synnott 83–84). Thus, whereas it is possible to maintain that sight depends on the properties of light, sound on vibrations, taste on sensations such as bitterness or sweetness, touch on the physiological and sociocultural polyvalence of skin, olfaction would seem to elude compartmentalization. Aristotle was very possibly the first to point out the uncategorizable nature of smell by placing it in the liminal zone between the so-called God-like senses (sight and hearing) and the animal-like ones (touch and taste). Centuries later, Hegel attributes the lowest place in his sensory hierarchy to the olfactory experience, the nose representing, he argues, a secondary function of being in both the animal and the human spheres. Freud, for his part, simply describes smell as "the characteristic *animal* sense" (185).

Robert Adams advances the proposition that olfaction is popularly associated not just with animality but also, more damningly, with obscenity. This, he maintains, is confirmed by the fact that "for many people," it "has aspects of bestial sexual behaviour summarized in the image of two dogs mutually sniffing" each other's genitals (Adams 24). Perhaps what is most unsettling about the sense of smell, apart from its association with lust, sensuality, primitive conduct and lack of sophistication, Synnott opines, is that we are all subliminally aware of its vital role as "a major component in the *moral* construction of the self" (Synnott 193) — a means of tracing lines of demarcation between the proper and the improper, the moral and the immoral, the pristine and the putrid. This is, at the most basic level, exemplified by the cultural expectation that it is not enough for things to be clean: they must smell good, too. Nonetheless, the centrality of olfactory structures is not sufficient to elide the concept of smell as a disturbing threat to both personal and collective boundaries. Smell violates any unitary construct through phenomena of constant and frequently untoward emanation and inhalation. We can by and large choose what to touch or taste; sights and sounds, for their part, may impose themselves upon us, yet cannot penetrate our bodies quite as literally as smells do; when it comes to smell, however, we find ourselves both absorbing and emitting olfactory traces in flagrantly uncontrollable ways. The unruly character of olfaction is underscored by recurring contradictions and paradoxes in the history of smell and of its cultural regulation. For example, the ideal of disinfection as a means to purity coexists with the fear of contagion. On the one hand, disinfection is regarded as a welcome way of drawing unhealthy miasmas from the body for healing purposes. On the other hand, the dispersion of unsound smells into a shared environment is dreaded as a source of lethal contamination. The art of the *parfumier*, to which Calvino's tale devotes ample attention, is itself paradoxical, in that the artificial concoction of scents is viewed both as a means of concealing putatively unbecoming odors and of disclosing their wearers' intimate identities. Underlying both paradoxes is a deep uneasiness about the fundamental phenomenon of emanation, whereby smell is simultaneously perceived as healthy — in that it bears witness to the purging of the body — and polluting — in that it is capable of penetrating other clean bodies and thus infecting them, possibly beyond repair.

Alain Corbin, in his matchless attempt to reconstruct a history of smell and thus rehabilitate this Cinderella of the sensorium, emphasizes the ethical and social connotations of the olfactory experience. Its decline in importance since the beginning of the modern period, in particular, can be related to urban anxieties about both physical and moral maladies. Indeed, the equation between stench and disease advocated by sanitary reformers is concurrently endorsed by social theorists: the crusade against unpleasant effluvia thus also becomes a zealous campaign against moral and verbal grossness, led by the conviction that the sources of malodorousness and indecency alike may be situated with the Great Unwashed. Smells deriving from the excretory and menstrual functions have, needless to say, been demonized above all others. The sanitization of smell operates along lines redolent of Michel Foucault's writings, and especially *Discipline and Punish* (1975), insofar as the basic pairing of stench and illness, of the physically and the spiritually unwholesome, becomes the legitimizing principle for strategies of strict societal disciplining and for the related production of "docile bodies" (Foucault 136). As Corbin argues, gradual changes can be perceived in the cultural tabooing of smells. If, to begin with, it was "excrement, mud, ooze and corpses" that "provoked panic" (Corbin 229), progressively, "fear of the obtrusive presence of a dangerous human swamp replaced the obsession with carrion and ooze" and "instinct, animality and organic stench became traits of the masses.... Far from the odor of the masses, the bourgeoisie set out, albeit clumsily, to purify the breath of the house: rooms had to be aired after a maid had stayed in them for an extended period," while the "fragrant alleys of the bourgeois garden revived amorous dialogue" (230–231).

The erotic potentialities of increasingly sophisticated scents, their ability to titillate through the subtle interplay of proximity and distance, presence and absence, and, above all, the notion of olfactory experience as a process of deferral and perpetuation of desire are central to "The Name, the Nose." The segment of the story situated in *fin-de-siècle* Paris vividly dramatizes the dynamics of desire and postponement, by emphasizing the ambiguous nature of the longed-for object as both absent — she is nameless and faceless — and present — by virtue of her distinctive, individualizing scent. The lover's pursuit is accordingly presented as an admixture of primitive drives, namely, the atavistic instinct to seek one's mate by olfactory means, and socialized behavior, as evinced by his stature as a "man of the world" (Calvino 2009a, 68), at home in the night life of the French capital and in its great *parfumeries*. Especially problematic, in this context, is the relationship between olfaction and memory. The proverbial transience of olfactory sensations would seem to defy any attempt to file them mnemonically in any organized fashion. Yet, there is plenty of evidence for the power held by smells to stir unconscious memories and evoke indelible and synesthetically colorful mental pictures. Calvino's tale records both poles of this paradox. In the nineteenth-century portion of "The Name, the Nose," in particular, the narrator stresses simultaneously the momentous role played by smells as the only available means of keeping the beloved alive in his memory, and the difficulty of articulating verbally the exact qualities of her scent. "But how could I put into words the languid, fierce sensation I had felt the previous night," the narrator laments, "when ... a streaked, rippling cloud had assailed my nostrils, as if I were breathing in the soul of a tigress?" (70).

As Madame Odile offers the doting gentleman sample after sample of her precious merchandise, he sadly realizes that what he is expecting of the lady is an unaccomplishable feat: attaching a label to an impression that cannot be fixed either in the nose or in memory: "at one point of the spectrum, there was a gap, a secret fold where there lurked that perfume which, for me, was a complete woman" (71). This description succinctly encapsulates the tenor of Calvino's entire vision — a vision wherein any meaning which human beings may aspire to emanates not from scenarios of plenitude but rather from gaps, holes, fissures and baffling pockets of nothingness. In fact, the sensation of wholeness itself — if and when it can even be experienced at all — issues from a brave acceptance of what remains indomitably elusive or altogether absent. The whole, ideally complete and completing object of desire may only be perceived as missing, as a hole or lacuna, insofar as the promise of plenitude belongs to an illusory realm whereas to love in the real world is always to lack, to pursue a goal whose attainment is continually deferred. This state of affairs can be viewed, in Lacanian terms, as an unhealable tension between Imaginary fantasies of fulfillment and a Symbolic reality of deprivation. The conflict informs Calvino's entire triptych, as each amorous pursuit of a nameless object of desire culminates in death — that is, in a metaphorical affirmation of the subject's inability ever to retrieve a scenario of infantile wholeness. The desired object is, in a sense, always already dead, unattainable, lost, invisible. Indeed, the endings of all of the three fragments constituting "The Name, the Nose" indicate that by the time the longed-for object is reached, desire itself has shifted beyond any prospect of consummation. In the climax of the *fin-de-siècle* strand, the protagonist discovers that at the very time the lady of his fantasies was supposedly dancing, surrounded by the exotic glamour of a masked ball, she actually had, according to official records, already drawn her last breath. Similarly, his prehistoric ancestor, who has recently attained to the status of *Homo erectus* and is keen on making the most of it by sniffing the air with alacrity, finds that the irresistible scent he has been pursuing rises from a pit swamped with decomposing carcasses. The protagonist's present-day avatar likewise retraces the odor that has kindled his desire to the sickening aroma of a morgue.

The omnipresent feeling of unfulfillment that insistently blights the erotic quests undertaken by the male narrators of the three novellas included in *Under the Jaguar Sun* harks back to the atmosphere of Calvino's earlier collection *Difficult Loves*, originally published in 1957. Already exhibiting extraordinary sensitivity to the vagaries of the sensorium in all its manifestations, *Difficult Loves* deals dispassionately with the ineradicable absurdity haunting humanity's feeble attempts at communication. Chronicling the ordeals of character types ranging from a soldier to a poet, from a bather to a reader, from a crook to a photographer (to name but a few), *Difficult Loves* bravely returns time and again to one elemental concern: people's perverse proclivity to erect barriers, both consciously and unconsciously, against the possibility of embarking on forms of emotional exchange that could alter their lives radically and thus alleviate their daily exposure to loneliness and tedium. Calvino shows scarce interest in the phases of the romantic curve traditionally prioritized by stories, poems and songs — i.e., the zenith were the lover's pursuit is crowned with triumph or the nadir where love fails and loss looms large. By contrast, he attends closely to the shadowy frontier where the orthodox amatory trajectory is boldly reversed and potential lovers fail to meet at all. Whether this results from their being the right people at the wrong time or else the wrong people at the right time is ultimately immaterial. What does matter is the lacerating recognition that nothing fuels desire more prodigally than its very frustration even before it has had a chance of being properly grasped. In the process, the languages of the senses make audacious forays into hitherto uncharted territory, and hence unleash their most imaginative tropes at the very point where their opportunities for free expression would seem to be most brutally stunted. These bold gestures on the part of an otherwise neglected sensorium frequently give rise, throughout *Difficult Loves*, to delicate celebrations of human creativity and of the imagination's heroic resilience in the face of all sorts of enemies — above all, isolation, melancholia and boredom. However, there are also many times when the senses, overwhelmed by shapeless waves of humanity, end up weaving a discourse so intricate, dense and eventually cumbersome as to communicate only one, extreme message: the terminal impossibility of communication within a graphic "tangle from which even the tiniest white spaces" by and by vanish until "only the black remain[s], the most total black, impenetrable, desperate as a scream" (Calvino 1999, 108).

Calvino's fascination with the reconceptualization of the very history of the senses also resonates throughout *The Road to San Giovanni* (posthumously released in 1990). This text superficially presents itself as a simple diary or collection of autobiographical pieces but gradually reveals its true identity as a multilayered chronicle of Calvino's commitment to a painstaking exploration of the sensorium not solely as a physical instrument but also as a daring creator of largely unpredictable aesthetic and cognitive experiences. *The Road to San Giovanni* foregrounds this vital aspect of Calvino's philosophy right from the start, devoting its first chapter to the writer's reflections on his personal history and literary aspirations. The titular road, in this context, rises well above the status of an inert geographical fixture to acquire a vibrant life of its own as the agency that simultaneously connects and separates the rural and the urban worlds. This liminal domain is veritably saturated with sensory impressions and memories that do not serve a merely decorative purpose. Nor do they simply supply the author with a pretext for yielding something of a Joycean stream of infantile recollections. In fact, they operate as the structural launch pad for a resolutely unsentimental analysis of much more considerable breadth and depth.

Two contrasting, yet also complementary, attitudes to the realm of the senses are assiduously explored throughout the book with reference to the figures of Calvino's father and of the author himself as a child. The former, a highly competent natural scientist sensitive to the tiniest manifestation of organic life on his estate, interacts symbiotically with his habitat and keeps it within clearly defined spatial and experiential boundaries. For the young Calvino, conversely, "the world, the map of the planet, began on the other side of our house and went downwards, everything else being a blank space, with no marks and no meaning" (Calvino 2009b, 3–4). While the father focuses incessantly on his immediate environment, the son longs for "the cinema screen to pass through, the page to turn that leads into a world where all words and shapes become real" (7). The distance separating the two key characters is captured, rhetorically, by their association with two principal sets of recurring words, both of which carry distinctive sensory and sensuous connotations. The father — whose solid personality is presented as a dominant throughout the text — is repeatedly linked with terms pertaining to the land and its cultivation, plants, woods and hunting. All of these words feature quite frequently to consolidate the significance of the paternal figure as an imposing presence. The young Calvino, for his part, is posited as a weaker textual function and the words that more clearly define him, such as "city," make more sporadic, albeit regular, appearances. The power balance between father and son is thus elliptically portrayed as a concurrently emotive and semiotic tug of war engaging tow discrete physical domains and their corresponding sensory properties, with an unequivocally greater aura of corporeality emanating from the country-oriented patriarch than from his city-driven offspring.

Father and son are posited as mirror images of each other. Relatedly, their conflicting approaches to the languages of the senses are specularly balanced: radically different, yet mutually completing and hence inseparable. This is borne out by the two characters' intrinsic affinity as human beings who ultimately pursue the same goal — the achievement of a sense of belonging, rootedness or connection to the world — and, more importantly still, do so not out of some abstract notion of duty but out of "fierce passion" and of a keen apprehension of the raw "pain of existence" (11). As the quotidian interaction of father and son is dispassionately recorded with a care for even marginal and seemingly trivial sense impressions (e.g., those associated with taking out the rubbish), it becomes increasingly clear that Calvino had to confront and negotiate what could easily look like a double defeat. Not only could it be claimed that he had failed as a son, at least in principle, by not following in his father's footsteps; it could also be argued that his pursuit of an artistic career inevitably condemned him to a fate of perpetual exile that starkly contradicted his desire, akin to the paternal drive, to belong. "I was already what I am," the writer reflects, "a citizen of cities and of history — still without city or history and suffering from it" (20). Ironically, it is precisely from the cultivation of his art that Calvino admits to having gradually regained, "in a world that was already lost," a "relationship" and hence a sense of "meaning" (22).

In a metaphorical sense, the "road to San Giovanni" could be regarded as the inceptive stage of Calvino's entire creative journey — an adventure, as chronicled in this book, that takes as a major and profoundly inspirational point of departure a bold rewriting of history. From the writer's first attempts to resist the demands of social realism onward, this project never demurs from an opportunity to let the real be flooded by the metamorphic, and often unruly, forces of the fantastic at its most eccentric. A gallery of mock-historical figures that issue entirely from Calvino's idiosyncratic imagination, yet feel strangely familiar to any reader even vaguely acquainted with the worlds of romance, epic and the picaresque saga, sustains this daring revisionist enterprise. With an agile display of experimental verve, the author then ventures into a virtually uncharted territory of cosmic magnitude, bending the rules and mores of classic science fiction to speculate about the genesis of the universe itself from the viewpoint of a transtemporal and purely hypothetical but nonetheless endearingly palpable narratorial voice. Seeking to enhance further the scope of his existential voyage, Calvino subsequently explores another speculative domain of unmappable breadth and complexity, that of the city as not solely an architectural and societal construct but also a metaphor for interrelated concepts of humanity and embodiment. In a desire to pursue the proposition, already articulated in the context of his city-related work, that no structure — no matter how stable it may seem to be — is immune to explosion, Calvino also exposes with deconstructive glee the self-dismantling tendencies inherent in all codes, discourses and systems of signs. The ironic subversion of the epic form, retraceable to the Renaissance, fuels Calvino's ambition to memorable effect. At the basis of every ostensibly crystallized system, one will sooner or later discern a fluid motion analogous to the unrelenting flow of sap from vegetation to stone lovingly captured by the pre–Columbian sculptures so congenial to Calvino's aesthetic mission and personal artistic taste.

It is to advance his increasingly radical interrogation of totalizing structures that the writer then channels his creative energies into a painstaking — and often painful, though jocularly absurd — metaphysical reflection on the mechanisms of perception, conceptualization and cognition, thereby engaging with the very fundamentals of being. The conviction that putatively all-encompassing systems underpinned by rigorous analysis sooner or later give way to randomness and chaos acquires unprecedented intensity. This message is communicated by recourse to two complementary narrative vehicles: a verbal diorama of anatomical dissections of the analytical mind at its most perversely — and self-defeatingly — punctilious, and an encyclopedic constellation of textual forms designed to demarcate the territory of the narratable only to reveal, inexorably, its indomitable inexhaustibility. It is, arguably, in order to stretch further the boundaries of his critique of taxonomic mentalities that in the closing part of his tragically and prematurely mutilated career Calvino turns to focus more pointedly than ever before on the languages of the sensorium. At this stage, the claims to epistemological excellence alleged by classic binary logic are not only deflated but rendered paltry or even unfounded altogether.

As Calvino's genius asserts itself through a unique handling of the extraordinary, it is often — and no less strikingly — by recourse to quite ordinary, inconspicuous, prosaic or even banal materials that it succeeds in conveying a visionary galaxy of marvels of a kind which only the very young seem spontaneously able to sense and contemplate. In the process, the author tirelessly reminds us that writing and reading — and, by implication, the entire universe of literature and even of the artistic imagination at large — are inconceivable without a commodious openness to the disparate levels of reality at work within them and hence to the diverse configurations of truth they elliptically yield. Never losing sight of the inextricability of intellectual pleasure and sensuous pleasure, and indeed often proposing that each partakes of the other, Calvino does not make it his key priority to perturb the reader as though this were an objective worth pursuing for its own sake. In fact, the destabilization of conventions toward which practically all of his writings are geared is at all times intertwined with the production of spaces for entertainment and fun. Calvino's works, in other words, tend to unsettle us by amusing us, and to amuse us by unsettling us in equal measures. By making the dark and the frightening at least partially a trigger for delight, Calvino assigns them a role analogous to the one played by the bogeyman in games where kids derive pleasure from the experience of feeling scared. However, the dark and the frightening also persistently communicate a sobering message which, to stick with the ludic metaphor, brings to mind James Joyce's cautionary words: "Children may just as well play as not. The ogre will come in any case" (Joyce, III, 144).

This study has hopefully succeeded in documenting that a major constant throughout the nearly four decades of Calvino's literary productivity is a sustained, albeit kaleidoscopically diversified, investigation of the viability, scope and powers of human knowledge. This proclivity should not be regarded as an indicator of the writer's underlying desire to debunk the value of knowledge incontrovertibly. In fact, the argument here pursued works on the premise that the very opposite is the case. What Calvino actually endeavored to expose right from the start, and increasingly as time went by, was not the speciousness of knowledge per se. His target, rather, was the abusive distortion suffered by knowledge in the hands of societies hell-bent on effacing its significance as the always provisional outcome of speculation and questioning, and attendant reduction to a sealed commodity measured according to purely functional and utilitarian concerns. It is for this reason that Calvino's works and philosophy are here posited as the source of inspiration for a sorely needed critical examination of that stifling doxa: a project to be embarked upon by us — as his student, scholars, fans or, quite simply and perhaps most importantly, as his *readers*.

Bibliography

Adams, R. M. 1986. "The Nose Knows." *The New York Review*, 20 November.

Ariosto, L. 1975. *Orlando Furioso, Parts I and II*. Trans. B. Reynolds. London: Penguin.

Ballard, J.G. 1995. [1973.] *Crash*. London: Vintage.

Barthes, R. 1967. "Science Versus Literature." *Times Literary Supplement*, 28 September.

Barthes, R. 1985. *The Responsibility of Forms: Critical Essays on Music, Art, and Representation*. Trans. R. Howard. New York: Hill and Wang.

Barthes, R. 1990a. *The Pleasure of the Text*. Trans. R. Miller. Oxford: Blackwell.

Barthes, R. 1990b. *A Lover's Discourse*. Trans. R. Howard. London: Penguin.

Baudrillard, J. 1991. "Simulacra and Science Fiction." *Science Fiction Studies*. vol. 18, part 3. November.

Benjamin, W. 1978. *Reflections*. Trans. E. Jephcott. New York: Schocken.

Benjamin, W. 1985. *Illuminations*. Trans. H. Zohn. New York: Schocken.

Benussi, C. 1989. *Introduzione a Calvino*. Milan: Laterza and Figli.

Bonura, G. 1973. *Invito alla lettura di Italo Calvino*. Milan: Mursia.

Borges, J.L. 1970. *Labyrinths*. Trans. J.E. Irby. Harmondsworth: Penguin.

Borutti, S. 1987. "Metafisica dei sensi e filosofia involontaria nell'ultimo Calvino." *Autografo* 4, March.

Boyer, M.C. 1996. *CyberCities: Visual Perception in the Age of Electronic Communication*. New York: Princeton Architectural.

Brand, C.P. 1974. *Ludovico Ariosto*. Edinburgh: Edinburgh University Press.

Butler, A., C. Van Cleave and S. Stirling. 1996. *The Art Book*. London: Phaidon.

Calligaris, C. 1985. *Italo Calvino*. Milan: Mursia.

Calvino, I. 1956. *Fiabe Italiane*. Turin: Giulio Einaudi.

Calvino, I. 1957. [1947.] *The Path to the Nest of Spiders*. Trans. A. Colquhoun. Boston: Beacon.

Calvino, I. 1975. [1963.] *The Watcher and Other Stories*. Fort Washington, PA: Harvest.

Calvino, I. 1978. [1973.] *The Castle of Crossed Destinies*. Trans. W. Weaver. London: Pan.

Calvino, I. 1979. "Interview." *La Repubblica*. 24 October.

Calvino, I. 1983. [1949.] *Adam, One Afternoon, and Other Stories*. Trans. A. Colquhoun and P. Wright. London: Picador.

Calvino, I. 1983. "The Written and the Unwritten Word." *New York Review*. 12 May.

Calvino, I. 1987. [1980, 1982.] *The Literature Machine*. Trans. P. Creagh. London: Secker and Warburg.

Calvino, I. 1988. *Sulla Fiaba*, Turin: Giulio Einaudi.

Calvino, I. 1992. [1960.] *Our Ancestors*. Trans. A. Colquhoun. London: Minerva.

Calvino, I. 1993. [1979.] *If On a Winter's Night a Traveler*. Trans. W. Weaver. London: Everyman's Library.

Calvino, I. 1994. [1983.] *Mr. Palomar*. Trans. W. Weaver. London: Minerva.

Calvino, I. 1995. [1970.] *Orlando Furioso di Ludovico Ariosto raccontato da Italo Calvino*. Milan: Mondadori.

Calvino, I. 1996. [1988.] *Six Memos for the Next Millennium*. Trans. P. Creagh. London: Vintage.

Calvino, I. 1996a. [1992.] *Numbers in the Dark*. Trans. T. Parks. London: Vintage.

Calvino, I. 1997. [1972.] *Invisible Cities*. Trans. W. Weaver. London: Vintage.

Calvino, I. 1997a. [1963.] *Marcovaldo or The Seasons in the City*. Trans. W. Weaver. London: Minerva.

Calvino, I. 1999. [1957, 1958, 1970, 1971, 1964.] *Difficult Loves; Smog; A Plunge into Real Estate*. Trans. W. Weaver and D.S. Carne-Ross. London: Vintage.

Calvino, I. 2002. [1994.] *The Hermit in Paris*. Trans. M. McLaughlin. London: Jonathan Cape.

Calvino, I. 2009. [1965, 1967.] *The Complete Cosmicomics*. Trans. W. Weaver, M. McLaughlin and T. Parks. London: Penguin.

Calvino, I. 2009a. [1986.] *Under the Jaguar Sun*. Trans. W. Weaver. London: Penguin.

Calvino, I. 2009b. [1990.] *The Road to San Giovanni*. Trans. T. Parks. London: Penguin.

Campbell, J. 1964. *Occidental Mythology*. Vol. I. New York: Viking.

Cannon, J. 1981. *Italo Calvino: Writer and Critic*. Ravenna, Italy: Longo.

Cook, A. S., and G.A. Hawk. 1992. *Shamanism and the Esoteric Tradition*. St. Paul, MN: Llewellyn.

Corbin, A. 1986. *The Foul and the Fragrant: Odor and the Social Imagination*. London: Picador.

de Bono, E. 1978. "Lateral Thinking and Science Fiction." In *Explorations of the Marvellous*, edited by P. Nicholls. Glasgow: Fontana/Collins.

de Certeau, M. 1984. *The Practice of Everyday Life*. Trans. S. Rendall. Berkeley and London: University of California Press.

Deleuze, G. 1994. *Difference and Repetition*. Trans. P. Patton. London: Athlone.

Derrida, J. 1978. *Writing and Difference*. Trans. A. Bass. London: Routledge.

Derrida, J. 1981. *Positions*. Trans. A. Bass. Chicago: Chicago University Press.

Derrida, J. 1984. *Of Grammatology*. Trans. G. C. Spivak. Baltimore and London: Johns Hopkins University Press.

Dick, P.K. 1978. "Man, Android and Machine." In *Explorations of the Marvellous*, edited by P. Nicholls. Glasgow: Fontana/Collins.

Donato, E. 1980 "The Museum's Furnace." In *Textual Strategies*, edited by J.V. Harari. London: Methuen.

Downs, R.M. and J.T. Meyer. 1978. "Geography and the Mind: An Exploration of Perceptual Geography." *American Behavioral Scientist* 22(1).

Eco, U. 1968. *La Struttura Assente* Milan: Bompiani.

Esquivel, L. 1992. [1989.] *Like Water for Hot Chocolate*. Trans. C. and T. Christensen. New York: Doubleday.

Fenton, S. 1990. *Fortune-Telling by Tarot Cards*. London: Aquarian.

Flusser, V. 1992. "Key Words," edited by A. Müller-Pohle and B. Neubauer.

http://www.equivalence.com/labor/lab_vf_glo_e.shtml.

Fontana, D. 1993. *The Secret Language of Symbols*. London: Pavilion.

Foucault, M. 1975. *Discipline and Punish: The Birth of the Prison*. New York: Random House.

Fournel, P. 1985. "Italo Calvino: cahiers d'exercise." *Magazine Litteraire*, June.

Fredericks, C. 1982. *The Future of Eternity*. Bloomington: Indiana University Press.

Frye, N. 1957. *Anatomy of Criticism: Four Essays*. Princeton, NJ: Princeton University Press.

Gabriele, T. 1994. *Italo Calvino: Eros and Language*. London: Associated University Presses.

Grosz, E. 1995. "Women, *Chora*, Dwelling." In *Postmodern Cities and Spaces*, edited by S. Watson and K. Gibson. Oxford: Blackwell.

Habermas, J. 1995. *Postmetaphysical Thinking: Philosophical Essays* Trans. W.M. Hohengarten. Cambridge: Polity.

Heaney, S. 1985. "The Sensual Philosopher." *The New York Times*. http://www.nytimes.com/books/98/12/20/specials/heaney-calvino.html.

Hebdige, D. 1986–1987. "The Encyclopaedia of Tlon." *Block* 12.

Heidegger, M. 1962. *Being and Time*. Trans. J. Macquarrie and E. Robinson. Oxford: Blackwell.

Huhtamo, E. 1996. "From Kaleidoscomaniac to Cybernerd." In *Electronic Culture*, edited by T. Druckrey. New York: Aperture.

Hume, K. 1992. *Calvino's Fictions: Cogito and Cosmos*. Oxford: Clarendon.

Hutcheon, L. 2002. *The Politics of Postmodernism*. London and New York: Routledge.

"Invisible Author." 2002. *Times Online*. December 18. http://www.timesonline.co.uk/tol/arts_and_entertainment/books/article803024.ece.

Jacques, F. 1991. *Difference and Subjectivity*. Trans. A. Rothwell. New Haven, CT, and London: Yale University Press.

Jones, E. 1992. "On the Vampire." In *Vampyres*, edited by C. Frayling. London: Faber.

Joyce, J. 1957. *Letters*. New York: Viking.

Ker, W.P. 1957. *Epic and Romance: Essays on Medieval Literature*. New York: Dover.

Kirk, W. 1963. "Problems of Geography." *Geography* 48: 357–71.

Lacan, J. 1977. *Écrits—A Selection*. Trans. A. Sheridan. London: Tavistock.

Lacan, J. 1990. "God and the *Jouissance* of Woman. A Love Letter." In *Feminine Sexuality: Jacques Lacan and the Ecole Freudienne*, edited by J. Mitchell and J. Rose. London: Macmillan.

Leach, E. 1972. "Anthropological Aspects of Language: Animal Categories and Verbal Abuse." In *Mythology: Selected Readings*, edited by P. Maranda. Harmondsworth: Penguin.

Lechte, J. 1995. "(Not) Belonging in Postmodern Space." In *Postmodern Cities and Spaces*, edited by S. Watson and K. Gibson. Oxford: Blackwell.

Lefebvre, H. 1991. [1974.] *The Production of Space*. Oxford, Blackwell.

Lodge, D. 1985. *Small World: An Academic Romance*. London: Penguin.

McLaughlin, M. 1998. *Italo Calvino*. Edinburgh: Edinburgh University Press.

McLeod, M. 1994. "Undressing Aritecture." In *Architecture in Fashion*, edited by D. Faush, P. Singley, R. El-Khoury and Z. Efrat. New York: Princeton Architectural.

Manguel, A. 1997. *A History of Reading*. London: Flamingo/HarperCollins.

Massey, D. 1975. "Behavioural Research." *Area* 7.

Mumford, L. 1991. [1961.] *The City in History*. Harmondsworth: Penguin.

Nascimbeni, G. 1984. "Colloquio con lo scrittore in occasione dell'uscita di *Cosmicomiche vecchie e nuove*." *Corriere della Sera*. 5 December.

Negroponte, N. 1995. *Being Digital*. New York: Alfred A. Knopf.

Norris, C., and A. Benjamin. 1988. *What is Deconstruction?* London: Academy, and New York: St. Martin's.

Ouspensky, P. D. 1985. *The Symbolism of the Tarot*. Sydney: View.

Ozick, C. 1988. "Mouth, Ear, Nose." *New York Times Book Review*. 23 October.

Piaget, J., and B. Inhelder. 1969. *The Psychology of the Child*. Trans. H. Weaver. New York: Basic.

Pile, S. 1996. *The Body and the City: Psychoanalysis, Space and Subjectivity*. London: Routledge.

Porro, M. 2007. "Images and Scientific Knowledge in Calvino." In *Image, Eye and Art in Calvino: Writing Visibility*, edited by B. Grundtvig, M.L. McLaughlin and L. Waage Petersen. Oxford: Modern Humanities Research Association.

Propp, V. 1968. [1922.] *The Morphology of the Folktale*. Austin: University of Texas Press.

Punter, D. 1985. *The Hidden Script*. London: Routledge and Kegan Paul.

Raban, J. 1974. *Soft City*. London: Hamish Hamilton.

Redfield, M.W. 1989. "Humanizing De Man." *Diacritics*, Summer.

Richardson, M. 1992. "The Psychoanalysis of Count Dracula." In *Vampyres*, edited by C. Frayling. London: Faber.

Scarry, E. 1985. *The Body in Pain*. New York: Oxford University Press.

Sheckley, R. 1978. "The Search for the Marvellous." In *Explorations of the Marvellous*, edited by P. Nicholls. Glasgow: Fontana/Collins.

Stallybrass, P., and A. White. 1986. *The Politics and Poetics of Transgression*. London: Methuen.

Synnott, A. 1993. *The Body Social: Symbolism, Self and Society*. London and New York: Routledge.

Tester, K. 1994. *The Flâneur*. London: Routledge.

Vidler, A. 1990. "The Building in Pain: The Body and Architecture in Post-Modern Culture." *AA Files* 19 (Spring): 3–10.

Weaver, W. "Calvino and His Cities." http://www.des.emory.edu/mfp/calvino/calweaver.html.

Weiss, B. 1993. *Understanding Italo Calvino*. Columbia: University of South Carolina Press.

Willett, J. 1964. *Brecht on Theatre*. New York: Hill and Wang.

Wilson, E. 1995. "The Invisible *Flaneur*." In *Postmodern Cities and Spaces*, edited by S. Watson and K. Gibson. Oxford: Blackwell.

Winterson, J. 1997. *Gut Symmetries*. London: Granta.

Winterson, J. 2009. "An Exploration of Seminal Novelist Italo Calvino, Through His Writing." *Times Online*. May 7. http://entertainment.timesonline.co.uk/tol/arts_and_entertainment/books/fiction/article6243460.ece.

Wittgenstein, L. 1974. [1922.] *Tractatus Logico-Philosophicus*. Trans. D.F. Pears and B.F. McGuiness. London: Routledge and Kegan Paul.

Woolley, B. 1993. *Virtual Worlds* London: Penguin.

Index

Adam, One Afternoon, and Other Stories 7–8
Adams, R.M. 188
Antonello da Messina 158
Arabian Nights 63
Ariosto, L. 13, 34–35, 40, 98–102, 121–125
Aristotle 175

Ballard, J.G. 60–61
Baron in the Trees 11, 17, 20–21, 23, 26–27, 29, 31, 36–37, 38
Barthes, R. 7, 31–33, 35–36, 37, 48, 161, 186
Baudelaire, C. 85
Baudrillard, J. 144–145
Benjamin, A. 88
Benjamin, W. 85, 149–150, 164, 165–166, 171
Benussi, C. 137, 176
Blackadder 38
Boccaccio, G. 90
Boiardo, M.M. 34
Bonura, G. 26
Borges, J.L. 94, 150
Borutti, S. 182–183
Boyer, M.C. 69, 77–78, 85
Brand, C.P. 101
Brecht, B. 24
Butler, A. 158

Calligaris, C. 55, 58, 90
Campbell, J. 51
Candide 18
Cannon, J. 40, 120, 168–169
The Canterbury Tales 90
The Castle of Crossed Destinies 13, 90–125, 126
Cervantes, M. 10, 43
Chanson de Roland 34
Chaucer, G. 90
The Cloven Viscount 11, 17, 19–20, 21, 23, 25–26, 30, 37, 126, 136
Cook, A.S. 105–106
Coover, R. 14–15
Corbin, A. 189
Cosmicomics 12, 41–65, 118, 126, 144
Crash 60–61

The Decameron 90
de Bergerac, C. 10
de Bono, E. 139–140

de Certeau, M. 83–84
Deleuze, G. 185
Derrida, J. 39, 58–59, 88, 186
de Saussure, F. 72, 92, 110
Descartes, R. 20, 175
Dick, P.K. 55, 139
Diderot, D. 21
Difficult Loves 14, 191–192
Donato, E. 150
Downs, R.M. 86–87

Eco, U. 120
Einstein, A. 5, 48
Eisenman, P. 88–89
Eliot, T.S. 115
Esquivel, L. 184

Fenton, S. 93, 106
Fiabe Italiane 62
Ficino, M. 106
Flusser, V. 3
Fontana, D. 93, 106, 119–120, 113
Foucault, M. 189
Fournel, P. 130, 174
Fredericks, C. 42–43, 47
Freud, S. 113, 188
Frye, N. 35, 53

Gabriele, T. 31
Galilei, G. 49
Grosz, E. 80–81

Habermas, J. 20, 159–160, 163–164, 169
Hawk, G.A. 105–106
Heaney, S. 128
Hebdige, D. 94
Hegel, G.W.F. 188
Heidegger, M. 74
Heisenberg, W. 48
The Hermit in Paris 9
Himmelblau, C. 79
Histoire de notre image 110
Hoengarten, M. 20
Huhtamo, E. 158
Hume, K. 163, 179, 181, 183
Hutcheon, L. 23–24

If on a Winter's Night a Traveler 13–14, 121, 142, 146–173
Inhelder, B. 137
Invisible Cities 4, 12, 66–89, 121, 126, 147, 168

Jacques, F. 27–28
Jones, E. 29
Joyce, J. 195

Keats, J. 137
Ker, W.P. 33
Kirk, W. 85
Kundera, M. 10

Lacan, J. 36, 53–54, 113
Lautréamont, Comte de 149
Leach, E. 78
Lechte, J. 85
Lefebvre, H. 81–82
Leopardi, G. 10
Lévi, E. 107
Lévi-Strauss, C. 39
Like Water for Hot Chocolate 184
Lodge, D. 33
Lucretius 10

Mallarmé, S. 170
Manguel, A. 150–151, 153, 155–156, 158, 165, 170
Marcovaldo: Or the Seasons in the City 14, 178–179
Massey, D. 85
McLaughlin, M. 7
McLeod, M. 88
Metamorphoses 10
Meyer, J.T. 86–87
Mr. Palomar 4, 13, 15–16, 121, 126–140, 143
Moakley, G. 106
The Motel of Crossed Destinies 104
Mumford, L. 80, 82–83

Nascimbeni, G. 174
Negroponte, N. 77
The Non-Existent Knight 11, 17, 22–23, 27–30, 31, 37–38, 39–40
Norris, C. 88
Numbers in the Dark 13, 140–145

Orlando Furioso 13, 34–35, 40, 98–102, 121–125
Orlamdo Innamorato 34
Our Ancestors 11–12, 17–40, 121, 143, 178
Ouspensky, P.D. 108, 112, 113, 116, 117
Ovid 10, 109
Ozick, C. 184

The Path to the Nest of Spiders 7
Petrarch, F. 106
Piaget, J. 137

Pile, S. 83, 84–85
Plato 175
Porro, M. 48
Propp, V. 64
Punter, D. 61

Raban, J. 77
Raccontato da Italo Calvino 34–35, 117–118, 121–125
Ramelli, A. 155
Redfield, M.W. 156
De rerum natura 10
Reynolds, B. 100
Richardson, M. 30
Richardson, S. 23
The Road to San Giovanni 14, 192–194

Scarry, E. 79
Shakespeare, W. 10, 111, 114, 116, 119
Sheckley, R. 49
Six Memos for the Next Millennium 9–15, 48, 49, 52, 63, 99, 100, 105, 109–110, 133–135, 137, 142, 147, 177
Stallybrass, P. 179–80
Stevenson, R.L. 18–19
Stirling, S. 158
Synnott, A. 175, 187–188
Sulla Fiaba 62–64

The Tavern of Crossed Destinies 90, 91, 96, 97, 113, 120
Tester, K. 85
Time and the Hunter 4, 12, 14, 41–65, 118, 126, 144, 170
Triumphs 106

Ultimo Viene il Corvo 7–8
The Unbearable Lightness of Being 10
Under the Jaguar Sun 14, 112, 121, 129, 130, 174–191

Valéry, P. 12
Van Cleave, C. 158
Verlaine, P. 170
Vidler, A. 79
Virel, A. 110
Voltaire 18, 43

Washington, P. 159
The Waste Land 115
The Watcher and Other Stories 8
Weaver, W. 73
Weiss, B. 8, 126
White, A. 79–80
Willett, J. 49
Wilson, E. 85
Winterson, J. 8–9, 43, 67
Wittgenstein, L. 66
Woolley, B. 102–103, 142

www.ingramcontent.com/pod-product-compliance
Ingram Content Group UK Ltd.
Pitfield, Milton Keynes, MK11 3LW, UK
UKHW042006140426
5217IPUK00015B/1015